Dickens and Heredity

When Like Begets Like

Goldie Morgentaler
Assistant Professor of English
University of Lethbridge
Alberta, Canada

First published in Great Britain 2000 by
MACMILLAN PRESS LTD
Houndmills, Basingstoke, Hampshire RG21 6XS and London
Companies and representatives throughout the world

A catalogue record for this book is available from the British Library.

ISBN 0–333–74723–2

First published in the United States of America 2000 by
ST. MARTIN'S PRESS, INC.,
Scholarly and Reference Division,
175 Fifth Avenue, New York, N.Y. 10010

ISBN 0–312–22493–1

Library of Congress Cataloging-in-Publication Data
Morgentaler, Goldie, 1950–
Dickens and heredity : when like begets like / Goldie Morgentaler.
p. cm.
Includes bibliographical references and index.
ISBN 0–312–22493–1 (cloth)
1. Dickens, Charles, 1812–1870—Knowledge—Science. 2. Heredity
in literature. 3. Literature and science—England—History—19th
century. 4. Darwin, Charles, 1809–1882—Influence. 5. Parent and
child in literature. 6. Family in literature. I. Title.
PR4592.H44M67   1999
823'.8—dc21   99–22231
                                                      CIP

This book is printed on paper suitable for recycling and made from fully managed and sustained forest sources.

10   9   8   7   6   5   4   3   2
09   08   07   06   05   04   03   02   01   00

Printed and bound in Great Britain by
Antony Rowe Ltd, Chippenham, Wiltshire

For my mother,
Chava Rosenfarb,
mit groiser libshaft

Contents

Preface

Charles Dickens was fascinated by heredity. There is not a single one of his novels which does not carry some statement, no matter how playful or incidental, about the amazing resemblances between children and their parents. Yet this aspect of Dickens's fiction has received very little critical attention, and there has been no systematic inquiry into what Dickens understood by heredity, nor why he was so insistent on drawing attention to hereditary resemblances in his fiction. What follows, then, is an attempt to rectify that omission by focusing on hereditary issues in Dickens's novels.

By heredity, I mean the biological process by which traits are transmitted from parent to child. I intend to demonstrate that this seemingly self-evident process lends itself to larger philosophical concerns, that it implies an attitude towards the formation of personal identity, towards issues of descent, of history, and of time. Since whatever lives inherits, to contemplate heredity means to contemplate the very root and essence of life.

The mechanics of heredity, the laws which govern it, the way it works to produce resemblance and the implications of genetic transmission have only become known in the twentieth century. But it is not necessary to know how heredity works in order to appreciate that it does work, that children resemble their parents and that this resemblance is the outer manifestation of what is commonly called a "blood tie." This blood tie forms the basis of all familial, and by extension, all social relationships. It lies at the heart of all idealized allusions to the Family of Man or to the universality of human destiny.

Because the mechanics of hereditary transmission were not understood in Dickens's time, contemporary theories were all more or less incorrect. Yet when applied to literature even a mistaken theory can reap philosophical and aesthetic rewards. It is my purpose here to suggest how Dickens translated the hereditary ideas of his time into his fiction, and to outline some of the broader implications which arise out of that translation.

Towards this end, I begin with a historical overview of what has traditionally been thought on the subject of hereditary transmission. This first chapter consists of two parts, roughly divided between the "scientific" and the "cultural." It will become evident, however, that the two categories are not distinct and that there is a good deal of overlap between them, since many hereditary theories formerly assumed to have scientific validity would today be classed within the cultural sphere of popular belief rather than the scientific realm of objective reality. In fact, one of the difficulties in apprehending hereditary beliefs of the nineteenth century is the need to disregard all twentieth-century assumptions. Nothing fades more quickly than a disproved scientific theory and resurrecting such theories without contamination from subsequent knowledge often requires an imaginative leap.

It is my contention that three theories of heredity had a particular impact on Dickens's fiction. These three are preformation, blended heredity (later adapted by Darwin as pangenesis), and reproduction. Preformation offered a historical model of regularity and duplication through time, which had great appeal for Dickens. Blended heredity suggested that children could simultaneously resemble both their mother and their father, an idea which occurs several times in the novels. Reproduction afforded Dickens the opportunity of tying hereditary issues to aesthetics through the visual pun of the portrait.

Allied to these scientific theories are more abstract concepts gleaned from the cultural traditions of the West. The first of these arises out of the pantheistic beliefs inherent in all folk cultures. This is the assumption that life is formed through magical transformation or spontaneous generation, that humans may spring from rocks or turn into stars. Metamorphosis of this type negates heredity, because it defines progenitors as irrelevant. Opposed to this is the model of heredity found in the Bible, in which the insistence on genealogies defines descent as analogous to history, and defines time as progressive and evolving rather than cyclical.

The chapters which follow attempt to apply these scientific and cultural models of heredity to Dickens's thematic concerns in his novels. Chapters 2 to 4 focus on the personal aspects of heredity, on its application to the individual. They attempt to discover how Dickens understood the formation of the self. My contention is that Dickens tended to define positive moral qualities as being hereditable, but he was extremely reluctant to ascribe a hereditary basis to evil.

Chapters 5 and 6 examine how Dickens expanded his understanding of heredity into the public domain. Chapter 5 discusses the social implications of heredity as these relate to issues of class, race, and ethnic origin. Chapter 6 focuses on the Darwinian revolution and its effects on Dickens's last three novels.

One of my contentions throughout this work is that Dickens's understanding of heredity and his designation of goodness as a hereditary quality were not constant throughout his career. In Chapters 2 and 3, I demonstrate that there is a progressive change in Dickens's attitude towards heredity as he matures, that the absolute determinism of the early novels gives way in his middle period to a looser model, and then disappears altogether after 1859, the year in which Darwin publishes *The Origin of Species*. In Chapter 6 I return to this argument, but this time seeking to relate Dickens's disenchantment with heredity to broader issues which arise out of Darwin's evolutionary theory – for instance, the preoccupation with regeneration, with disintegration, and with death as a biological process.

In *Great Expectations* and *Our Mutual Friend*, the two novels which Dickens wrote after 1859, heredity very nearly disappears as a factor in the formation of the self, and this annihilates the thematics of cohesion and integrity which Dickens metaphorically associated with heredity. These give way to what I would call the poetics of disintegration. In *The Mystery of Edwin Drood*, there seems to be a reanimation of interest in heredity, but in this last novel, which Dickens did not live long enough to complete, heredity seems to exist almost exclusively within the context of sterility and death. At the same time, the accident of Dickens's death has ensured that *Edwin Drood* will exist forever within the framework of cyclical time, waiting for an ending which never comes. That – however unintended – is as good a symbol as any for heredity itself, living on without end for as long as there is life, representing, in Thomas Hardy's words, "the eternal thing in Man."

Acknowledgements

This book began as a dissertation for McGill University, under the direction of Michael Bristol, who, though not a Dickensian, agreed to guide the project when it was little more than an amorphous, unarticulated gleam in its author's eye. Thanks too must go to Maggie Kilgour, also of the English Department at McGill University, who, though similarly not a Dickensian, gamely put up with Dickens at numerous ethnic restaurants over a variety of exotic dishes – and never once complained of indigestion.

As for those who are Dickensians, a great debt of gratitude must go first and foremost to John Jordan, master of the (Dickens) Universe and head of the Dickens Project at the University of California, Santa Cruz, who was the manuscript's first "outside" reader, who encouraged its publication and so is its unofficial godfather, and whose kindness and support have remained constant ever since. A special word of thanks must go as well to Jerome Meckier of the University of Kentucky for taking a newly minted Dickens scholar under his wing and going out of his way to offer help and professional support, to say nothing of numerous epistolary discussions of *Great Expectations*. A section of Chapter 6 has appeared in *Studies in English Literature: 1500–1900* (Autumn 1998), whose editor, Robert Patten, has often heartened me with a few well-chosen and much-appreciated words of approbation. And I cannot omit a word of thanks to John Glavin of Georgetown University for his several invitations to speak at the Dickens Universe conference – and for being John Glavin. There are many other scholars and lovers of Dickens, too numerous to mention here by name, who have cheered me on over the years and proved to me that a passion for Dickens need not be lonely. I thank them all.

On a more personal level, I wish to express my gratitude to my brother, Dr Abraham Morgentaler, Associate Professor of Surgery at Harvard Medical School and director of the male infertility program at Beth Israel Hospital in Boston, for sharing with me some of his expertise on reproductive matters, and especially for his close reading of the first chapter. And thanks as well to Dr Philip Shulman for reading drafts of several chapters, for haunting bookstores for my sake, and keeping me up to date and well-supplied with books, journals and encouragement, for being a friend in need and in deed. A major thanks also to Douglas Jensen of Thornton Steward, North Yorkshire, England for plowing through Victorian novels of every size and description in search of hereditary references, for reading and rereading every single chapter of this book, tracking down quotations, drawing endless cover designs and for his affection, patience and kindness. And my heartfelt gratitude to Jonathan Seldin, mathematician extraordinaire, for computer help, proofreading and all-around emotional support.

Above all, this work being devoted to the subject of heredity, I would like to thank my mother, without whom none of it would have been possible – not the work and not the author. It is to her that I dedicate this book.

Heredity

I am the family face;
Flesh perishes, I live on,
Projecting trait and trace
Through time to times anon,
And leaping from place to place
Over oblivion.

The years-heired feature that can
In curve and voice and eye
Despise the human span
Of durance – that is I;
The eternal thing in man,
That heeds no call to die.

Thomas Hardy

. . . All true classification is genealogical . . . Community of descent
is the hidden bond which naturalists have been unconsciously seeking,
and not some unknown plan of creation, or the enunciation of
general propositions, and the mere putting together and separating
objects more or less alike.

Charles Darwin, *The Origin of Species*

1
Whatever Lives Inherits: a Historical Overview of the Hereditary Puzzle

I

In an essay on *David Copperfield*, Q. D. Leavis noted that this novel illustrates "the new scientific interest in heredity characteristic of Victorian literature, and a corresponding new interest in what determines conduct."[1] She does not elaborate on this statement nor cite any further evidence to back it up, yet she is certainly correct in pointing to "the new scientific interest in heredity characteristic of Victorian literature," despite the fact that heredity was hardly a new subject in the nineteenth century, nor – from the vantage point of the twentieth century – was the knowledge surrounding it particularly sound. In fact, as late as the 1860s, the decade after Darwin published *The Origin of Species*, scientific knowledge about heredity remained vague and insubstantial. It was so vague that scientists were not even aware of what they needed to know, and the work of Gregor Mendel, who in that decade published his findings on the laws of heredity, was totally ignored. Nevertheless, Leavis is correct in ascribing to Victorian literature a new emphasis on heredity as a factor in the formation of the self. The reason for this new emphasis, and the evolving assumptions about human nature that it foreshadows, can best be understood when placed against the backdrop of what went before.

Agriculture and animal husbandry, both successfully practiced among
the ancients, provide clear evidence that the mechanics of hereditary laws need not be understood in order to be applied. For example,
while the sexuality of plants was not discovered until the seventeenth century, the ancient Assyrians of the seventh and eighth
centuries BCE were carefully cross-pollinating the date palm, maintaining a stable and regular ratio between male and female trees.
Similarly, biblical injunctions against hybridization, such as those
found in Deuteronomy and Leviticus, indicate that the practice was
widespread in the ancient world.[2]

The attempt to improve the stock was not limited to agriculture.
Most ancient cultures had theories on how best to improve their
own progeny. Some cultures held that in-breeding was beneficial.
The Egyptian pharaohs married sisters or half-sisters, while the Greeks
looked favourably upon the union of uncles and nieces. Other peoples
held other degrees of kinship to be desirable. Bestiality too had its
proponents as a means of improving the human bloodline. Some
ancient peoples held intercourse with animals in such high regard
that it was a part of their religious ceremonies, while others – notably
the ancient Hebrews – abhorred it to the point of decreeing it a
capital offense.

Thus from earliest times, people have not only known about
heredity but have tried to control it. Eugenics is not a modern
concept. It was practiced among the ancient Greeks, most notably
in Sparta, where private life was dissolved, marriage frowned upon,
and advantageous matings with many suitable partners actively
encouraged and sponsored by the state, all in the cause of produc-
ing strong and healthy offspring. Those infants deemed less than
perfectly sound were simply eliminated.

In fact, the manipulation of hereditary endowment is often
a primary element in utopias, both ancient and modern. In *The
Republic*, Plato advocates a scheme similar to that of the Spartans
for the propagation of the Guardians, his ruling class. Moreover,
Plato's prescription for the conception and successful rearing of
children contains many allusions to the best techniques for raising
hunting dogs, race horses, and game birds. This suggests that, for
Plato at least, there was no essential distinction between human
and animal physiology, and that as far as hereditary laws were
concerned, he felt no compunction about generalizing from one
species to another.

Plato also believed that the relative contribution of each parent to the formation of the child depended on the level of his or her emotional involvement at the time of conception. The degree of enthusiasm would determine whether the child resembled its mother or its father. The belief that external circumstances at the moment of conception – such as the degree of pleasure taken in the sexual act – have an effect on the hereditary endowment of the child is a prime example of the confusion between inner and outer states that was to nip at the heels of the hereditary puzzle for most of its history.[3] The widespread acceptance until this century of the inheritance of acquired characteristics is another manifestation of the same confusion.

The Roman poet Lucretius concurred with Plato about the manner in which offspring come to resemble their parents, although his formulation had more of the dramatic about it. Lucretius believed that children resemble their parents because, "at their making, the seeds that course through the limbs under the impulse of Venus were dashed together by the collusion of mutual passion in which neither party was master or mastered."[4]

Something similar was suggested by the medieval cleric Isidore, who claimed that "newborns resemble fathers if the semen of the fathers is potent, and resemble mothers if the mothers' semen is potent."[5] The idea that the resemblance conferred by heredity is linked to a sexual contest between the parents – a reified battle of the sexes – whether this be described as a contest of emotional states as Plato suggested, or one of contending seeds, as proposed by Lucretius and Isidore, was obviously popular from the time of the Greeks into the medieval era.

Another model of generation was supplied by Aristotle, who claimed that in the formation of a living being, the male represented the active efficient cause, the female the passive material cause. In other words, the female provided the raw material while the male supplied the blueprint, and the female incubated the embryonic material which the male fashioned. In this analogy, the earthy material body derived from the female, the ethereal insubstantial soul derived from the male.

The Greeks originated many of the beliefs about heredity that were to recur during the centuries which followed the dissolution of the classical world. (One of the most interesting examples of this kind of recurrence is Darwin's adoption of the theory of pangenesis to explain heredity. Pangenesis, the view that each part of the body contributes to the hereditary endowment of the individual, was a

hypothesis originally propounded by Hippocrates.) The equation of
fertility with innate heat also originated with the Greeks. Empedocles
thought that the sex of children was determined by the amount of
heat in the womb, and Aristotle thought that females resulted from
a deficiency of such heat. Mostly, however, the heat that causes
fertility was thought to be located in male sperm. Aristotle, following Greek prejudice generally, thought that a small penis was a
better indicator of fertility than a large one, because the semen,
having a shorter distance to travel to the womb, was in less danger
of cooling.[6]

The Greek equation of innate heat with the insemination of life
was carried over into Christian Europe. God was thought to have
located this life-giving heat in two places, male seed and the sun.
The heat in male seed allowed it to activate and mould the matter
contained in female seed; otherwise, wrote Montaigne, women would
be apt to bring forth shapeless lumps of flesh.[7] By the same token,
heat from the sun activated the elements and permitted them to
give life to myriad creatures through spontaneous generation. The
equation of the vital force with heat was corroborated by observation, since dead bodies lose their warmth and grow cold.

Aristotle's theories, which essentially allotted to the male pride of
place in generation, were widely accepted until the seventeenth
century, when they were challenged by William Harvey. In 1651,
Harvey, having demonstrated the circulation of the blood and the
action of the heart as a pump, turned his attention to a more in-
tractable subject and published *De Generatione*, an attempt to solve
the riddle of how life begins. In his introduction, Harvey gave a
cogent summary of the state of knowledge – and its confusions –
up to that time:

> Physicians following Galen teach that from the semen of the
> male and female mingled in coition the offspring is produced
> and it resembles one or the other, according to the preponder-
> ance of this or that; and further that in virtue of the same
> predominance it is either male or female. Sometimes they de-
> clare the semen masculinum as the efficient cause and the semen
> feminum as supplying the matter, and sometimes they advocate
> precisely the opposite doctrine. Aristotle, one of nature's most
> diligent enquirers, however affirms the principles of generation

to be the male and female, she contributing the matter, he the form, and that immediately after the sexual act the vital principle and the first particle of the future foetus, viz. the heart in animals that have red blood, are formed from the menstrual blood in the uterus.[8]

Harvey's dismissive vagueness about the "this or that" is due to the fact that he is about to disagree with the traditional Aristotelian account of generation. Harvey's own contribution to the scientific history of heredity was the dictum *omne vivum ex ovo*, i.e. whatever lives must come from the egg, which suggested that mammalian reproduction was to be understood as analogous to the egg-production of hens and fish.

In 1667, this assertion was echoed by Nicolaus Steno who further proclaimed that the female testicles in mammals were not the equivalent of the male organs of the same name but instead were comparable to the ovaries of all types of oviparous animals, and should be designated by the same name. By insisting on the difference in biological function between the male and female reproductive organs, Steno began the trend towards an understanding of men and women as opposite sexes rather than as superior and inferior examples of the same sex.[9] In 1672, Regnier de Graaf confirmed the assumptions of both Harvey and Steno by discovering the ovarian follicles.

The seventeenth century, in which Harvey, Steno, and de Graaf lived, saw the beginning of a change in the general apprehension of the living world and its development. Up to that time Christian Europe had considered the formation of a human being as an act of God which echoed the creation of the first man. In *The Logic of Life*, François Jacob, winner of the 1965 Nobel Prize for medicine, formulates the attitude as follows:

> Until the seventeenth century, the formation of a being remained immediately subject to the will of the Creator. It had no roots in the past. The generation of every plant and every animal was, to some degree, a unique, isolated event, independent of any other creation, rather like the production of a work of art by man.[10]

But if the formation of a human being was seen as a unique event occurring entirely in the present, how then to account for the fact that lines of descent and succession clearly played an important role in the ordering of society from earliest times? When the social station of human beings is defined according to ancestral bloodlines and every child occupies a definite social position from birth based on the position of its parents, when, furthermore, there is an evident resemblance between parent and child – how then does one explain that each being is also seen as a unique example of God's creation and therefore without a past?

Jacob suggests that the solution to the paradox lies in the medieval habit of thinking by analogy:

> Certain bodies look alike because they have the same qualities. Conversely, similarity expresses common qualities. The resemblance of a plant to the eye is just the sign that it should be used for treating diseases of the eyes. The very nature of things is hidden behind similitudes. Thus the resemblance of a child to its parents is only a special aspect of all those by which beings and things are linked.[11]

Therefore, presumably, the resemblance of parents and children to each other was merely a sign of their analogous formation as God's creatures.

If the resemblance of a child to its parents could be explained through the use of analogy, the variations that differentiated progenitors and offspring were attributed to maternal impression. This meant that the physical, mental, and/or behavioral destiny of the developing fetus was thought to be affected by the experiences of its mother during pregnancy. In this sense, no human being was ever as powerful as a pregnant woman. "Women's imagination," said Paracelsus, "resembles divine power, its external desires imprint themselves on the child."[12] The theory of maternal impressions – one of the most popular beliefs in the study of procreation – had wide currency in the ancient world, and is thought to have originated with a lost text of Empedocles. Hippocrates is said to have saved an Athenian princess from charges of adultery by claiming that her child was black, not because of the mother's infidelity, but because she had the picture of an Ethiopian in her bedchamber.[13]

Every feeling of the mother, every errant fantasy, or untoward occurrence was thought to influence the development of the child. In this way, variations between adult and offspring would be accounted for. This type of belief declared the contiguity of inside and outside. Positing the susceptibility of pregnant women to external influences allowed the outer world of sensation to have a bearing on the destiny and development of the individual. Human development was thus seen as precariously dependent on the haphazard influence of environment. But the influence of outside stimulation on the development of the infant in the womb was essentially seen as a negative effect. The belief in maternal impressions set up a dialectic in which the birth of normal children was expressed as an unproblematic hereditary endowment bequeathed by God, thus an invisible natural inner process, while deformities were laid at the door of the mother's susceptibility to outside impression.[14] If a woman brought forth a monstrous child, the fault lay, not in nature, which always functioned normally, but in the woman, who was assumed to have sinned in some way – usually through acts of bestiality. As François Jacob puts it, "Physical or moral, each divergence from nature produces unnatural fruit. Nature too has its morality."[15]

During the seventeenth and eighteenth centuries some of the thinking concerning the deity's place in the scheme of conception began to change. Until this time, the production of its own kind by a living organism had not been taken to express a law of nature. Instead, it was thought that the most important event in generation was the implantation of the soul in the body. This equation of the mystery of life with metaphysical impulse predates Christianity. Both Aristotle and Galen had accounted for vital activity by assuming it to be controlled by "souls" or "faculties." By the time of the Enlightenment, however, the generation of a living being was no longer considered to be an isolated event. Instead it had come to be seen as a demonstration of laws that expressed the regularity of the universe. It became the means through which form was maintained over time and the permanence of species assured.[16]

The concept of species had arisen at the end of the seventeenth century from the need of naturalists to base their classifications on the reality of nature. Dividing living things into species allowed the messy profusion of the natural world to be slotted into neat compartments, making it more amenable to study, and confirming the existence of a rational world which functioned along orderly mechanistic principles.

The favourite trope of the Enlightenment was to compare the workings of Nature to those of a machine. Discoveries, such as Harvey's, that the heart worked like a pump to ensure the circulation of blood through the body, and that blood itself, being liquid, followed the laws of hydraulics, only confirmed the general impression of the mechanical function of nature. (The study of hydraulics – the action of fluids under pressure – dates from the seventeenth century. A priest named Edmé Marriot, one of the founders of the French Academy, was stimulated by his interest in the waterworks at Versailles to publish a thesis in 1686 on the theory and practice of hydrodynamics.)

Descartes was among the first, and was certainly the most influential, of the philosophers to advocate the theory of the "animal machine." He declared that the physical world was essentially mechanical, and that all change was due to a rearrangement of the particles of matter. The bodies of organisms were therefore nothing more than physical structures governed by the laws of mechanics.

This change in the way Nature was perceived led inevitably to a changed attitude towards God and his relationship to the living world. It no longer seemed reasonable to suppose that God's hand was at work in every detail of natural activity. The "clock-maker God" of the deists was still the Creator of the Universe, but now the act of creation had been pushed a step back. God was no longer defined as an active agent engaged in the ongoing process of creation, but as the initiator of a pattern, a pattern which, once given its original impulse, remained constant throughout the centuries. The God of the Enlightenment had set the world in motion, and decreed its development. It followed, then, that the form of the natural world was perfect, permanent, preordained, and impervious to alteration or modification.

The lines dividing the various species were consequently assumed to be fixed and immutable, so that no species was in danger of merging with any other and thus confusing the taxonomy. Classification by species was dependent on notions of heredity, since the very concept of species was based on the assumption that each succeeding generation always produced its like.

This type of classification established a bond between the contemporary world and its biblical origin, subsuming and erasing all definitions of time as an evolving historical process through the insistence on the permanence of living forms. In this way, the biblical moment of creation was identical with present time, and the natural world of the Bible was made visible in the here-and-now. Generation could be seen as another expression of the regularity of nature, a reassuring stability to place against the relentless advance of time.

François Jacob explains how analogies from the inanimate world of machines could be thought to apply perfectly to the living world of Nature by suggesting that until the end of the eighteenth century there was no clear distinction between beings and things. The animate and inanimate worlds were contiguous, with no break between the two and no acceptable definition for distinguishing them.[17] The steam engine was thought to be the best model for describing a living body since it had a source of heat that required feeding, as well as a cooling system and devices for adjusting the various operations. In effect, the mechanistic view of nature merely turned on its head the pantheism of earlier times. Whereas pre-Christian Europeans had ascribed to all things, animate and inanimate, the properties of life, the deists' emphasis on mechanism ascribed to all things, whether living or not, the properties of machines.

By the end of the seventeenth century all females were acknowledged to possess eggs, although these were often referred to as "testicles," thus illustrating the linguistic confusion between male and female reproductive systems that persisted in both medical and popular circles until well into the seventeenth century. At the same time, refinements in the technology of the microscope had revealed the existence of spermatozoa in male semen.

These two related discoveries gave rise to the next important theory in the history of heredity, that of preformation. Because living things at this time were only comprehensible through their visible structures, it became necessary to determine how these structures were maintained from one generation to the next. Obviously, the structure itself could not disappear but had to remain constant and relatively intact throughout the process of transmission. The idea that growth entailed the constant subdivision and multiplication of cells was not a concept available to the scientific mind of the seventeenth and eighteenth centuries. It was therefore assumed that a living organism had to exist as a minute version of its eventual adult self. Since the structure could not disappear, it had to persist in capsule form either in the seed or in the egg in order to be passed on to future generations. The fertilizing contact of egg and sperm triggered the growth of the capsule, known most commonly as the "germ," and so began the development of the organism.

Postulating the existence of a germ moved the process of generation back one step. Life was now defined as originating in the distant past with the creation of the germ, rather than in the present at the moment of sexual contact. Parents were now perceived as little more than the activating agents of the germs they carried. In fact, preformation deprived sexual activity of its procreative purpose, at the same time as it diverted scholarly attention to the origin and organization of the germ, which now required explanation.

The problem then became how to account for the germ getting inside the parent in the first place. The solution was to consider that the germs of all organisms, past, present, and future, had always existed, that they had been formed at the time of Creation, and were only awaiting the moment of activation by fertilization. The preformed germ in turn contained within itself the germs of its own future children, who contained the germs of their children, and so forth. Thus all future generations lay encapsulated within the reproductive organs of the first parent.

But which parent was it? Since the organism was conceived as existing preformed and intact within the germ, it could not be a product of the combined contribution of male and female but had rather to be located entirely within either the male seed or the female egg. In the beginning, and until the role and function of semen were better understood, most preformationists were ovists, believing that the germ was located in the egg. The discovery of parthenogenesis served to confirm this. The fact that certain species of insect could multiply without sexual contact allowed for a scientific recasting and reaffirmation of the biblical story of the first mother in Genesis.

Now all of humanity was seen to spring from the loins of Eve in the most literal sense, since all generations that ever were and ever would be had existed as encapsulated germs in her ovaries. In the words of Elizabeth Gasking: "The first female of every species contained within herself all future generations of her kind. Each generation in turn would come to maturity, and when all the created germs had reached adult form the species would become extinct."[18] This Russian-doll concept became known as "emboîtement"; it complemented and completed the theory of preformation.

When the role of the spermatozoa was more clearly understood, however, the animalcule – as the spermatozoon was called – was seized on by many scientists as a more acceptable location for the germ than the egg. Proponents of this view were called "animalcultists" and their theory had the advantage over that of the ovists in restoring the male to his previous supreme position in generation.[19] Either way, however, whether one believed that the germ was located in the male or in the female, preformation remained a theory of generation that was essentially sexless, since the new organism was not formed through sexual contact but merely activated that way.

The theory of preformation was first introduced into scientific literature in a monograph on insects published in 1669 by the Dutch naturalist Jan Swammerdam. It immediately won wide acceptance and dominated most of the scientific work done on generation for the next one hundred and fifty years. Some twentieth-century commentators have been aghast at its reception and its longevity. "That such an apparently ridiculous theory was discussed seriously for over a century seems incredible," sniffs Peter Bowler.[20] It has been argued, however – notably by Stephen J. Gould – that the preformationist view of science was not that different from our own, in the sense that preformationists were mechanists who insisted on a material cause for all phenomena, but were hampered by the limited knowledge of their own era.[21]

Preformation also provides excellent proof of how ideological needs may dictate what is perceived regardless of any inherent logic supplied by "facts." The widespread acceptance of the preformation theory suggests that it accorded well with the intellectual outlook of the age in which it circulated. Preformation confirmed not only the existence of God, but also the substantial accuracy of biblical revelation. It enhanced and strengthened the notion of the fixity of species at the same time as it reinforced the mechanistic bias of the era. Preformation stipulated that God had created all individuals of all species at the beginning of time, thus initiating the pattern. Problems of individual development and differentiation were thus reduced to a matter of growth, which was regarded as a mechanical process.

The preformationist notion of how growth occurred was essentially static, in that all stages of development were perceived as identical, except for their size. In other words, the young were understood to be little more than miniaturized versions of their future full-grown selves. (Against this may be set the later models of growth as a process of gradual development through accretion.) This idea was not peculiar to theorists of generation, but existed in the general culture as well. The notion of the child as miniature adult has a lengthy historical pedigree ranging all the way from medieval paintings of children with adult features to the late 1880s when Frances Hodgson Burnett published *Little Lord Fauntleroy*. Anger at the assumption that children are merely small versions of adults constitutes one of the major themes in Dickens's fiction.

The invention of the microscope and the discovery of microscopic life seemed further to confirm the findings of preformation, since it was now evident that minuteness of the type required to imagine germs encased within germs was decidedly possible. The invention of the microscope also signalled the end of the belief in spontaneous generation, which now succumbed to the weight of observation. In 1668, Francesco Redi had demonstrated that maggots do not arise spontaneously from decaying meat but from the eggs laid by adult flies. In yet another illustration of how profitably science and literature may interact, it was said of Redi that he was inspired to perform his experiments on decaying meat by reading Homer's *Iliad*. The description of the Fall of Troy led him to wonder why Homer's heroes were always so anxious to protect the bodies of their slain comrades from flies and worms.[22]

François Jacob notes that the significance of preformation lay in the fact that it marked a change in thinking about the provenance of the child. The germ holding the living organism may have been formed by God at the beginning of time, but that made the future being all the more dependent on the sexual congress of its parents to kickstart the process and so assist in its development. The individual was no longer understood as an isolated and unique creation independent of others. On the contrary, he was now part of the warp and woof of a larger design that included all living beings of his own species, who had been created in the germ along the same pattern at the identical time. Preformation deprived the process of creation of its loneliness, but also of its momentousness.

In addition, the previous tension between invisible inner processes and overpowering external influences was now resolved in favour of what was internal. As Jacob observes:

> The idea of pre-existence fitted in naturally with the concept of species. If the germ preformed in the begetter had been formed at the time of Creation together with all those of its species, no place remained for any outside intervention during generation, for irregularities due to the fantasies of parents or sins against nature. Generations could succeed generations, always identical ...The species became a collection of germs, a reserve fund of copies made on the same pattern.[23]

It was a picture of the living world as contained and static within a fixed framework that was reassuring in its regularity, but also rigid in its insistence on orderly descent and uniformity. Preformation may have explained the continuity of type from one generation to the next, the unity between the parts of an organism, and the orderly differentiation that is observed when a new individual appears. But it could not explain variation, and variation is – to quote Elizabeth Gasking – "so general that no biologist can deny it."[24]

The belief in preformation and the fixity of species persisted throughout the eighteenth century, but not without cracks of skepticism here and there. In 1742 Linnaeus, the most famous and influential of the eighteenth century taxonomists, recognized a variety of toadflax as a new species, and gradually came to abandon his belief that all extant species had been created as-is at the beginning of time. By 1760, he was suggesting that God had merely created a few species in each group and that hybridization had produced many of the other species that he catalogued – an idea that was clearly anathema to preformationists.

Nor was the challenge posed by hybridization limited to plants. The spread of the slave trade in the eighteenth century with its attendant sexual abuses resulted in the birth of children of mixed racial parentage. It began to be noticed that such children tended to inherit from both parents, and that their skin colour, in particular, was often of a blended hue. Could God have foreseen miscegenation at the beginning of time, or approved of it to the extent of creating germs that displayed mixed traits of black and white? (The fixity and distinctness of races was thought to be as permanent and unalterable as that of species.) The existence of children of mixed race focused greater attention on the fact that offspring seem to inherit some features from one parent and some from the other. As the eighteenth century progressed the problem of family likeness became another reason to doubt preformation. A child who resembles both parents casts doubt on the entire theory, since such a blend of hereditary endowment means that the child could not have existed in totality preformed in the germ at the beginning of time.

In 1745, the French mathematician and astronomer Pierre de Maupertuis published *Vénus physique*, which contained an essay called "Une dissertation physique à l'occasion du Nègre Blanc." Maupertuis's essay treated the problem of hereditary traits – in this case albinoism among blacks – remaining hidden through several generations, then suddenly reappearing. The white Negro was an example of this phenomenon, since neither a white mother nor a white father was necessary in order for the trait of white skin to appear. Maupertuis wrote: " . . . Elements which represent the condition of an ancestor rather than the immediate parent may enter into the union forming the embryo and so produce a resemblance to that ancestor rather than to the parent."[25]

In a similar vein, Maupertuis investigated the phenomenon of polydactyly as an inherited trait in a family. He traced a family tree through four generations and produced mathematical evidence to show that the trait of having six fingers was inherited. Evidence of this type of inheritance, which could be passed on to children of either sex by parents of either sex, constituted a severe blow against the theory of preformation.

Some of Maupertuis's theorizing has a decidedly Darwinian ring to it, since his primary interest lay in the mechanics of variation. Maupertuis believed that new forms must arise as the result of chance changes in the form or arrangement of the seminal particles. He also believed that mutations were the ultimate source of novelty. Once a new trait appeared it might become a true variety by repeated generation, or disappear as the result of interbreeding with normal individuals.[26]

Maupertuis's work was largely overlooked because of the eminence of his countryman and contemporary, the naturalist George de Buffon. Buffon was primarily interested in problems of growth and regeneration – Gasking suggests that he came close to inferring the cell theory – whereas Maupertuis had concentrated on the inheritance of variations. On account of the wide influence of Buffon's work, problems of inheritance were dropped from scientific investigation and were not considered important again until after Darwin's *The Origin of Species* had been published.[27]

By the middle of the eighteenth century, preformation had been largely discredited as a viable theory, succumbing to a welter of observable facts – children resembling both parents, the occurrence of deviations, the intermediate appearance of hybrids – that could no longer be ignored. The entire subject of generation and the organization of living matter was in chaos, and would remain so until it was replaced by the notion of reproduction.

The fading of the idea that the individual – or his parts – exists in miniature in the germ was accompanied by the rise of a new ideology which signalled yet another change in the way nature was conceived. The perfecting of the microscope made possible the embryological studies of K. F. Wolff. Wolff, a German physiologist, theorized that the embryo does not exist fully formed in the womb, but develops in a self-determined way out of a mass of undifferentiated tissue. This way of looking at generation has become known as epigenesis, the belief that the embryo develops as a new creation through the action of the environment on the protoplasm. It is growth by incremental stages rather than preformation. Or, in Stephen J. Gould's formulation: "Embryology is addition and differentiation, not mere unfolding."[28] This conception, with its emphasis on the gradual development of the individual in the womb, fitted in perfectly with the new intellectual climate of Romanticism which arose in the late eighteenth century.

Romanticism affected scientific discovery in much the same way as it affected literature and the arts. It expunged the mechanistic outlook of the preceding era, and replaced it with a philosophy which, among other things, defined nature as unruly, wild, and uncontrollable, at the same time decreeing that the individual, not the collective, was the measure of all things.

François Jacob defines the corresponding changes in the scientific world as follows:

> ...At the end of the eighteenth century there was a change in the relations between the exterior and the interior, between the surface and the depth, and between organs and functions of a living being. What became accessible to comparative investigation was a system of relationships in the depth of a living organism designed to make it function. Behind the visible forms could be glimpsed the profile of a secret architecture imposed by the necessity of living.[29]

This redefinition of inner and outer with its increasing emphasis on the inner workings of the individual – an emphasis which in literature and the arts generally was translated into an active focus on the emotions and on psychological development – was in science spurred on by new discoveries in the physiological functions of the body.

Elizabeth Gasking points out that when a scientific subject has produced a secure theory that accords reasonably well with the facts, then that theory is not likely to be influenced by changes in the intellectual climate. A good example of this is Newtonian mechanics, which many Romantic philosophers disapproved of but which remained largely untouched by the new views. In biology, however, where scientific theories were less secure, Romanticism inspired changes that were profound and far-reaching. The German philosophers Herder, Fichte, Schelling, and Hegel saw the universe, not as a machine produced by a Creator who then remained a spectator, but rather as a living whole in which the Spirit or Will was constantly present. The biologists who adopted these philosophical views were called vitalists.

> Many of them regarded it as axiomatic that the phenomena they observed could not be explained by any underlying causal physico-chemical processes. Instead they looked for an explanation of a radically different kind, which had more in common with the Aristotelian idea of a formal cause. Nature could only be understood by studying the diversity of its forms, but these forms were all variations of a limited number of ideal types or archetypes which, like the Platonic idea, were never fully realised in the actual organisms.[30]

It may be imagined, then, that vitalism and mechanism are at two opposite philosophical poles. Vitalism is associated with the mystical tendency in science which sees living things as being invested with a spark of life that is not quantifiable and cannot be reduced to its component parts.[31]

The Romantic philosophers also emphasized that individuals and institutions could not be understood without a knowledge of their historical development. This led to an interest in history generally with a particular emphasis on the history of beliefs, customs, traditions, races and peoples. As far as the natural sciences were concerned this new interest in history translated into a belief that living things too had a history, and the corresponding idea – promoted by examinations of fossils – that animals and plants alive today might differ from those which had existed in earlier times.

The Romantic movement had a profound effect on early nineteenth-century biology. Its insistence on generalized descriptions and explanations in terms of a historical sequence of forms started several fruitful lines of inquiry, most notably embryology. Its effect can be seen in K. F. Wolff's theory that the embryo develops in a self-determined way. Epigenesis and the notion of the progressive elaboration of the fertilized egg cell helped to undermine the earlier belief in preformation.[32]

But not completely. Wolff's observations may have paved the way for the development of cell theory, and his scientific discoveries certainly heralded a new, non-mechanistic outlook on nature, but none of this disproved preformation once and for all. By the 1760s, preformation in a new ovist version had once again become popular, and remained so until the dawn of the nineteenth century. The reason for this was its acceptance by three of the top naturalists of the time, Haller, Bonnet, and Spallanzani. Each scientist, by supporting the theory, encouraged the others to do likewise, and by presenting a united front they convinced most of their contemporaries. The late eighteenth-century version of preformation was known to a large public, and remnants of this belief lasted into the early nineteenth century.

The late eighteenth century also saw a revival of interest in the Great Chain of Being, which was now rethought in terms of the increased diversity of knowledge about geology in general and fossils in particular.

The Chain of Being was originally a Greek method of classification for the natural world. It posited that all living things could be arranged on a metaphorical ladder with the simplest organisms at the bottom and the most complex – Man invariably occupied the apex – at the top. As a philosophical concept the Chain of Being tended to emphasize the unity and interdependence of living beings, as well as their subservience to one Creator. But while the Chain kept species separate and distinct, it did seem to imply a progressive evolution from one step of the ladder to the next.

The Chain's practical value from a historical point of view lay in the fact that it served as the basis for the classification systems of the eighteenth-century naturalists, and as such proved a boon to the study of biology. In its pure form, the Chain of Being reaffirmed the immutability of species, while providing still more proof of the productive potential of God. Yet the necessity of demonstrating and substantiating the deity's creative accomplishment stimulated the study of taxonomy and variation.

Loren Eiseley suggests that because the Chain of Being implied an ascendency from lower forms to more complex ones, eighteenth-century scholars were less shocked by the proximity of apes to Man than their counterparts would be a century later.[33] This was because belief in the fixity of species guaranteed that there could be no perceived blood relationship between man and beast, and so the question of physical kinship could not arise in the way it did later in response to Darwin.

One person to exploit the Chain of Being for his theory was Jean Baptiste Lamarck. Lamarck felt that Nature, ideally, always arranged itself on an ascending scale from the simplest organism to the most complex. He believed that variation consistently proceeds from the rudimentary to the detailed, that it is constantly striving to attain perfection. But this perfection is seldom, if ever, attained, because of the presence of the physical environment, which shifts with time and circumstance, forcing living organisms to adapt in order to survive. This leads to changes in behavior and habit which eventually influence the physical structure of the organism. The abstract perfection of the Chain of Being is thus being constantly undermined by changing environmental circumstances, which force animals into adaptive strategies in order to survive. To account for these adaptive strategies, Lamarck proposed a theory which postulated that environment had a direct effect on heredity. The mechanism which he outlined as leading to the adaptive influence of environment on heredity has come to be known as "the inheritance of acquired characteristics."

The inheritance of acquired characteristics was certainly not original with Lamarck. It is, in fact, one of the most traditional and universal explanations for the workings of heredity, and can be found in the mythologies and popular beliefs of all cultures. The writings of antiquity are replete with the stories of children perpetuating through inheritance the accidents that occurred to their parents. Lamarck erected his system on the possibility of such inheritance, making it the mechanism that explained local transformations and allowed organisms to adapt themselves fully to their surroundings. Even Darwin, who made evolution rest on spontaneous fluctuations in large populations, accepted a form of the inheritance of acquired characteristics through his championing of pangenesis, which permitted external conditions to directly influence hereditary characteristics. It was not until the discovery of germ plasm in the 1880s, which in turn led to the discovery of chromosomes, that the possibility of inheriting acquired characteristics was ever seriously questioned.[34]

Lamarck died in 1829, but during his lifetime a dramatic change had occurred in the way that generation was understood. In fact, the word "generation" had by the nineteenth century begun to fall out of use. It was replaced by "reproduction," a term which incorporated a new way of thinking about the origins of life. In fact, "reproduction" filled the conceptual void so completely that "generation," in the sense of giving life to offspring, has largely fallen out of modern usage.[35] Reproduction confers a past on living things by implicitly linking them to their forebears, their "producers." The word was originally used to designate the phenomenon that occurs in certain animals of regenerating limbs to replace those lost to amputation. In other words, that which had existed previously was re-produced. This sense of the word was eventually expanded by Buffon, writing in 1748, to indicate the generation of living things.[36]

For much of our history – in fact until the Darwinian revolution in the middle of the nineteenth century – the living world was considered as a system controlled from the outside. The concept of reproduction helped to change that by defining the existence of each human being as the direct result of the sexual actions of his or her parents. The physical, mental, and emotional make-up of the individual was now seen to have a direct relationship to the same characteristics in the parents. How this relationship came about biologically was still a mystery at the dawn of the nineteenth century – as indeed it would be at the dawn of the twentieth – but what was now beyond doubt was that a close bond tied children to parents in a way that had not previously been imagined. The physiological lines of heredity had been disentangled to the extent of recognizing a physical, and not merely a legal, a customary, or even a biblical link between the generations. The concept of reproduction conferred a physical past on each living thing, tying the individual to his parents, and beyond his parents to grandparents and ancestors.

Thus, at the beginning of the nineteenth century living creatures were no longer seen as isolated structures standing above and beyond the natural world, but were integrated into nature, the product of generations which had gone before. The attitude towards time itself had changed. The history of the earth was increasingly seen in relation to the history of living things on the earth, and that history, when extrapolated from fossils, seemed increasingly unstable and impermanent. The problem of species had expanded to include questions about the origins of humanity as a whole, about mankind's place within nature, about the reasons for racial difference, and the proper relationship of the various races to one another.

*   *   *

The 1830s, when Dickens first began to publish, was a decade particularly rife with speculation and debate over human origins. Adrian Desmond maintains that the evolutionary theories imported during this decade from France to England had disturbing social and political associations which precluded their being widely accepted in England. The British gentry, already alarmed by the French revolution of 1789, became even more reactionary in the 1830s following the July revolution in Paris in 1830, which had seen revolutionaries co-opting Lamarck's ideas to the service of their own democratic agitation.[37]

Despite the reactionary mood, the new sciences of paleontology and chemistry stimulated inquiry into the history of living things, and most especially into the question of how humans fitted into the natural design. Between 1830 and 1833, Charles Lyell published his three-volume *Principles of Geology*, which cast doubt on the reliability of the Bible as a means of accounting for the geological history of the earth. In 1837 – the year in which Dickens began to serialize *Oliver Twist* – there appeared an expanded five-volume edition of James Cowles Pritchard's *Researches into the Physical History of Man*. This book was concerned with the question of race among humans, which Pritchard attempted to reconcile with scriptural teaching.

The intense and continuing interest in books like William Lawrence's *Lectures* – which had been published and suppressed in 1819[38] – and Pritchard's *Researches* – to say nothing of Robert Chambers's best-selling *Vestiges of the Natural History of Creation*, which appeared in 1844 – all indicate a keen public appetite throughout the early decades of the nineteenth century for more knowledge about the origins of life.

But this fascination with origins and races swamped further inquiries into the nature of heredity, which was now relegated to the specialized domain of horticulturists and animal breeders. While observations about heredity had accumulated and multiplied by the nineteenth century, heredity itself ceased to be an object of scientific investigation. Theories of how it worked and why it worked were vague and unsatisfactory. Scientific researchers in the first half of the century may have focused on questions of human origin, but they did so without any clear sense that such questions were intimately tied to the riddle of hereditary transmission. In François Jacob's formulation, the nineteenth century could contemplate heredity, but it could not analyze it.[39]

The vagueness of nineteenth-century notions about heredity proved a particular handicap to Darwin. In his theory of evolution, successful adaptations are gradually incorporated into the biological make-up of species by means of hereditary transmission. Because the mechanics of heredity were unknown during Darwin's lifetime – despite the fact that Mendel published his laws in the decade immediately following the appearance of *The Origin of Species* – Darwin had difficulty defending his theory against those who charged that "blended" heredity would eradicate any advantages that selection might confer.

Scientific debate of the nineteenth century focused not only on the question of human origins, but also on the mechanics of sexual reproduction, specifically on the role of the male in generation. By this time, the female contribution to the reproductive process was generally acknowledged and understood, but the importance of sperm and the manner in which it interacted with the egg – if, indeed, it did so at all – was still a matter for conjecture and controversy. This debate had serious repercussions for the social interaction of the sexes during the nineteenth century.[40] Since the female role in reproduction was not in dispute, reproduction came to be seen as primarily a female activity and this in turn contributed to the belief in the separate functions of the sexes.

Scientific assumptions about what was "natural" merged with social customs in furthering the division of the sexes along lines assumed to be dictated by biology. The German zoologist Rudolph Leuckart pointed out in 1851 that the differing sex organs of male and female decreed a division of tasks depending on these organs, so that a single individual was scarcely capable of fulfilling both roles with equal facility.[41] This neatly formulates and rationalizes the widespread assumption of inherent biological difference between the sexes which is characteristic of the Victorian era. The male sphere encompassed the public domain, whereas the natural sphere for women was the domestic: women were responsible for procreation, the care and nurturing of children, the maintenance of the household. Dickens laid at his wife's door the entire blame for the fact that they had too many children – nine who survived to adulthood – and her fertility was one of the factors in the couple's eventual separation. Later, he blamed his troubles on his male children, accusing them of shiftlessness and a lack of energy inherited from their mother. But the Victorian understanding of biology contained a paradox. While the woman was thought to be primarily responsible for the processes of generation, it was the man who was assumed to play the primary role in heredity. This notion harks back to the theories of Aristotle and to the doctrine of maternal impressions which held that children most often resemble their fathers, because the mother transfers to the foetus the features of the man she sees at the moment of conception. In Victorian times the father was considered the primary actor in the drama of passing on physical characteristics – although even in this the Victorians were not consistent. Legally, however, there was no doubt about who was the important parent: the father had sole rights over the offspring of any legitimate union. As long as the role of the sperm in reproduction was unclear, Victorian attitudes towards heredity remained a jumble of contradictions and confusions.

At the same time, nineteenth-century literature began to show signs of an ever greater interest in the dramatic possibilities of heredity. The ramifications of the child's hereditary attachment to its parents began to be more and more emphasized. Jane Austen's *Pride and Prejudice*, in which each of the five daughters is a variation on either the silliness of the mother or the cynicism of the father, is just one example of this. The fondness of Victorian fiction for the representative figures of the foundling, the orphan, and the bastard is another.

The orderly world of the seventeenth- and eighteenth-century mechanist had broken down. God might still be said to watch over each individual, but the extent to which He was now understood to be actively responsible for the formation of personality had degenerated to a matter of rhetoric. What J. Hillis Miller has referred to as the "godless" quality of Victorian fiction, in which omniscient authors have perfect knowledge of a world they did not create, is a symptom of the advances in science which I have outlined here.[42] For Victorian authors, tracing resemblances between generations became a way of internalizing the godhead, locating not only the power of creation but also the ability to determine and predict future conduct within the invisible and mysterious processes of biological inheritance.

II

Dickens lived in a society organized along class lines with a hereditary monarch at its apex, and a vast underbelly of disenfranchised poor at its base. He was born in 1812 and died in 1870, and while the decades prior to his birth and in the early part of his life were times of great ferment in scientific circles, this ferment affected relatively small numbers of people.[43] Far more influential in terms of elaborating and disseminating notions of heredity was the popular and literary culture of the time. Fairy tales, legends, ballads, proverbs, superstitions, the heritage of Greek and Roman classical tradition, the teachings of the Bible, the plays of Shakespeare – all of these had an effect on the common perception. This meant that on the subject of heredity, Dickens was heir to a long and influential history of cultural assumptions about the meaning and mechanics of hereditary transmission, without necessarily being conscious of the fact. In this section, I would like to look at some of these assumptions, especially those to be found in the two major sources of western cultural tradition.

The cultural heritage of Western Europe may be loosely divided between the legacy of classical Greece, disseminated by the Roman Empire, and the legacy of the ancient Hebrews, disseminated by the Christian church. These two sources merged in various ways throughout European history and so nourished the wellsprings of modern tradition. The models of heredity advanced by these two cultures were fundamentally opposed – an opposition vitally tied to the fact that the Greeks were pantheistic and the Hebrews monotheistic.

Pantheistic societies, like that of the ancient Greeks, collapse the distinctions between the human and the natural world, so that Man is not viewed as separate from his environment, but as an integral and functional part of it. The mythologies of most peoples are full of legends that assert this type of kinship between species, and most European folklores contain tales of animal brides or husbands, while an entire class of British folk ballad features anthropomorphic animals who are half-human and half-animal. Furthermore, some form of totemic tradition, which defines human beings as descended from animal ancestors, appears to be nearly universal among primitive peoples. Such traditions certainly existed in Britain: the Scottish McCodrum family and the Irish Keneelys claimed seals as the ancestors of their clans.

The belief in crosses between two species was just as common as the belief in crosses between Man and beast. John Locke, the seventeenth-century philosopher, reported seeing a chimera which he asserted to be the offspring of a mouse and a cat. In the mid-East, camels were thought to be especially likely to engage in experimental matings. The giraffe was thought to be a mix of a camel and a leopard, while the mating of a camel and a sparrow produced an ostrich.[44]

As these examples suggest, the most important way in which popular belief integrates the human animal into the natural world is to imagine his or her sexual union with individuals of different species. The resulting offspring partake equally of the characteristics of both their parents, thus erasing all lines of integrity between one species and another. The centaurs, satyrs, and minotaurs of Greek mythology are half-human and half-animal, personifying a view of the world which defines nature as fluid and multiple, a place where all mergers are possible. At the same time, these dual creatures are not examples of "blended" heredity. Their two halves are kept recognizably distinct, one part welded to the other. Integration consists of the fact that the two disparate selves exist within the same entity.

The belief that the categories of nature are infinitely dissoluble is closely tied to the creed of magical transformation, which forms an essential part of Greek mythology – as indeed it does of most pantheistic mythologies. The possibility of unlimited transformation implies a worldview that is infinitely metamorphic and pliable, lacking a sense of fixed division between entities. Such an outlook rests on the assumption that all objects are in a constant state of potential change, which means that magical transformation undermines the supremacy and inviolability of the human form by decreeing it to be no more than another shape to be shifted.

The existence of such metamorphic beliefs means that classical Greek mythology eliminates heredity altogether as a significant factor in the development of life. This is in keeping with the mythology's presentation of other biological processes as floating free of all temporal and physical constraints. In the Greek myths birth may occur in the normal way – or it may not – and it may be defined as a female activity – or it may not. Thus Athena springs full-grown and fully armored from Zeus' head, and to retaliate for this appropriation of feminine function, Zeus' wife Hera conceives and delivers the god Hephaestus by herself. (Both of these instances might be called early examples of parthenogenesis.) Cadmus sows the ground with dragon's teeth and a race of armed men is engendered in the furrows.

In other words, all objects are equally viable and equally capable of engendering life. Transformation from one mode of being into another is not only possible but universally imminent. Where magical metamorphosis is the mechanism underlying development, heredity – that is, the relationship of transmission from parent to child – loses all validity. The fact that an individual may be instantly transformed into a star, a spider, a stone, a tree at the whim of the gods – the fact that the gods may just as easily transform themselves – means that the form one inhabits is not understood as a constant handed down from parent to child, but is viewed instead as an interim casing perpetually on the brink of being sloughed off. In addition, the fact that sexual contact between humans and animals, or even between humans and the elements – I am thinking of the shower of golden rain in the legend of Zeus and Danaë – may result in offspring, means that hereditary factors are worthless as a means of indicating genealogy or origin. The idea that like must consistently reproduce like, or that there is a family connection between the thing engendered and its progenitor is totally foreign to a scheme of creation which defines all objects as equally vital and equally fertile. In a pantheistic vision of the world, magical transformation takes the place of hereditary transmission.

Leonard Barkan suggests that metamorphosis renders all things numinous, designating every object in the universe as containing not merely a spark of life, but also a mystical and metaphorical meaning.[45] Myths which seek to explain origins do so in terms of how an individual – invariably a human – was transformed into something else: Arachne into a spider, Narcissus into a flower. Once transformed, the spider goes on to become the ancestor of generations of spiders, as the flower does of generations of flowers, but we know that this constant reproduction of like by like is not inevitable, that should some god will another transformation, the spider may be returned to her original human shape or may even be transformed into another shape. Yet because the original ancestor is designated as human, there exists an ancillary suggestion in myths of origin that while the human form may be transmuted into any number of other forms, it nevertheless supplies the prototype for the rest of the natural world. All objects are thus personified and humanized at their source.

Magical transformation obliterates the significance – and the inevitability – of life's processes. Birth and death may occur in the Greek myths, but the existential impact of these events is muted by the idea of progression from one shape into another. In Gillian Beer's words, "Metamorphosis bypasses death. The concept expresses continuance, survival, the essential self transposed but not obliterated by transformation."[46]

Allied to this subversion of actual biological processes is the obliteration of all notions which define time as a historical juggernaut aimed into the future. Chronological conceptions of time are closely tied to hereditary imperatives, and the world of the ancient Greeks and Romans took little note of such temporal constraints. Instead, classical tradition viewed time as infinitely malleable. It may be expanded or contracted, stopped altogether or simply collapsed into one temporal unit so that past, present, and future become one. For example, according to Roman laws of succession in the Augustan Age, the son was considered to be his own father for purposes of inheritance. He was designated as "heres sui ipsius" (his own heir), and so entitled to take his father's place without a handover of property or legacy. He, in effect, became his own father.[47]

In his essay on time and the chronotope in the novel, Mikhail Bakhtin notes that in the early Greek adventure novels, time is not defined as an element which brings change, either internal or external. The plot begins when the hero and heroine meet and fall in love; they then go through a series of trials and adventures, which do not take place in chronological time, since there is no developmental effect. Hero and heroine do not age, nor do their personalities undergo any alteration because of the experiences they have just lived through. They are the same both essentially and chronologically at the end of their adventures as they were at the beginning.[48]

The action in these adventure tales is governed by chance. Protagonists in classical literature seldom take the initiative. They rarely even fall in love on their own. (Eros is responsible for that.) Instead they are the pawns of fate, at the mercy of divine whim or chance occurrence. Bakhtin relates this emphasis on chance to subsequent developments in the European novel:

> Whenever Greek adventure-time appears in the subsequent development of the European novel, initiative is handed over to chance, which controls meetings and failures to meet – either as an impersonal, anonymous force in the novel or as fate, as divine foresight, as romantic "villains" or romantic "secret benefactors."[49]

Bakhtin mentions Walter Scott's historical novels as examples, but he might as easily have suggested Dickens, whose reliance on coincidence and accident is just as marked.

The classical tradition's abrogation of the imperatives of time, with its attendant diminution of the importance of human genealogy, flies in the face of Judeo-Christian belief. Shape-changing means that the human form is less important than its potential for infinite variability. Such an idea is untenable in a monotheistic conception of the world which defines the human body as the sanctified replica of the divine corpus.

The Hebrew Bible is an account of the relationship of a particular people to its God, a relationship traced back to its beginnings through genealogy and projected forward through descent. It is the first elaborated account of a monotheistic religion, and the relationship which it establishes between the children of Israel and their God is a familial one. God creates Man in his own image. Genesis 1: 27 in fact stipulates that He creates both man and woman in His image, and exhorts them to be fruitful and multiply. The human relationship to the deity is thus established on the basis of physical resemblance. Moreover, the human resemblance to God is the result of an act of parthenogenetic creation. One of the attributes of the Jewish God is that he is a father to the children of Israel, and this attribute underlines the state of kinship between Man and his Maker.

The connection between God and Israel speaks to the issue of biological paternity in another way as well. It is a relationship based entirely on faith, a fact underlined by the prohibition against graven images which ensures the abstract quality of the Hebrew conception of monotheism. In this it echoes the actual relationship of fathers to their offspring, a relationship which until the twentieth century was based on no verifiable evidence, and so required a leap of faith on the part of both fathers and their progeny to cement the bond of paternity. (The severity of biblical laws against female promiscuity, and especially against adultery, are directly related to the male need to ensure paternity by restricting a woman's sexual access to other men.) It is thus possible to assert, as Thomas Laqueur does in *Making Sex*, that the Judaic insistence that God cannot be seen but must be accepted on faith is analogous to the blind faith required to assume that a given man is the father of a given child. Fatherhood, Freud had argued in *Moses and Monotheism*, is a supposition based on inference, while motherhood is based on knowledge derived from the "lowly senses." Fatherhood is thus, according to Freud, the conquest of intellectuality over sensuality, of the refined and abstract over the sensory and material.[50]

The frequent genealogies of the Hebrew Bible expand the paternal metaphor still further by broadening it into a relationship that includes all human societies. These genealogies reaffirm the implicit message of the story of Genesis, namely that all nations, tribes, clans, families, and individuals are ultimately descended from a single paternal deity. This type of relationship, which establishes kinship by tracing lines of descent, has an inclusive familial function in the sense that it defines all male members of a given group – artisans, musicians, poets – as part of a hereditary family by virtue of their station in life. "All those in hereditary professions were linked through some ancient ancestor and whoever joined such a group was as a matter of course included in the genealogy even if he did not actually stem from its line."[51] The New Testament writers for their part appropriated genealogies as a means of justifying Jesus as the Messiah by establishing his descent from the House of David, the hereditary line which, according to Isaiah's prophecy, would give birth to the Messiah.

Genealogies, then, despite the seeming lack of imaginative scope permitted by long dry lists of family names, actually carry a pronounced ideological punch, and as such have metaphoric uses when adapted to fiction. Dickens exploits this type of genealogy in *The Old Curiosity Shop*, his most obvious attempt to portray apotheosis. By tracing the saintly Little Nell back to the mother and grandmothers who preceded her, women who were all noted for their virtuous goodness, Dickens reverses the thrust of the Old Testament genealogies, which tend to point backwards to the greatness of a vanished ancestor. By suggesting that the highest point of this exceptional female line is achieved in the person of Little Nell – for whom all previous generations were just preparation – Dickens allies himself with the ideological focus of the New Testament genealogies, which suggest that the outstanding personalities of past generations anticipate the arrival of the Messiah in the present. In this way, Dickens draws a subtle connection between his heroine and the figure of Jesus.

The biblical insistence on genealogies is closely allied to its obsessive concern with time. Biblical characters are constantly identified by their ages. We know how old Sarah was when God opened her womb (ninety) and the age of her husband Abraham at the same time (one hundred). We know how old Methuselah was at death (969 years). This concern with time is closely linked to the biblical notions of generation and heredity. Biblical time is chronological and historical, never cyclical. Time moves in one direction only, towards the future, and its advance is measured in generations. The opening verses from Exodus – "And Joseph died, and all his brethren, and all that generation ... Now there arose up a new king over Egypt, which knew not Joseph" (Exod. 1: 6–8) – represent an unequivocal statement of the passage of time, and the beginning of a new episode in the historical chronicle.[52]

In the Bible people are born and they die. The span of their lives may be hyperbolically extended to hundreds of years, but once they die they are dead. In contrast to the mythologies of pantheistic peoples, there is little explicit mention of an afterlife in the Hebrew Testament. In Greek myths, human beings either go to Hades after death, or they are transformed into something else – Cadmus and his wife become serpents. In the Hebrew Bible, only the actual human life span is important, and immortality is achieved through children, through the multiplication of seed and the proliferation of descendants. Fertility and sterility are matters for divine intervention. God will step in and open a womb when necessary – as it is in the case of three of the four matriarchs – and He will bless his favourites by making their seed as plentiful as the grains of sand.

The Hebrew Bible is also the source of the western belief in hereditary taint, best expressed in the language of the second commandment: "I the Lord thy God am a jealous God, visiting the iniquity of the fathers upon the children unto the third and fourth generation of them that hate me" (Exod. 20: 5 or Deut. 5: 9). This type of curse assumes that the state of culpability, if not the act itself, may be transmitted from parent to child through more than one generation. A slightly different logic underlies the injunction that "A bastard shall not enter into the congregation of the Lord; even to their tenth generation shall they not enter into the congregation of the Lord for ever" (Deut. 23: 2). Here the problem is related to the uncertain hereditary components represented by the offspring of an unlawful union. Here too, however, the stain of the initial transgression is transmissible to several generations.

The Christian doctrine of Original Sin takes this view of inherited stain and generalizes it to all of humanity. Since Adam is the father of mankind, when he falls, the penalty of his disobedience is visited upon all the succeeding generations of his descendents. The thumbnail definition of Original Sin in *Brewer's Dictionary of Phrase and Fable* makes the hereditary connection explicit:

> [Original Sin is] that corruption which is born with us, and is the inheritance of all the offspring of Adam. Theology teaches that as Adam was founder of his race, when Adam fell the taint and penalty of his disobedience passed to all his posterity.[53]

Only through the Second Coming of the Messiah, in the person of Jesus, will this hereditary culpability be lifted. Or, in Gillian Beer's formulation: "... Man – the son of God, [is] cast out of his inheritance by his forebears' sin and restored to it by the intercession of the immediate heir."[54] What Beer is enunciating here is one of the prototypical plots of heredity, the plot of concealed aristocratic lineage, in which the protagonist, having been separated from his noble parents at birth, grows up in a degenerate state, until the machinations of the plot eventually restore him to his rightful patrimony.

The hereditary drama as played out in monotheistic religions centers on the conflict between free will and determinism. I will take my example from Judaism, but the same dilemma occurs whenever the exigencies of belief in divine intercession are confronted with the realities imposed by the physical fact of heredity. The Bible claims that it is the immediate action of the Creator's will which influences and moulds Man and his destiny. Echoing this, the Talmud unequivocally announces that marriages are preordained: forty days before a child is born its mate is decided upon. At the same time, however, the Talmud lays down laws as to what a man should look for in a prospective bride, insisting that no hereditary faults should run in her family. The Talmud discourages the marriage of the physically unfit, since the children of such a union are born weak, and marriage between a man and woman who are either very short or very tall is discouraged, lest the children be born either too short or too tall. The Talmud also urges that a man seeking a wife should marry the daughter of a man of character, because as the tree, so the fruit.

All these prescriptions and caveats point to the central tension between free will and determinism. If the match has been preordained by heaven, then it is not clear why so much effort should go into finding the proper unblemished spouse. Obviously, then, the fact that something has been preordained does not preclude the need for human intervention in the choice of options. This type of dilemma – summed up in Judaism by the paradoxical aphorism, "everything is predestined but the will is free" – is played out in Dickens's novels in slightly different terms. There, the element of determinism is located in the bloodline that is passed from one generation to the next, while free will resides in the ability of the individual to surpass his or her hereditary endowment and so disarm its prescriptive grip.

In the foregoing I have attempted to simplify the complex metaphor of hereditary transmission by dividing it into two abstract models. The first model, informed by a pantheistic and animistic worldview, is amorphous, fluid, and multiple, recognizing no boundaries of time or of substance, and no distinction between the living and the inanimate. In this version the characteristics that we would normally ascribe to heredity are subsumed by the process of magical transformation. Human development is here confounded with fantasy, linked to the irrational, associated with the individualistic, and defined by the purely imaginative. Time is presented as circular and regenerative. What dies is eventually reborn.

The second hereditary model is a more realistic presentation tied to actual life processes. In this version heredity is inextricably linked to chronology and to historical development. Here the distinction between categories is steadfastly maintained, while heredity itself is perceived as an internal process, immune to outside forces, progressive, inviolable, deterministic. This second model speaks to issues of family, of inclusion (or exclusion), of succession. Where the first model presents human nature as individual, unfettered, spontaneous, multiple, and blessed with infinite possibility, the second model presents human nature as part of a whole. It is a portrait of Man in his connections, as part of society, part of a generation, part of a genealogy and a history, part of a class and a race. In this second model, heredity stands as a metaphor for the stability of orderly succession, for the rational apprehension of the universe and of humankind's place within it.

It will be my contention throughout the following chapters that both of these models of heredity, simplified polarities though they may be, can be found within the great Victorian edifice of Charles Dickens's novels, where they clash and contend, or – more rarely – complement each other. I will further argue that mediating between these two philosophical constructs, giving weight first to one and then to the other side of the equation, are the scientific beliefs of Dickens's time, such notions as preformation, blended heredity, and reproduction, culminating in the evolutionary theories of Darwin in the last decade of Dickens's life.

Part I
Heredity and the Individual

2
The Inheritance of Goodness: the Early Books

For most of his career, Dickens was fascinated by the subject of heredity. Allusions to heredity occur frequently – almost obsessively – in the novels: "He had stamped his likeness on a little boy," "My girls are pictures of their dear mother," both from *The Pickwick Papers*. "Humanity is a happy lot when we can repeat ourselves in others" (*Barnaby Rudge*). "In this daughter the mother lived again" (*The Old Curiosity Shop*). "He would be as like his father as it's possible to be, if he was not so like his mother too" (*David Copperfield*). And these few quotes barely skim the top of the barrel. Phrases such as "the express image," "the living copy," "the speaking likeness" occur over and over again, defining the relationship between parents and children as one of near-perfect duplication.

Dickens's hereditary views seem to have been influenced by the various remnants of earlier beliefs which were still current in the nineteenth century. The doctrine of maternal impressions, for instance, appears in *Barnaby Rudge*, and there is mention of the inheritance of acquired characteristics in the novels as well. In *The Pickwick Papers*, Dickens describes a meeting of the United Grand Junction Ebenezer Temperance Association. One of the newly reformed tee-totallers is "Betsey Martin, widow, one child and one eye. Goes out charring and washing, by the day; never had more than one eye, but knows her mother drank bottled stout and shouldn't wonder if that caused it . . ." (PP, 547). This is clearly intended as a joke and is in line with a subsequent reference to the deleterious effect of alcohol on the longevity of wooden legs. Yet, despite the widespread acceptance of the inheritance of acquired characteristics during his lifetime, Dickens made very little use of this belief in his novels.

His preferred hereditary models tended to be "hard," that is he liked to conceive of heredity as being impervious to external influence.

However, there was another aspect of Lamarck's theory which did find an answering echo in Dickens's philosophy. This is the notion, derived from the Chain of Being, that there is an inherent perfectibility in Nature, a perfectibility which exists despite the repeated subversions of time and environment. This vision of an immaculate ideal encrusted in the dross of ordinary human life lies very close to the heart of the Dickensian universe.

The theories of the deists also found their way into Dickens's fiction, and their influence can be felt most strongly in his literary style. The Dickensian world is one in which inanimate objects are endowed with a vitality indistinguishable from that of living beings. And the opposite is true as well. The sort of mechanistic imagery that confuses animal and machine can also be found in Dickens's fiction, for instance in the description of the elephantine factories in *Hard Times*. There is even an allusion to the deists' Watchmaker God, embodied in the clock in *Dombey and Son* which ticks away young Paul's life. As John Carey suggests, Dickens's imagination was most engaged by "the border country between people and things" and he tended to increase the population of this region by likening inanimate objects to people and people to inanimate objects.[1]

But the most striking thing about Dickens's conception of heredity is that he tends to define moral qualities as being hereditable. In the early novels, virtue, grace, and goodness are hereditable characteristics, amenable, like blue eyes, to being passed on from parent to child. Evil, on the other hand, tends to die out with the malefactor, and is seldom passed on to progeny. That Dickens conceived of moral qualities as being transmissible is not really surprising, since, as Juliet McMaster points out, he tended to equate morality with looks.[2] It being demonstrable that physical characteristics are passed on from parent to child, it follows that the moral qualities which those characteristics represent should be equally the stuff of hereditary transmission.

Dickens's tendency to define moral qualities as hereditable can be seen in its purest form in the novels which feature children as protagonists. These novels, taken chronologically, also serve as the best illustration of how Dickens's views on heredity changed over the course of his career until, under the impetus of the Darwinian revolution, heredity ceased to play any role in his depiction of the formation of the self.

Oliver Twist

The first avatar of childish goodness in Dickens's novels is, of course, Oliver Twist. Oliver is a foundling – or to use Dickens's ironic pun, a "fondling" – born in a parish workhouse to an unwed mother who dies within hours of his birth. As far as the world is concerned, Oliver has no identity other than the one imposed on him by external circumstances: he is illegitimate, illiterate, and impoverished, just another "item of mortality," a member of the vast Victorian underclass of the disenfranchised and marginalized. Oliver is brought up in the workhouse and charged to the care of the parish. At the age of nine he is put out to work. He runs away to London, where he falls in among thieves, prostitutes, and murderers. Yet despite these unpromising beginnings, Oliver Twist remains the quintessential little gentleman, a model of honesty and integrity whose character is untouched by his environment and unblemished by the slightest hint of moral stain.

Oliver Twist is a fairy tale in which the magical element is located within the domain of heredity. It is his biological inheritance which protects Oliver from the corrupting effects of his surroundings, and it is this same biological inheritance which ensures his happy ending, safely ensconced within the middle-class milieu of his parents.

Dickens signals the importance of heredity very early in the novel. In the second chapter, he describes Oliver on his ninth birthday: "Nature or inheritance had implanted a good sturdy spirit in Oliver's breast." Nature, here made synonymous with inheritance, is no sooner invoked than it is put in opposition to external circumstances: "It [the sturdy spirit] had had plenty of room to expand, thanks to the spare diet of the establishment, and perhaps to this circumstance may be attributed [Oliver's] having any ninth birthday at all" (OT, 49). In other words, the mysterious force designated as inheritance or nature is from the beginning presented as shielding Oliver from the vicissitudes of life.

Oliver may be described as an "item of mortality," but heredity endows him with a predetermined invincibility which cancels out the implications of that phrase. Because of this Oliver requires neither education nor experience to instruct him; he is incorruptible from birth. Not even exposure to the malignant Fagin can shake his imperviousness to temptation, and this despite the fact that the other boys in Fagin's troop, whose personal histories are as little exalted as Oliver's but who lack the distinguishing features of his biological inheritance, have taken to stealing without compunction. This fact illustrates the negative side of viewing heredity as the sole determinant of personality – its dependence on chance. If heredity is destiny, it is a destiny wholly determined by luck. Genealogy may comfort the dispossessed, but only if their lineage is more distinguished than their station. Without Oliver's exalted bloodline to immunize and protect them, Fagin's other boys turn out to be no more than criminals-in-waiting.

Oliver, on the other hand, exists in virtual isolation from his environment. Unlike his friend Dick who dies as a consequence of early privation, Oliver does not succumb to the physical consequences of the neglect he suffers in the workhouse. Nor does he lose his innocence prematurely, like the Artful Dodger, who is Oliver's age but acts much older due to the hardening and aging effects of a life of crime. Furthermore, all the other positive characters in the novel turn out to be either close friends of Oliver's parents or related to them by blood, thus forming a charmed circle of the privileged to which Oliver inherently belongs. Oliver's parents, we learn at the end, were good people acting out of the best motives; their love for each other was a true love, despite the fact that circumstances prevented their marrying.

The fact that Oliver is illegitimate puts an interesting twist on what would otherwise be a most unimaginative portrayal of virtue. In fact, Dickens seems to insist that Oliver's goodness is directly linked to his illegitimacy, a link which is strengthened when it becomes apparent that one of the novel's three villains, Oliver's half-brother Monks – whose moral and physical degeneracy is emphasized – is the legitimate child of his parents. (Oliver's bastardy is contrasted as well with that of the obnoxious charity-boy Noah Claypole who "could trace his genealogy all the way back to his parents" (OT, 77).)

The fact that Oliver's father was not married to his mother means that Oliver himself constitutes the living proof of his parents' sexual transgression. In the novel's words, he is "the offspring of a guilty and most miserable love" (OT, 440). Oliver's very existence is therefore defined as inherently tainted, at least according to the accepted views of religion, law, and society. But all of these constitute nothing more than "the feeble censure of the world" (OT, 457); they are definitions of morality imposed from the outside. The novel places this external morality in opposition to the inner workings of heredity, which is defined as the physical transmission to Oliver of his parents' moral essence. Oliver inherits what his parents were, not what they did. Virtue that has been biologically transmitted is inviolable; it cannot be affected by external circumstances.

But why is Oliver distinguished by this sort of inheritance? Why is his illegitimacy more privileged – and more emphasized – than that of the novel's other children? One answer has to do with class. The other children in the workhouse and in Fagin's school, most of whom may be assumed to be just as illegitimate as Oliver, all descend from the lower classes, so that they grow up within the milieu of their parents. But Oliver is deracinated when placed in such degraded circumstances. He is by right – that is, by biological right, by the right of his bloodline – a member of the middle class.[3] What Oliver inherits from his parents is more than just their moral essence, it is their moral essence as defined by their social class. Virtue in *Oliver Twist* is a middle-class characteristic, bound up with such traits as respectability, honesty, hard work, personal honor, and a good command of English.

Yet Oliver's virtue is portrayed as more transcendent than this. What seems to bestow grace on Oliver is the fact that his parents loved each other, and that he is the product of that love. This sets him apart from his half-brother Monks, who is the offspring of the father's unholy (because coerced) – but legal – union with Monks's mother. Monks is legitimate, evil, and degenerate; Oliver is a bastard, but good and innocent.

That it is love which accounts for the distinction between the half-brothers is not as fanciful or sentimental a notion as it may at first appear. The Victorians assumed that such matters as the state of mind of the parents and the degree of their affection for one another at the time of conception had a bearing on the personality of the engendered child.[4] The fact that Oliver's parents loved each other makes their son a love child in the full sense of the word, with the result that, shielded by the grace of his heredity, Oliver emerges from the near-starvation and brutalization of the workhouse, from the miserliness and mistreatment of his employers, and from the company of thieves, prostitutes, and murderers, unscathed and unscarred.

This means that heredity, as it is presented in *Oliver Twist*, is a biological process of supernatural potential. Oliver is what he has inherited. Everything about his personality, everything about his history is dependent on and has been predetermined by the virtue which he has inherited. Dickens made clear in his preface to the novel that Oliver is intended to be a figure of grace: " . . . I wished to show, in little Oliver, the principle of Good surviving through every adverse circumstance and triumphing at last."[5] In other words, Oliver is to be a symbolic protagonist, functioning within a realistic framework. This means that the grace bestowed on Oliver is not to be understood as a metaphysical construct, however much it may be an allegorical one. Dickens never suggests that Oliver's transcendence springs spontaneously from the hand of God. Instead he makes it a matter of biology, thereby locating it within the sphere of human interaction – and what is more to the point, of human sexual interaction.

Nevertheless, the contradiction between the supernatural and the realistic persists, despite Dickens's attempts to account for Oliver's nature through human agency. The magical qualities which Dickens attributes to heredity – its ability to shield and protect, its perpetuation of the good despite a moral vacuum – suggest a metaphysical construction imposed on a physical process. This uneasy alliance is not far removed from the vitalism of those late eighteenth- and early nineteenth-century scientists who were inspired by Romanticism. Vitalism assumed the existence of a vital force in living things that was distinct from all physical and chemical processes. This mysterious force controlled the form and development of the organism. Vitalism suggested that metaphysical factors lay beyond and above the rational and material processes of heredity. Dickens developed a similar belief about the mysterious forces at play in generation and translated it into a doctrine that I would call mystical heredity.

Mystical heredity is the intuitive apprehension of kinship on the part of characters who have no other rational reason to believe that they are related. In *Oliver Twist* mystical heredity occurs in the scene where Oliver reacts with instinctive emotion to the portrait of his mother hanging on the wall of his bedroom at Mr Brownlow's house. Oliver has no way of knowing that this is a portrait of his mother, but the mysterious workings of heredity are enough to make him sense a connection. Says Oliver, " . . . The eyes look so sorrowful; and where I sit, they seem fixed upon me . . . as if it was alive and wanted to speak to me, but couldn't" (OT, 129).[6]

This same chapter ends with a description of Oliver's uncanny resemblance to the portrait. He is called its "living copy": "The eyes, the head, the mouth; every feature was the same. The expression was, for the instant, so precisely alike, that the minutest line seemed copied with an accuracy which was perfectly unearthly" (OT, 132). The portrait of Oliver's mother serves as a trope for the relationship between art and life. Oliver's mother is dead, but she lives on in her portrait in much the same way as she lives on in Oliver, who is the living copy of both the portrait and the woman whose likeness the portrait represents. Portraits in Dickens's fiction do the work of genealogy by demonstrating the persistence of features from one generation to the next. In this manner, Dickens expands the term "reproduction" to its fullest metaphoric potential. "Reproduction" had supplanted "generation" in the late eighteenth century as the term used to denote procreation, and the dual sense of the word, encompassing both biological and artistic re-creation was well-established by Dickens's time.[7] (The extent to which Dickens connected portraiture to reproductive issues can be seen in *Bleak House*, where a failed likeness of Sir Leicester Dedlock is referred to as "a fearful abortion" (BH, 853).)

Dickens's figurative use of the concept of reproduction relates the biological activity of engendering life to the artistic faculty of reproducing it. By insisting on the resemblance of living beings to the portraits of their progenitors, Dickens highlights the interplay between life and art, and raises philosophical concerns about the relationship of facsimile to original, and about the value of art as an imitation of life. Portraits are permanent records of family features which are simultaneously preserved through time and shielded from the ravages of time. Heredity is the natural equivalent of portraiture, preserving family features over the course of generations and maintaining them intact despite the passing of time.

Dickens thus adapts the concept of reproduction to his own ends by extending it into a visual pun. In his fiction he frequently uses family portraits not merely as signals of hereditary relationships, but also as decoders of the mysteries of connection. Portraits in the novels often hint at heretofore unacknowledged family ties, thus making visible on canvas the hidden bonds which link one character to another. This is especially evident in such novels as *Oliver Twist* and *Bleak House*, where the protagonist is ignorant of his or her origins.

The portrait of Oliver's mother is the first of several such genealogically significant portraits in the novels. But in this case Dickens adds an interesting complication: the portrait of Oliver's mother was painted by Oliver's father, thus enhancing the procreative symbolism of a portrait which not only serves to identify an unknown son, but also ensures that the mother's features will remain forever fresh in his memory. By this act of reproduction, the father collapses the distinction between artistic and biological productivity, a procreative duality that is given yet another twist, when Dickens, at the end of the novel, assigns to himself as narrator the role of a painter. There he speaks of "painting" Rose Maylie as "the life and joy of the fireside circle" and of "painting" the happy love that exists between Rose and her dead sister's child (OT, 479). The irony of using the verb "to paint" in this context is obvious. Neither of the two things which the narrator would like to paint can be rendered visually because they are abstractions. They require painting in words not pictures. Yet through the verb "painting" one art form is melded into another and both are related to artistic representation and to the engendering mind of a male author.

Artistic reproduction is the transferring of resemblance from one medium to another. Biological reproduction is the transferring of resemblance from one generation to another. In all of Dickens's depictions of the hereditary relationship, resemblance is the key element. In a case like that of *Oliver Twist*, where heredity is so vital in determining the protagonist's personality and protecting him from the evil effects of the life he leads and the company he keeps, Dickens insists on his resembling both parents (OT, 438–9). Oliver's resemblance to his mother is so strong that it is evident to Mr Brownlow, Oliver's protector, as soon as he lays eyes on the boy for the first time. What is even more astonishing is that Mr Brownlow had never actually met Oliver's mother but knew her features from a portrait.

Yet Oliver's physical resemblance to his father is no less striking. "Even when I first saw [Oliver] in all his dirt and misery, there was a lingering expression in his face that came upon me like a glimpse of some old friend flashing on one in a vivid dream" (OT, 438). Again, the speaker is Mr Brownlow, but this time the reference is to Oliver's father, who had been his old friend. What is more, the villain Monks realizes that Oliver is his half-brother through being struck by the boy's resemblance to their common father (OT, 439), even though, again, Monks had never laid eyes on Oliver before.

This emphasis on the physical resemblance between generations is Dickens's favourite device for indicating hereditary relationships. So important is resemblance to him as a way of demonstrating kinship that he often appears to be exaggerating its extent beyond the realm of the probable. Such a strong resemblance to both parents as we are asked to believe existed between Oliver and his mother and father may seem very unlikely. Yet, in this instance, Dickens is not indulging his penchant for imaginative exaggeration, but accurately reflecting the beliefs of his own time.

The replicating likeness described in *Oliver Twist* is symptomatic of the confusion prevalent throughout the nineteenth century on the subject of heredity. The theory of blended heredity – which was essentially an attempt to account for the contribution of both sexes to the biological endowment of their offspring – suggested that children represented amalgams or alloys of the characteristics of their parents. Each parent was thought to pass on all of his or her characteristics through the blood, and the resulting child was therefore a blend of the two endowments. As late as 1895, Eduard von Hartmann was writing in his book *The Sexes Compared* that during pregnancy the father's blood, containing all his qualities, mixed permanently with the blood of the mother, who then passed the mixed blood on to the fetus.[8] Such a conception of heredity presupposes carbon-copy resemblance, which is another reason why this type of duplication is so often linked in Dickens's novels to its closest artistic analogue – portraiture.

Physical resemblance is the most obvious manifestation of family connection. Of all the qualities which may be passed from parent to child, the one about which there can be the least empirical doubt is looks. It is clear to all who have eyes to see that there is a similarity of feature between parents and children. The problem for the naturalists of Dickens's time, who had no conception of genes or particulate inheritance, was how to account for this perpetuation of features. Scientific opinions during Dickens's youth favoured theories of fixity and immutability. This was a holdover from the generally accepted eighteenth-century belief – enunciated, but later abandoned by Linnaeus – that the number of species had not changed since the Creation.

Hereditary endowment was therefore seen as the means of maintaining, stabilizing, and perpetuating immutability. Belief in heredity's fixed properties was so firmly established that a naturalist like William Lawrence, otherwise an advocate of variation in nature, could nonetheless write: "The offspring of sexual unions is marked with all the bodily characteristics of the parents."[9] Hereditary transmission, which maintained and stabilized characteristics from generation to generation, was therefore thought to perpetuate family features more or less intact, while the idea that heredity represented a blending or fusing of the traits of both parents would account for the fact that Oliver simultaneously resembles both his mother and his father.

Resemblance is also related to another aspect of Dickens's fictional technique. As Juliet McMaster points out in *Dickens the Designer*, for Dickens, appearances are synonymous with moral qualities, an equation of inner and outer states which Dickens borrows from folk tale. Thus, beauty is equated with goodness, ugliness with depravity, and a character's external features serve as a reliable guide to his or her inner essence[10] (for instance, the description of Florence, the heroine of *Dombey and Son*, "whose guileless heart was mirrored in the beauty of her face" (DS, 320)). It should come as no surprise, then, that Oliver, despite his many experiences of hardship and misery, remains sweet and innocent, just as he remains a beautiful child, uncoarsened and unspoiled by life's depredations. Oliver's physical beauty is the outer sign of his inner grace.

That Oliver's beauty bespeaks a genteel and gracious parentage is made manifest through the machinations of Dickens's plot, which is primarily concerned with relocating Oliver within his proper genealogical niche. In this sense, the novel constitutes a journey backwards. Dickens subtitles *Oliver Twist*, "the parish boy's progress," but the only progress he describes is one which turns back on itself by returning the protagonist to his roots. At the same time, Oliver's various adventures are merely steps on the way towards externalizing an inner reality, which is the reality of his essential nobility. The world at large must eventually acknowledge the dispossessed orphan's rightful place in society. That place has been his all along by virtue of his inner nature, but it has been obscured by external circumstances. The novel is thus a tale of hidden origin, culminating in the restoration of the outcast to his proper station. As such it sets up a tension between inner and outer states, between what is essence and what is appearance that testifies to Dickens's early understanding of human identity as a thing innate and inborn.

Oliver's speech and moral qualities are all portrayed as part of his essential self, a self which is eclipsed by the unfortunate circumstances into which Oliver is born. These circumstances dictate how the workhouse foundling is treated by those around him. External circumstances may have no bearing on internal identity, which has been fixed at birth, but they do nevertheless constitute a form of identity, an identity imposed from the outside. The relationship of the outer world to the essential self is symbolized in the novel –

as it is elsewhere in Dickens's fiction – by clothing, as, for instance, in the following description of Oliver soon after his birth:

> What an excellent example of the power of dress young Oliver Twist was! Wrapped in the blanket which had hitherto formed his only covering, he might have been the child of a nobleman or a beggar; – it would have been hard for the haughtiest stranger to have fixed his station in society. But now that he was enveloped in the old calico robes, which had grown yellow in the same service, he was badged and ticketed, and fell into his place at once – a parish child – the orphan of a workhouse – the humble half-starved drudge – to be cuffed and buffeted through the world, – despised by all, and pitied by none.   (OT, 47)

Like speech and good manners, clothing is an indicator of social status, but unlike the first two, clothing represents disposable identity, a matter of things being put on or taken off. Clothes are a false indicator of the essential self because they may disguise as well as reveal, and they are infinitely malleable. More than one person may dress in the same clothes. The essence of inborn identity remains constant no matter how it is dressed, or as Juliet McMaster writes, "Clothing mediates between the individual soul and the social function."[11] In this respect it is interesting that the first items which Fagin teaches his young charges to steal are pocket handkerchiefs, another indication of how unreliable clothing is as a clue to true identity.[12] Clothing in *Oliver Twist* bespeaks the symbolic blindness of society, which is easily misled by external appearance, and cannot recognize inherent worth when it lies behind a shabby exterior. (The inconsistent relationship of clothes to essential identity is given a ghoulish twist in *Barnaby Rudge* where Dennis the Hangman "inherits" the clothes of those whom he has executed.)

Dickens returns repeatedly to the plot of hidden identity as a narrative device. It is related to two of his favourite themes – resurrection and interconnection. Because the plot of hidden identity privileges the internal over the external, it is essentially an attempt to idealize the mysteries of biological inheritance. The plot of hidden identity relies on heredity as the mechanism by which nobility is encoded into the personalities of the disinherited, the orphaned, the illegitimate, and the outcast. It assumes that human relationships are essentially familial, and that this family connection lives on in the blood of offspring even after death has cut the tie to the previous generation. It is a myth of the self in the sense that it places every individual, no matter how solitary, within the social context of a historical family. The problem for the narrative is to resurrect the protagonist's family out of the mists of time, to clarify the line of descent until it emerges from the obfuscating shadows of present confusion. Identity is conferred on the protagonist through his relationship to his own past, since the plot of hidden identity is perforce connected to time. That is why there are so few truly autonomous beings in the Dickensian universe. Every individual has a history, and every history is familial.

The Old Curiosity Shop

The extent to which Dickens defines heredity as existing in intimate relationship to time can be illustrated by the following quote from *Oliver Twist*:

> The boy stirred, and smiled in his sleep, as though these marks of pity and compassion had awakened some pleasant dream of a love and affection he had never known. Thus, a strain of gentle music, or the rippling of water in a silent place, or the odour of a flower, or the mention of a familiar word, will sometimes call up sudden dim remembrances of scenes that never were, in this life; which vanish like a breath; which some brief memory of a happier existence, long gone by, would seem to have awakened; which no voluntary exertion of the mind can ever recall.
>
> (OT, 268)

The "scenes that never were in this life" presupposes scenes that were in another life. But while this may constitute a reference to the Wordsworthian notion of pre-existence as Cates Baldridge suggests,[13] I would propose that there is another hereditary model at work here, whose presence is made explicit in *The Old Curiosity Shop*. This model is preformation, a theory in which every generation constitutes a repetition of the generation that went before, so that all generations are more or less identical. What happens to those alive today may be supposed to have happened to others like them in earlier times. Oliver's sense of feeling something that he could only have experienced in another lifetime is an allusion to this form of cyclical history.

Because it defined generation as a process that was both regular and repetitive, preformation appealed to Dickens as a way of accounting for human virtue without having to resort to supernatural explanations. If virtue was defined as a hereditable quality, then it fell within the domain of human agency, and if heredity was understood as a process of near-perfect duplication from one generation to the next, then virtue might be propagated and perpetuated through descent.

The Old Curiosity Shop offers the best example of this kind of thinking. This novel – Dickens's fourth – again features a saintly child at the center of its narrative. This time the child is a girl, and while she, like Oliver, is orphaned, there is no suggestion of illegitimacy in her background. Little Nell's circumstances are more comfortable than Oliver's. She has a home of her own, and a family in the person of her grandfather, who is the owner of the old curiosity shop of the title. But Nell's grandfather gambles away his money. Hounded out of their shop by their creditor, the villainous dwarf Quilp, Nell and her grandfather take to wandering around the countryside until Nell succumbs to the hardships of a life overburdened with adult care, and dies at age 14, followed soon after by her grandfather.

The basic dynamic of the relationship between Nell and her grandfather is that of reversal. She, the chronological child, takes care of the old man who should be taking care of her, so that youth and age change places – a favourite Dickensian motif. While this makes Nell's situation as pathetic as Oliver's was, it lacks the dimension of abandonment that characterized Oliver's initial desolation, that vulnerable sense of being cut off from one's source of identity. Instead Nell's sanctity is located in upholding the demands of family and in taking premature responsibility for those from whom she springs.

Dickens accounts for this unusual – almost unnatural – sense of family obligation on Nell's part by relating it to the girl's bloodline. She springs from a line of sweet-natured angelic women, whose ancestry is demonstrated through the metaphor of a picture gallery, thus repeating – and expanding – the trope of hereditary resemblance and its relationship to portraiture that Dickens first introduced in *Oliver Twist*.

"If you have seen the picture-gallery of any one old family, you will remember how the same face and figure – often the fairest and slightest of them all – come upon you in different generations;

and how you trace the same sweet girl through a long line of
portraits – never growing old or changing – the Good Angel of
the race – abiding by them in all reverses – redeeming all their
sins – " (OCS, 637)

In this description, Dickens wraps the metaphysical aspects of
goodness within the concrete form of an inherited trait through
his punning allusion to reproduction as both a human and an artistic process. Here unequivocally is Dickens's presentation of goodness
as a hereditary trait that is simultaneously physical and moral. The
passage is one of the clearest statements in Victorian literature of
the manner in which qualities once assumed to derive from God
and to have religious significance, such as goodness or grace, have
been reassigned to human agency, including so celestial a category
as the angelic.

This repetitive encapsulation with its model of the generations
succeeding one another with little or no variation is at the heart
of the preformation theory. More than this, each daughter in the
line essentially functions as a reanimation of the mother: "In this
daughter the mother lived again . . . her breathing image" (OCS,
637) is how Dickens puts it.

This exalted picture gallery has a more down-to-earth analogue
in *The Old Curiosity Shop*'s other portrait gallery, Mrs Jarley's waxworks, which also deals with resemblance and reproduction, this
time of the three-dimensional variety. "There were so many of them
[the wax figures] with their great glassy eyes – and, as they stood
one behind the other all about [Nell's] bed, they looked so like
living creatures and yet so unlike in their grim stillness and silence . . ." (OCS, 289).

The wax works may comprise the artificial side of resemblance,
yet their attraction lies in the fact that they counterfeit life. Says
Mrs Jarley: "I've seen wax-work quite like life, and I've certainly
seen some life that was exactly like wax-work" (OCS, 272). This
reproductive confusion between the living and the inanimate significantly extends to Nell herself, who is referred to as "a wax-work
child" (OCS, 308). In the passage quoted in the previous paragraph,
the wax figures even stand behind one another in a parody of the
hereditary model offered by the picture gallery in which the same
sweet female figure recurs in all generations.

What is significant about these reproductive models in *The Old
Curiosity Shop* is that they are almost exclusively feminine. The wax

figures in the novel may occasionally represent men, but they are the property of the motherly Mrs Jarley, who appears to be an echo of the real-life Marie Tussaud. And Madame Tussaud herself was not the only woman to be involved with waxworks in England. When she arrived in the country from France in 1802, two other women were already operating wax galleries there.[14] Certainly *The Old Curiosity Shop* attaches a feminine connotation to the waxworks. Not only are they owned and operated by Mrs Jarley and demonstrated by Little Nell, but the clientele includes "a great many young ladies' boarding schools" (OCS, 288). It is difficult to avoid the conclusion that the wax figures, being reproductions of actual human beings, belong properly to the domain of the feminine.

But in *The Old Curiosity Shop* the metaphor of the portrait gallery is also feminine, thus negating Marie-Hélène Huet's suggestion that unlike waxworks, portraiture is primarily a masculine art.[15] It was certainly masculine in *Oliver Twist* where the mother is the model and the father is the painter, but in *The Old Curiosity Shop* the portrait-gallery analogy of hereditary transmission applies specifically to women. What this means is that the goodness attributed to little Nell acquires the added dimension of sexual innocence, this being the particular form of transcendence appropriate to a female child. We are told that Nell's mother dies

> . . . leaving to her father's care two orphans: one a son of ten or twelve years old; the other a girl . . . the same in helplessness, in age, in form, in feature – as she had been herself when her young mother died.
> . . . The boy grew like his father in mind and person; the girl so like her mother, that when the old man had her on his knee, and looked into her mild blue eyes, he felt as if awakening from a wretched dream, and his daughter were a little child again.
>
> (OCS, 637–8)

In other words, boys take after fathers, girls after mothers. Each mother and daughter is so alike that even their personal histories are near duplicates. And so it goes back through time, each female generation representing a copy of the one before.

But this tracing of a strand of female virtue back through time leads Dickens into a bind. He portrays Nell as the final product of a hereditary line of female angels – "the Good Angel of the race" – all of whom are defined as similarly vulnerable and innocent. Yet

the innocence of Nell's grandmother and mother is undermined
by sexual experience, an experience which they must have in order
to carry on the line. There is thus an insoluble paradox at the
heart of a definition which sees female virtue as synonymous with
the sexual innocence of angels, since each woman must engage in
sexual relations in order to pass on the trait of sexual purity.

The corrupting effect of sexual knowledge on virtuous women is
suggested by the fact that the women from whom Nell is descended
either die young – like Nell's grandmother – or marry men who
mistreat them – like Nell's mother – and then die young. Nell is
the culmination of this line, its apotheosis and finest product. As
such, the logic of equating innocence with sexual purity decrees
that she die a virgin, so that she may finally fulfill the destiny of
her line by remaining inviolate and pure – despite being constantly
exposed to sexual threats. But this also means that she represents
the extinction of her line and of the particular redemptive strain
of female virtue which it represents. His heroine's premature death
may be an indication of Dickens's belief that saintliness of the type
Nell personifies is too fragile to survive for long in this world, but
it is also an apparent contradiction of Dickens's intention to present
goodness as immanent in human affairs through the agency of
hereditary transmission.

Because Nell is a special case, an example of goodness so exquisite that it cannot survive to propagate itself, Dickens offers another,
more mundane instance of the inheritance of goodness in *The Old
Curiosity Shop* – but it is a very odd example. The Garlands are a
family of three, the two parents and an only child, a son. Abel
Garland is 28 years old when we meet him. Being the sole offspring of parents who married late in life, he is overprotected, so
that despite having reached the age of majority, Abel has been away
from his parents only once in his life, and the experience was so
traumatic that he fell ill.

There is certainly something unsettling in Dickens's description
of the Garland family. What we seem to have is an unhealthy,
smothering, overly close relationship between a grown child and
his parents. Dickens hints at this in his description of the family
group:

> Mr Abel, who had a quaint old-fashioned air about him, looked
> nearly of the same age as his father, and bore a wonderful re-
> semblance to him in face and figure, though wanting something

of his full, round cheerfulness, and substituting in its place a
timid reserve. In all other respects, in the neatness of the dress,
and even in the club foot, he and the old gentleman were precisely alike.   (OCS, 167–8)

The Garlands are presented sentimentally as the prototype of a
secure and happy family group, yet the physical resemblances drawn
between Abel and his father suggest something a good deal less
wholesome. Steven Marcus was one of the first critics to draw attention to the anomalies in this family group. Abel is a "grown-up
baby," grumbles Marcus, who has "placidly inherited his father's
little club foot, thereby affirming the transmission to him of a kind
of grace of affliction." In addition, Dickens complacently writes that
father and son appear to be the same age, although the chronological gap must be considerable, since Abel is the son of his father's
old age. Marcus calls Abel's relationship to his father "a cheerily
willed abasement of self before an absurd image of authority."[16]
This willed abasement of self is reproduced in Nell's relationship
with her grandfather.

There is much justice in Marcus's complaint, but what he fails to
notice is that Dickens depicts Abel and his parents as bound to
one another through love. This love is similar in kind to the in-
sidiously destructive affection which binds Nell to her grandfather,
but in the case of the Garlands, Dickens presents a positive outcome to the affective side of family life. Dickens, in this novel, is
still concerned to prove, as he was in *Oliver Twist*, that the redemption of parents rests with their offspring. He draws what appears
to be an unhealthy portrait of a family only to deny the negative
implications of his description.

In this sense, Abel must be seen as a comic, watered-down stand-
in for Nell. As she was an innocent child forced too early into an
adult's role, so Abel is an innocent adult anachronistically clinging
to his childish role. They are two sides of the same coin. Abel's
childishness links him to Nell through their shared qualities of kind-
heartedness and innocence. What is more, because Abel is male,
Dickens may depict him as innocent while scanting the issue of
sexual threat; Abel may propagate his kind without losing or stain-
ing his integrity.

The result is that Abel, despite or because of being smothered
with love by his parents, turns out rather well. He finds the perfect
marriage partner in a girl who is as bashful as he is, and the two

settle down to raise a family, a fact which Dickens, as narrator, finds "pleasant to write down . . . because any propagation of goodness and benevolence is no small addition to the aristocracy of nature, and no small subject of rejoicing for mankind at large" (OCS, 667). The Garlands – in company with the novel's other positive secondary characters, the Nubbles, and Dick Swiveller and his wife, the Marchioness – perpetuate the quality of goodness as a hereditary trait, thus making up for the extinction of the line which Nell represents.

The ambiguous element in the description of the Garland family, the fact that father and son resemble each other so closely that the son even duplicates his father's club foot, constitutes another example of the theory of preformation and its link to the transmission of goodness as a hereditary quality. The very name Garland suggests a positive chain of descent. The Garlands' hereditary line is clearly not as exalted as Nell's – there is no suggestion that any angels will bloom on it, the hereditary club foot indicating an all too human blemish. But the blemish is physical not moral. The Garlands are redeemed by their kindness, and this kindness justifies their fertility, which in turn constitutes a hopeful sign for the future.

In fact, as Juliet McMaster points out, hereditary resemblances are especially notable among the good characters of this novel.[17] The Nubbles too resemble one another, and Barbara, the future wife of Kit Nubbles, is described as looking just like her mother. There is a sense in which all these positive characters make up in their fecundity for the sterility of Nell. With these less exalted but still admirable human characters Dickens wishes to fill the hereditary void he created by expunging Nell's line and with it the extraordinary virtue which she embodied.

Dombey and Son

Dickens's presentation of goodness in *The Old Curiosity Shop* is essentially optimistic, despite Little Nell's death. In all the early novels, he takes as a given the fact that virtue and benevolence exist, and he presents heredity as the mechanism by which these attributes are propagated and their redemptive qualities disseminated through the population and across the generations. But by the time he comes to write *Dombey and Son* in 1846, Dickens's opinions on the positive aspects of heredity have begun to alter, and his insistence on absolute determinism as a factor in the formation of the self is more muted.

Dombey and Son may be read as an extended fable of heredity in which the evil forces of male dynastic ambition are aligned against the gentler and more humane qualities of love and affection handed down by mother to daughter. The novel takes as its premise the assumption – common to scripture, the Victorians, and western culture generally – that the only worthwhile offspring a man can have is a son. (Dickens was writing at a time when it was common for the obstetrician's fee to be higher for delivering a boy.[18]) This assumption is turned on its head by a demonstration that the values of a male world, as symbolized by the ideologies of capitalism and technological progress, are corrupted and debased when they exclude the contributions of the feminine. The demonstration is effected through the figure of Mr Dombey, head of the mercantile house of Dombey and Son.

Mr Dombey wants a son in order to pass on to his descendants the wealth which his house has acquired over the generations. So imperious is this need within him – and so tied up is it with his own *amour propre* – that all other aspects of his life are made subservient to it. For Mr Dombey a son would be the living embodiment of all his ambitions – affective, dynastic, economic.

Here, for the first time, Dickens portrays physical resemblance – previously his most cherished trope for indicating the transmission of positive qualities from one generation to the next – as a negative, more conducive to the vanity of parents than the benefit of children. "You Angel," cries the spinsterish Miss Tox to the infant Paul, "you Picture of your own Papa!" (DS, 148). But the remark no longer carries the positive charge that such comparisons – mediated, here as elsewhere, through the metaphor of the portrait – had in the earlier novels. On the contrary, it is rife with dynastic implications, since so much of Mr Dombey's indomitable pride is wrapped up in molding his son into a true replica of himself.

Dickens makes explicit in the opening chapters that what Mr Dombey loves about his son is the fact that he is a son, and so resembles his father in a way that no daughter can. "Paul and myself will be able, when the time comes, to hold our own – the House in other words, will be able to hold its own, and maintain its own, and hand down its own of itself . . . " (DS, 102–3). Catherine Waters points out the "masturbatory grammar" of this passage, and suggests that it describes a process of male parthenogenesis, which excludes all intimations of the feminine from its apprehension of the world.[19]

That Mr Dombey's absorption in his son is a form of self-love animated primarily by considerations of gender can be seen in the analogous situation in *David Copperfield* where Betsey Trotwood storms out of David's young life when she discovers that he is a boy and not the girl whom she had hoped would carry her name. The point is made even more forcefully when Betsey greets the run-away David with the heavily symbolic gesture of chopping the air with her knife as she says, "no boys here!" In both cases, the adult is looking to duplicate his or her self in the child, a duplication achieved most obviously and definitively through the reiteration of sex. In both *Dombey and Son* and *David Copperfield* – novels from his middle period – Dickens presents an adult's preference for children of the same sex as a mark of selfishness and narcissism.

Egotism, and its near cousin, narcissism, are the unsavory aspects of heredity which Dickens dramatizes in *Dombey and Son*. Mr Dombey places such value on a male heir because he wants a copy of himself to love. He is so full of pride that the only other being to whom he is prepared to confide his heart is one he has created in his own image. In Mr Dombey, Dickens, for the first time, demonstrates the negative implications of defining heredity as the unsullied reproduction of identical traits: such a definition makes offspring valuable only to the extent that they resemble their parents.

It follows, then, that the novel should associate the abuses of hereditary determinism with gender. In *Dombey and Son*, both Paul and his sister Florence have their futures prearranged solely on the basis of their sex, as Mr Dombey makes clear when speaking of his son: "His way in life was clear and prepared, and marked out before he existed" (DS, 204). But Dickens does not regard this statement as boding well either for Paul or for his sister. The preordained course of the son's life will have such disastrous consequences that it constitutes, in effect, a death sentence. At the same time, Mr Dombey's intense focus on Paul deprives his sister of her right to equal consideration and affection. In the context of this novel, the predetermined path marked out for children of either sex is as calamitous for the favored son as it is for the neglected daughter.

Dickens mocks the implications of physical resemblance between the generations in *Dombey and Son's* opening paragraphs. There Mr Dombey's 48 years of life are contrasted to his son's 48 minutes.

Both father and new-born son are bald and have red faces; both are wrinkled. The irony, of course, lies in the fact that these apparent resemblances are nothing of the kind, and the assumption of genealogical regularity through the generations, with the infant representing just one more rung on the ladder of descent, is false. The idea that the species Dombey remains constant and paramount, preserving and perpetuating the family name, while its individual members are subsumed under the needs of the collective, hints again at the theory of preformation, but this time without approval.

When Paul is a little older, Dickens again contrasts father and son. Paul is described as Mr Dombey's "little image with an old, old face . . . The two so very much alike, and yet so monstrously contrasted" (DS, 151–2). Paul is his father's biological son, but as the passage makes clear, he is also his contrast. The resemblance of little Paul to his father, and to all the other Dombeys before him therefore exists and does not exist. There is a superficial quality to their connection, which marks it as ephemeral and illusory. Dickens emphasizes this by adding a supernatural dimension to Paul's identity, describing him as "a changeling" and "a young goblin," "one of those terrible little Beings in the Fairy tales, who at a hundred and fifty or two hundred years of age, fantastically represent the children for whom they have been substituted" (DS, 151). This suggests that Paul is the product of spontaneous generation, owing his existence to no parents or forebears.

But Dickens is merely being fanciful. Paul's uniqueness as a Dombey rests not on metaphysical explanations, but on his being his mother's child. And that mother was most emphatically not a Dombey, a point made forcefully by Mr Dombey's sister, Louisa, as Mrs Dombey lies dying (DS, 53). Mrs Dombey is Paul's forgotten parent – forgotten because she is female and forgotten because she is dead. For this reason it is easy to overlook the fact that both Paul and Florence actually inherit from her. Paul's physical and his emotional frailty are attributable to his mother, as is the mildness of his personality. But nothing binds mother and son more closely than their common fate: neither can survive for long in the Dombey air. Both are doomed to a premature demise.[20]

Paul's mother dies soon after his birth, while Paul catches a chill during his christening from which he never recovers. Dickens makes Paul more vulnerable to outside influences than his previous child protagonists, and his wilting and early death are far more convincing than Little Nell's, who is originally described as "chubby, rosy, cosy little Nell" (OCS, 125), indicating robust good health rather than physical frailty. It is not her environment that kills Little Nell, but rather Dickens's determination – a determination he arrived at mid-way through writing *The Old Curiosity Shop* – that she must die.[21] This is what accounts for the discrepancy between her early sturdiness and her later frailty. But Paul's apparent susceptibility to his environment is in fact an inherited quality, transmitted to him by his mother. That Paul, the Dombey son, should owe more in terms of biological inheritance to his mother than to his father adumbrates the novel's ideological intent, which is to champion women as equal and positive contributors to the rungs of genealogy.

Florence, too, has inherited from her mother. When the dying Paul sees a vision of heaven, he exclaims to his sister: "Mama is like you, Floy. I know her by the face!" (DS, 297). Here the transcendent – and transmissive – quality of female virtue is made abundantly clear. That the mildness of Florence's personality is similar to her mother's is remarked on by several characters, most ironically by the villain Carker (DS, 105, 686). In fact, the close bond between Florence and her brother is an indication of just how similar their natures are.

Steven Marcus suggests that it is Florence, not Paul, who is the figure of grace in this novel, and he compares her to Oliver Twist, suggesting that grace does not work miracles for Florence as it did for Oliver. Marcus defines grace in this novel as the ability to feel affection, to respond to people with fullness, to be able to love.[22] What Marcus does not say, but what is clear, is that Florence represents the female version of grace, with all the limitations this suggests – most notably, that for women, grace is biologically defined. As long as Florence is a girl, she has little power in the cold mercantile world of the Dombeys. It is only when she reaches sexual maturity and with it the potential for motherhood that she attains the kind of moral power which will eventually swamp and erase the masculine dominance of the unbending Dombeys.

Patricia Marks suggests that *Dombey and Son* is about the valorization of motherhood, and links this not only to the domestic drama of the Dombeys but also to the hints of imperialism present in the novel: Brittania, the motherland, exploits her colonial children.[23] The novel begins with the death of a mother and the banishing of her substitute; it ends with the reinstatement, through Florence, of the maternal principle. But Florence's fluctuating power as girl and mother suggests the limits of a grace that is defined biologically.

In its attempt to champion the female principle in generation, *Dombey and Son* focuses on the ways in which that principle can be corrupted and debased. The novel channels its critique of capitalism through the commercialization of the female body. In *Dombey and Son*, women are prized primarily for their biological functions, which may be bought and sold. Thus Mr Dombey hires Polly Toodle for her breast milk, just as he courts Edith for her reproductive potential as the mother of another son. Edith's cousin, Alice Marwood, represents the most common symbol of femaleness for hire – she is the "fallen woman," who has bartered her sexual favours for lucre. In a mercantile world where everything is a matter of trade – Mr Dombey is, after all, a merchant – women represent the most obvious example of human beings as commodities.

If everything has a price, then heredity too may be subjected to financial transaction. The corruption of human values through their association with money forms the subtext of *Dombey and Son*, and is most evident in Mr Dombey's courtship of Edith, which culminates in the businessman's vast wealth being laid out to purchase the future mother of another son. Edith is a widow when Mr Dombey is first introduced to her. His interest is piqued by her beauty and her pride – the latter because it so resembles his own – but his decision to make her his wife hinges on her fertility, about which he inquires immediately after meeting her. He learns then that she has been the mother of a son who died young, which makes her an ideal candidate for his purposes, since it means that she can have children – male children – and yet is unencumbered by any actual child.

As part of his courtship, Mr Dombey tests Edith's various accomplishments, asking her to play on an instrument or to draw, as if these activities were accurate indicators of her hereditary potential. Lawrence Stone has suggested that scientific advances in the eighteenth century had given the English a sense of control over their environment, and that this was most apparent in their enthusiasm for animal breeding. Success in breeding livestock and domestic pets led men to choose their wives as they would a brood mare, with great care for their hereditary endowments.[24] Mr Dombey's courtship of Edith certainly contains hints of a search for sound breeding stock, which makes it doubly interesting that his primary method of assessing hereditary suitability should be through artistic endeavors.

It is doubtful that Mr Dombey has any ambition to father a child who is musical or artistic. The purpose of his testing Edith's accomplishments is to measure her mastery of the proper social prerequisites for the position of being his wife. It is a testing for social attainments rather than artistic ability, but these attainments are nonetheless emblematic of hereditary potential. There is of course another, more psychological aspect to Dombey's testing of Edith – it is a means for him to assert his will over her by making her perform according to his wishes.[25] In this sense, it also serves as an indication of her future malleability and compliance – at least, Mr Dombey assumes it does.

This careful preliminary weighing of her external qualities makes Edith's intended adultery with Carker all the more devastating to Mr Dombey, since it would subvert his claims of future paternity, a matter so close to his heart that he even names one of his ships the *Son and Heir*. The inequality of Victorian divorce laws, which enforced the double standard by sanctioning the husband's adultery and condemning the wife's, was rationalized on just such grounds, namely that a wife's adultery threatened her husband's status as father. In thus rendering a man's paternal status problematic, a woman's infidelity was thought to attack his personal identity.[26]

By the same token, Edith's elopement with Carker is the only assertion of female rebellion possible in a society which defines and values women solely for their biological functions – just as her refusal to become Carker's mistress, even after she has eloped with him, reinforces the fact that the only freedom available to her is the freedom to dispose of her sexual favours as she sees fit. A woman's assertion of sexual freedom carries with it an implicit claim to equal status in the realm of biology, since it affirms her ability to determine the hereditary composition of her offspring. Dickens's championing of femininity in *Dombey and Son* does not extend so far as to allow Edith such powers of determination, so she remains childless.

The mercantile, mechanistic society depicted in *Dombey and Son* values women solely for their biological potential as the conduits of male inheritance, but in doing so it devalues and sterilizes what is best and most worthwhile in human nature. Assigning a price to women's biological functions negates the very qualities which Dickens defines as the highest attainments of femininity – affectionate empathy, tenderness, altruism, spirituality – qualities which Victorian sexual ideology designated as redemptive of the degeneracy of men. These female qualities Dickens locates in the idealized – and fertile – Florence.

Florence's lack of stature in her father's eyes is tied to her perceived lack of economic worth. From Mr Dombey's point of view, she has no market value. "But what was a girl to Dombey and Son! In the capital of the House's name and dignity such a child was merely a piece of base coin that couldn't be invested – a bad Boy – nothing more" (DS, 51). Florence's true value, of course, is priceless. She is one of Dickens's many female angels, a child rejected and unloved, who never rejects and never fails to love. Florence, in her unstinting kindness and affection, in her unwavering meekness and humility, is clearly an example of the intangible and unquantifiable worth of the best in human – and female – nature.

Florence's fertility ensures that the ideal elements of her personality will be passed on to succeeding generations. In fact, fertility in this novel, as elsewhere in Dickens's work, is a sign of blessing, of the expansive potential of heredity as a means of propagating the good. It also stands as an indication of the limits of capitalism, of the things which money cannot buy. Human fertility in *Dombey and Son* is implicitly contrasted to the unnatural breeding of money, as in the old Aristotelian prohibition against charging interest: "This term usury, which means the birth of money from money, is applied to the breeding of money from money because the offspring resembles the parent. Wherefore of all modes of making money this is the most unnatural."[27]

Fertility in this novel is the overriding female virtue, the natural result of an affectionate womanly heart. Dickens's unexpected and rather startling feminism here is, in fact, based on and confined to biological considerations. What he is actually championing is not social, political, or educational equality for women, but an appreciation of their biological worth. (Dickens makes Florence cleverer than her brother, but her intelligence is placed entirely at his service and channeled into being his tutor. It has no value in itself.) *Dombey and Son* seeks to establish the female claim as a force for good in the founding of a dynasty. Mr Dombey's dynastic ambitions foundered when he sought to ground them on his son. Through her fertility, Florence proves that a dynasty may spring just as well from the loins of a daughter, and that the result is a kinder, gentler, more loving line of descent.[28]

Clearly, Dickens's faith in hereditary endowment as a force for the propagation of good has not entirely dissipated in *Dombey and Son*.

His idealization of the family remains intact and is at the heart of the theme which Kathleen Tillotson identifies as integral to this novel – the sense of the past under assault by the present.[29] Viewed from this perspective, heredity becomes the conservative force standing in opposition to the anarchic thrust of technology. No matter what the abuses imposed on the new generation by the old, the repetitive nature of hereditary endowment still stands for a stabilizing and secure element at the heart of life, in contrast to the reckless advance of inhuman technology embodied in the railway. Trains, and the destruction they wreak on countryside and city, are emblematic of the ambiguous price of progress, with its headlong rush into a chaotic new world cut adrift from the certainties of the past. Heredity and the family relations it implies stands as the one secure, if imperfect, foundation for human continuity.

It is significant that the novel's villain, Carker, who dies so dramatically under the wheels of a train, has severed all connections to his own brother and sister. Not content with alienating his siblings, Carker also attempts to destroy Mr Dombey's second marriage by seducing Edith Dombey away from her husband. Carker is the novel's "modern man," the character most wedded to the elusive ideal of technological progress, and the one least impressed by family obligations and connections. It is fitting, therefore, that he should end under the wheels of a train. Tolstoy's Anna Karenina meets the same fate, and she too has sinned against the concept of family by committing adultery. Mr Dombey, on the other hand, full of selfishness and pride though he may be, is allowed to live long enough to realize his error. Mr Dombey's saving grace lies in his belief in the human – and hereditary – institution of the family, his mistake being the assumption that this institution is just an extended reflection of himself.

Closely tied to the themes of heredity and family in *Dombey and Son* are names.[30] On the one hand, names resemble clothing in being symbols of disposable identity, but they are also public manifestations of genealogy, either fencing off one family from the next, or indicating a conjunction. In *Dombey and Son*, names are intimately tied to both power and identity. The fact that Mr Dombey is the novel's primary dispenser of names suggests that one of the attributes of power is the ability to label and therefore to define the world in accordance with one's wishes. (God grants Adam, and through him Mankind, a similar power in Genesis 2.)

Mr Dombey changes Polly Toodle's name to the more respectable Richards, because he feels that the latter is more appropriate to her function as his son's nurse. Having purchased her services as wet-nurse, he feels that he has bought her name and identity as well. Polly, for her part, asks that the name-change be considered in her wages, underlining the extent to which names may be considered commodities. Similarly, once married to Edith, Mr Dombey expects her to be suitably impressed with the new name and new identity which he has bestowed upon her: "I have made you my wife. You bear my name. You are associated with my position and reputation" (DS, 651). In *Dombey and Son*, naming is linked to the corrupting influence of capitalism. Mr Dombey's money gives him power, his power allows him to impose names, and, therefore, to dispense identity. But, this sterile capitalistic power has its limits. Paul Dombey may have the same name as his father and grandfather, but that does not ensure that he will inherit their personalities – or their longevity.

But if names are not indicative of identity, they are – usually – indicative of genealogy. So, on the one hand, Dickens uses the imposition of names as a way of alluding to sham identities; on the other, he manipulates names to suggest the repetitive nature of generation. Thus at the end of *The Old Curiosity Shop*, when Kit Nubbles marries and has children, they are all named after the positive characters in the novel (OCS, 671). Only Little Nell has no one named after her. By leaving hers as the one name which is not repeated into the next generation, Dickens implies that Nell herself was too singular, too exquisite, to be reincarnated in another child of flesh and blood.

In *Dombey and Son*, Mr Dombey, who was named after his father, names his son after himself, while his daughter Florence names her son after her father and her brother. Thus little Paul Dombey, who is named after his father, is reincarnated again in his nephew Paul Gay, the son of his beloved sister Florence. In commenting on Paul's premature death, Dickens had written that all that remained of the boy was his name (DS, 113). But that turns out to be no small thing. Since names are recyclable from one generation to the next, they have memorializing qualities, so that, in a sense, Paul Dombey is revitalized by having his name conferred on his nephew. Dianne Sadoff, referring to the novel's end, writes that Florence carries the message to her father that genealogy binds and redeems because she herself has become a mother. Little Paul, her brother reborn, links her to her father; Little Florence, herself reborn, links her to herself and to her mother.[31]

As Sadoff notes, *Dombey and Son* ends, not only with a new little Paul, but also with a new little Florence, daughter of the original Florence. The repetitive naming from one generation to the next allows the now-humbled Mr Dombey to redeem himself through the third generation for the sins which he committed against the second. He loves his granddaughter Florence, "hoarding" her in his heart, to make up for the way he mistreated her mother. (One wonders if the verb "hoarding" is a sly allusion to the persistent economic basis of Mr Dombey's affections.) Nevertheless, it is curious that Dombey's love for his granddaughter remains secret, unlike his love for his grandson, which he displays to the world. Referring to the elder Dombey's love for his granddaughter, Dickens writes: "That story never goes about" (DS, 975), and one wonders if Dickens intended this secret affection to stand for the hidden and inexplicable processes of heredity which turn daughters – despite the lack of resemblance – into the legitimate heirs of their fathers.

The repetitive naming allows Dickens to work his happy ending by suggesting that each new generation affords the one before it an opportunity for expiation and exculpation. This is similar to the kind of reiteration that is inherent in preformation, and in fact Dickens's habit of repetitive naming is indicative of a worldview very much akin to that of preformation. Preformation wiped out all distinctions of time because it denied the existence of variation and, therefore, left no scope for change. When those who lived in the past are defined as identical to those who live today and to those who will live tomorrow, then past, present, and future become coterminous. The repetition of names from generation to generation has a similar effect, erasing distinctions between individuals and suggesting that there is a regularity and duplication in human affairs which allows a situation of injustice in one generation to be rectified in the next. In this sense, *Dombey and Son*, which for most of its narrative course had been concerned with demonstrating the damaging effects of too strong an emphasis on the imperatives of bloodline and genealogy, ends by resurrecting heredity as a positive force in human life.

3
The Inheritance of Goodness: David Copperfield and Pip

If, in *Dombey and Son*, Dickens appears to be torn between conflicting presentations of heredity as first a negative and then a positive force, *David Copperfield* signals a still more radical change. This novel marks a loosening of Dickens's belief in the prescriptive grip of inborn traits. Where previously Dickens had exploited resemblance as a trope for the discussion of positive genealogical transmission, in *David Copperfield*, resemblance, in the form of behavioral patterns modeled on parents and compulsively repeated over the course of a lifetime, alludes to psychological factors more than it does to inherited proclivities.

David Copperfield is presented as the autobiography of a successful novelist, but it is not a portrait of the artist as a young man. Dickens does not, as a rule, attribute talents to heredity, and certainly David's literary gift, which is essentially Dickens's own, is depicted in the novel as more the product of hard work and steadfast application than of inherited predilection. David's literary talents are, in fact, one of the few aspects of his personality which cannot be traced to his parents. Instead, they are ascribed to environmental factors, specifically the obsessive reading, "as if for life," in which David indulges to escape his miserable childhood. His literary abilities may account for David's success in later life, but there is not much speculation as to their origin, nor, for that matter, much emphasis on their importance.

In fact, David insists on keeping his profession incidental and marginal: "It is not my purpose, in this record, though in all other essentials it is my written memory, to pursue the history of my own fictions" (DC, 758). David's public career as author is scarcely touched upon, as if no true drama lay in that sphere of life. Instead the novel's focus is on the hero's progress from the immaturity of his youth to his sense of fulfillment in a second marriage. *David Copperfield* may be a bildungsroman, but the drama of David's education lies not in his intellectual or philosophical attainments, but in his emotional development.[1] The entire dramatic scope of this "autobiography" is confined to the private domain of affective relationships.

This focus on David's emotional development means that *David Copperfield* is a novel which is vitally concerned with the question of what is inherent in human development and what is acquired.[2] The novel dramatizes the course of a life in which the emotional patterns established in childhood are repeated in adolescence and young manhood. The problem constantly before the reader throughout the enactment of these recurring patterns is to establish how much of David's personality is inherited – and therefore predetermined and immutable – and how much may be attributed to the effects of environment and experience. That environment and experience may have a modifying effect on the raw material of hereditary endowment had never before been a serious consideration for Dickens. (Little Nell and Paul Dombey may be susceptible to the dangers of their environments, but their essential selves remain unaffected.) In *David Copperfield*, for the first time, Dickens posits the question of nature versus nurture in terms of the difference between autonomy and determinism.

David is a posthumous child. His father, who died six months before his birth, lies buried beneath a white gravestone that is visible from his son's bedroom. Thus, in a scene which he would repeat in *Great Expectations* written some ten years later, Dickens begins his account of an unfolding life with a meditation on death, specifically on the death of a parent. In both *David Copperfield* and *Great Expectations*, the opening scenes near the parental graves serve simultaneously as a reminder of the end of life and of its source. But if parental gravestones establish an absence in the life of the child, they also suggest an enduring presence, a type of ghostly immortality conferred by the inherited material coursing through the veins of the living offspring of dead parents.

Thus, the opening scenes of *David Copperfield*, which establish

David's orphaned state, also raise the question of the abiding claims of the dead upon the living, and the manner in which such claims may be expressed.[3] Into David's unfolding life a certain quantity of raw hereditary matter has been poured, and this inheritance will influence the future course of his biography. Dickens has always portrayed heredity as destiny, and he seems to be extending this assumption into *David Copperfield*, with its opening declaration of the hero's orphaned state. The dead live on in their children, while the children's lives are played out under the long shadow cast by the dead.

This ongoing relationship between the dead and the living is made palpable in the early chapters. In fact, it is suggested in the novel's opening paragraphs, where David claims that, according to superstition, his birth in the small hours of a Friday night means that he has been fated to see ghosts and spirits. He no sooner makes this claim than he dismisses it, asserting that he has never yet come into this "inheritance" (DC, 49). In fact, the "autobiography" he is preparing to narrate takes as its theme the persistence of the past into the present, and the need to come to terms with and to assimilate the ghostly presence of past attachments. A further instance of this same theme occurs when we are told of David's boyhood fear that the dead have risen from their tombs in the graveyard which he can see from his bedroom window. This fear of the reanimated dead is linked to David's obsessive thoughts about his father.

David's reflections on the grave of his father, towards whom he feels an "indefinable compassion," are connected to his sense that with regard to his father "the doors of our house were – almost cruelly, it seemed to me sometimes – bolted and locked" (DC, 50–1). This Hamletic opening with its suggestion of a forsaken and outcast paternal spirit haunting a house that will soon see the introduction of an unwanted and – from the son's point of view – usurping stepfather, predicts, as well, David's own fate in the Murdstone ménage. In this way, Dickens prepares for future developments in this first section of the novel by introducing a theme that will see David duplicate in himself, and in the choices he makes in his life, the character flaws and mistakes of his parents.

If David's father represents the ghostly influence of the dead on the destinies of the living, his mother represents the parental influence which the child actually experiences. The fact of her being alive during David's childhood means that the role she plays in her son's development is based on his conscious awareness of her, so that her hereditary contribution to his make-up is superseded by her phenomenological essence. This is the first fictional statement by Dickens of the complicating effect which experience may have on hereditary endowment as a factor in human development.

As to what David actually learns from his mother, Q. D. Leavis sums it up as follows: "That David's love of his mother is the love of Woman, and that he is always looking for her image, a pettish, wilful, childish, loving playmate, is shown as the pattern of his emotional life."[4] In David's case the emotional attachment to his mother is intensified by the fact that his father is dead, and he has no siblings. There are no other family members to distract his mother's attention from her only son, nor his from her.

Clara Copperfield is thoroughly and determinedly girlish, making a virtue out of her immaturity. David's childhood adoration of her initiates a pattern that will culminate in his infatuation with Dora. In fact, the pattern emerges very early. No sooner has David arrived in Yarmouth than he thinks himself in love with Little Emily, a child of his own age. Here again Dickens is establishing for David a model – this time a model of attraction to girlishness – that he will repeat in later life. The roots of this attraction lie in his relationship to his mother.

David Copperfield therefore represents a new stage in Dickens's understanding of heredity and its influence. In this novel, repetitive behavior from one generation to the next may well be a product of inherited predisposition, but the possibility also exists that this behavior is learned, that individual proclivities may indicate a psychological response to actual life experience. Dickens has transformed his previous reliance on hereditary resemblance as a means of explicating personality to a stress on the duplication of behavioral patterns from one generation to the next. The shift away from presenting hereditary qualities as static reproductions – appropriately mediated through the iconography of portraiture – to a notion of the individual reproducing during the course of his life the emotional patterns he has learned in childhood, takes the definition of heredity into a new dimension. Thus, the novel dramatizes the course of a life in which the emotional patterns established in childhood are repeated in later life.

David's attachment to his mother and the unfortunate consequences which this too-close relationship has for his future is replicated in the relationships of the novel's other orphans to their parents. None

of *David Copperfield*'s many principals has a sibling, and all its domestic triangles are shattered by death, leaving the children orphaned
and intensifying the attachment to the surviving parent, who is
invariably of the opposite sex. David, Steerforth, and Uriah Heep
all suffer from unhealthy attachments to their mothers, while Agnes
Wakefield is the victim of her father's excessive love, as is Little
Emily of her uncle Peggotty's obsessive attachment. More significant still is the fact that this type of intense emotional bond between
parents and children of the opposite sex is plainly labeled as unhealthy. Agnes's father acknowledges that his love for his daughter
is diseased.

Stephen Kern writes that in the Victorian family, "Motherhood
was regarded as positive, supportive, and bisexual, while the father–
child relationship was conceived to be conflict-ridden, with a special
destructive sexual element in the father–daughter relation."[5] It is
interesting, therefore, that Dickens is so even-handed in apportioning
blame for unhealthy parent–child relationships in his novel.
Steerforth's mother is scarcely more commendable in her over-
indulgence of her son than Agnes's father is in his obsessive concern
for his daughter.

As for David himself, he is still, to a large extent, the sum of what
he has inherited from his parents, but this inheritance is no longer
entirely positive, as it was, for instance, for Oliver Twist or Little
Nell. Like Oliver, the child David is inherently honest, to say nothing
of scrupulous beyond his years. Having decided to run away from
the firm of Murdstone and Grinby, he nevertheless determines to
stay until he has worked the equivalent of his week's advance pay
because he was "unwilling to disgrace the memory I was going to
leave behind me" (DC, 233). But this innate honesty – and precocious worry about his good name – cannot protect David from
the perfidy of the adults he meets on his way to Dover, who frighten,
trick, cheat, and rob him of the few possessions he has.

Again, like Oliver, David is presented as bearing a strong resemblance to both his parents, or to use his aunt's words: "He would
be as like his father as it's possible to be, if he was not so like his
mother too" (DC, 248). But in this novel, being like both one's
parents does not strain credibility, because resemblance is no longer
defined as purely physical; it now includes learned behavior as well
as inherited predilection. What is more, being like one's parents

has become a mixed blessing. In David's case, his double indebtedness seems to have predisposed him to a double immaturity. He inherits his father's gullibility and his mother's malleability. He duplicates his father's attraction to "wax dolls," and remains, like his mother, passive and childish. Even David's attraction to Dora appears to have been predetermined, so closely does his marriage to her reproduce his own parents' "babes in the woods" union, down to the identical problems with housekeeping.

But Dickens has now come to distinguish physical inheritance from moral qualities. The distinction is made by Betsey Trotwood. She notes David's physical resemblance to his mother, then to his father, then specifies:

> But what I want you to be, Trot . . . I don't mean physically, but morally; you are very well physically – is a firm fellow. A fine firm fellow, with a will of your own. With resolution . . . With determination. With character, Trot – with strength of character that is not to be influenced, except on good reason, by anybody, or by anything. That's what I want you to be. That's what your father and mother might both have been, Heaven knows, and been the better for it. (DC, 332)

The assumption behind this speech is one which Dickens has not made before – that physical appearance has no relation to moral essence, that personality is subject to alteration through the free workings of the will and is not unalterably predetermined by inheritance. When David notes the resemblance between Steerforth and his mother, he says "All that I had ever seen in him of an unyielding wilful spirit, I saw in her." (DC, 531). Here again, while the resemblance is stressed, it is not clear that the culprit is heredity rather than a deliberate fostering on the part of the mother of a perverse nature in the son. Steerforth's resemblance to his mother is in fact presented as an egotistical attempt on her part to mould him in her own selfish image.

Similarly, while David's marriage to Dora duplicates his father's union with his mother, David's treatment of his child-wife also contains echoes of the Murdstone doctrine of marital firmness. This is learned behavior on David's part and suggests that David has modeled himself on someone he detests. Clearly Dickens has begun to move away from seeing heredity as the entire answer to the problem of human development.

In fact, the link between Mr Murdstone and David is very close, even though they are not connected by blood. Not only are Murdstone and David rivals for the same woman – David's mother – but they also share the same attraction to "wax dolls," as can be seen in Murdstone's subsequent targeting of another child-like young woman to be his wife, and his driving her mad through his repeated insistence on firmness. Murdstone, it is clear, is no more free from the obsessive repetition of emotional patterns than is David, and the fact causes him just as much distress, although David cannot see this. Murdstone's passionate grief over the death of David's mother seems to suggest that he is the type of man who cannot help killing the thing he loves. Yet, he is incapable of surmounting the destructive patterns of his behavior, patterns which are further complicated, in his case, by a severe brand of Christianity.[6]

Steerforth, the other important male character in the novel, is also subject to the obsessive repetition of destructive emotional patterns. He is the type of the seducer, playing a dangerous and deceitful game with women, which is ultimately self-defeating. In fact, Dickens hints at the tragic element in a personality which cannot overcome its own destructive tendencies – the need to be constantly charming others into admiration, followed by the wish to discard them once the conquest has been made. Steerforth's first success is with Rosa Dartle, his second – ironically – is with David himself in his boyish (and feminine) guise of "Daisy." Miss Mowcher is yet another victim of Steerforth's manipulative style. Finally there is the elopement with Little Emily. Steerforth's emotional pattern is clear, and it is just as obsessive as David's or Murdstone's.

It is left to David to prove that a break with the emotional past is possible. David is the first of Dickens's child protagonists to have the opportunity to be influenced by and to learn from events. He is shown as having the option of choice – and often choosing wrongly. What is more, his relative age at the time he makes his choices dictates how he should be judged. When he is still a child and his innocence and trust are taken advantage of by the waiter at the inn, who eats up all his food, it is clearly the waiter who is at fault. But when as a young man, and later as a married man, he continues to be taken advantage of by tradespeople, landladies and servants, his innocence becomes less pardonable. In fact, it ceases to be innocence and becomes gullibility. Similarly, when as a young boy, David inadvertently brings about Mr Mell's dismissal because of a wish to please his beloved Steerforth, it is difficult to condemn him entirely; but when as a young man he persists in being blind to his idol's faults and unwittingly abets Steerforth's designs on Little Emily, it is far more difficult to absolve him of guilt. Thus the very notion of innocence has undergone a change in *David Copperfield*. It is no longer a fixed trait, totally synonymous with goodness and vulnerability, but has become the plaything of perspective, admirable or condemnable depending on such relative factors as chronology and circumstance.

Yet despite the options for change available to his protagonist, Dickens's portrayal of autonomy in *David Copperfield* is problematic. David's recognition of his misguided affection for Dora and Steerforth, defined as the "mistaken impulses of an undisciplined heart," coupled with the shock of their premature deaths, leads him to a new understanding of himself and of the ways in which he has contributed to his own unhappiness. Having reached this understanding of himself, David proceeds to act on it by choosing Agnes for his second wife.

This means that Dickens locates the notion of self-determination in David's altered sense of what he requires in a wife. No longer does he look for a glorified child and playmate as a spouse. Instead, in Agnes, he finds the very model of maturity and responsibility who will be the proper helpmeet.[7] Agnes has in fact been there for David to love during most of the course of the novel. Other characters, such as Betsey Trotwood, are perfectly aware of her virtues and her suitability for David. Even David seems unconsciously aware of Agnes's suitability when he overreacts to the discovery that Uriah Heep has designs to marry her.

The fact that Agnes has been there all along and has hopelessly but faithfully loved David, despite his being blind to her wifely potential, is presented as part of the deterministic side of David's make-up. Agnes's precocious maturity makes her an ideal sister-figure, but, as Leavis points out, maturity in a woman is chilling to the younger David.[8] The Victorian ideal of womanhood called for something a good deal flightier, and David's experience with his mother, to say nothing of his inheritance from his father, predisposed him to fall for the attractions of a child-woman like Dora and to overlook the sterling qualities of an Agnes, for whom his affection is initially fraternal and asexual. Thus a mix of hereditary, cultural, and psychological forces predetermine David's attraction to Dora and stand in the way of his love for Agnes.

We are meant to understand that David finally breaks free of all such deterministic constraints when he recognizes Agnes's true worth, and decides to make her his wife. Dickens clearly intends this second choice of a wife to signal the possibility that self-determination may play a role in individual development. But because he portrays Agnes in such idealized terms that she scarcely seems to be real, the viability of this notion is difficult to accept. Agnes is seldom mentioned without reference to her sanctity, and this wrapping her in a mantle of religiosity only accentuates the impression of fantasy, implying that David has married an angel, not a flesh-and-blood woman. She is always portrayed as pointing upwards in the direction of heaven, and David always sees her in the remembered glow of a stained glass window. If it is difficult to accept the reality of Agnes, it is even more difficult to accept David's marriage to her as the solution to the problem of personal autonomy versus determinism.

Harry Stone suggests that at the heart of the difficulty with Agnes lies Dickens's separation of woman into a sexual partner on the one hand, and a companion and helpmate on the other. In fact, Agnes does not seem any more realistic or wise a choice than Dora was. But while Dickens was aware of what was wrong with David's choice of Dora, he seems not to have sensed that Agnes too is a form of wish-fulfillment.[9] Agnes is intended as the answer to David's "old unhappy loss or want of something" (DC, 890). But by turning her into a saint, Dickens nearly succeeds in throwing doubt on his own definition of maturity as marriage to the proper partner.

In *David Copperfield*, David is still very much influenced by his heredity and the novel itself is a chronicle of how patterns established in childhood and predetermined by heredity are repeated in adulthood. But *David Copperfield* also suggests that these childhood patterns may be broken through the wisdom conferred by self-knowledge. The novel portrays this self-knowledge – which it equates with maturity – as both possible and attainable. Once David has escaped the pattern of childishness that he has both inherited and learned from his parents, once he has disciplined his heart sufficiently to recognize who is and who is not worthy of its affections, he can settle into a fulfilled existence as a successful novelist and a successful family man. Indeed the novel is written from the standpoint of that achieved success, and as such it tempers a certain underlying sadness about the human condition with a hopeful view of human nature. Men, the novel seems to imply, may be far from perfect, but redemption is still possible through the love of a good woman. By the time Dickens came to write *Great Expectations*, even that hope was gone.

*   *   *

It would be a decade before Dickens again put a child at the center of a novel. When he did so in 1860, his thinking on the subject of heredity had expanded and changed. The novels written between *David Copperfield* and *Great Expectations* – *Bleak House*, *Hard Times*, *Little Dorrit*, *A Tale of Two Cities* – no longer take as their primary subject the developing identity of a single individual. Instead they focus on society as a whole, the various strands of narrative being gathered under the unifying umbrella of one overarching metaphor – the law suit, the prison, the French revolution, etc. These novels attempt to encompass all classes, their narratives moving from the highest rungs of the social ladder to the lowest, hinting at the common fate of all. This alteration in focus alters the manner in which Dickens presents heredity as both metaphor and narrative device. However, in 1860, ten years after the completion of *David Copperfield* – and one year after the publication of Darwin's *The Origin of Species* – Dickens again decided to place an individual at the center of a novel and to return once more to the subject of the single developing consciousness.

The proximity in time of Darwin's book to Dickens's novel had a major effect on Dickens's attitude towards heredity and his consequent depiction of how identity is formed. In my last chapter, I will examine in greater detail the Darwinian influences on Dickens's last three novels, beginning with *Great Expectations*, but here I would like to look only at the manner in which Dickens alters his understanding of the formation of the self in this novel.

Great Expectations constitutes a reassessment of *Oliver Twist* and *David Copperfield*, reversing the theme of hidden identity in the former, and re-examining the remaining traces of hereditary determinism in the latter. The most obvious points of comparison are between *David Copperfield* and *Great Expectations*, since both are "autobiographical" novels narrated in the first person by the central character. (Dickens himself was so worried about repeating the earlier novel in the later that he reread *David Copperfield* to make certain that his new book was original.) But *Great Expectations* does not so much echo *David Copperfield* as turn it inside out, negating many of the assumptions about human nature that Dickens had so confidently espoused in the earlier book.

In *Great Expectations*, Dickens takes the radical step of totally discarding heredity as a determining force in human development. In its place he substitutes experience, which he defines as encounters with other people. Pip is as complete a tabula rasa as Dickens ever created for a protagonist. We know nothing of his parents beyond what is reported of them on the inscriptions of their tombstones. Alexander Welsh notes that many of Dickens's novels begin with a thought of death immediately superimposed upon a birth, the birth being that of the novel's main character, and the death that of a parent.[10] This pattern is followed in *Oliver Twist, Dombey and Son, David Copperfield* and *Great Expectations*. As I suggested in my discussion of *David Copperfield*, such an opening tends to establish heredity as the prescriptive force in the unfolding life of the young child, alluding as it does to an absence that remains potent beyond the grave.

But such is not the case in *Great Expectations*. When the dead are invoked at the opening of this novel, it is specifically to deny their future influence on the protagonist, and to replace them with the convict, whose impact on the course of young Pip's life will be far more powerful than that of any blood relative. Pip's lack of hereditary connection makes him the most utterly desolate of Dickens's orphans. Not only are his parents dead, but they are utter blanks. There is not the least speculation throughout the course of the novel to enlighten Pip, or the reader, as to what they may have been like.

The result is that Pip must create himself out of whatever material happens his way, and we are first introduced to him on the very day when he begins the process of sorting out the "identity of things." It is on this particular afternoon in his seventh year that Pip first makes the acquaintance of Magwitch as the convict rises up from among the tombstones that mark the graves of Pip's parents and brothers. This terrifying apparition imprints himself on Pip's consciousness just seconds after the boy has come to the frightening realization that his existence is a thing separate and distinct from his surroundings. No sooner has the full impact of this existential loneliness impressed itself upon Pip than he begins to cry, and his crying rouses the terrible specter of the convict. Pip in a sense calls him forth, so that the convict rises from among the graves seemingly in answer to a need.

The nature of that need may be variously interpreted. It may be the need for a second father to replace the defunct original, and Magwitch will certainly play that role in Pip's life. Or it may be the need for a second self to fill the vacuum left by Pip's sudden consciousness of emptiness.[11] But it is also possible to read this opening from a Darwinian point of view. Pip's original awareness of himself as distinct and solitary, a creature existing apart from his surroundings, is given a check by Magwitch's sudden emergence from behind a tombstone. That check constitutes a reminder that there is no such thing as total distinctness in nature or human society, that all living creatures are fundamentally related and interdependent, from the simplest organisms to the highest, from the lowest classes to the most exalted – a proposition which the ensuing narrative will proceed to demonstrate.

So complete is Dickens's break with the notion of inherited personality in this novel that he purposely scrambles the kinship relations which he creates. The most obvious blood tie, that of Pip to his sister, is the one most devoid of any trace of family feeling and affection. The boy Pip reserves his love for his brother-in-law Joe, to whom he is related only by marriage. By a similar scrambling, Mr Pumblechook has been appropriated by Mrs Joe, Pip's sister, as her uncle, although in fact he is Joe's uncle not hers. And, despite his blood relation to the mild-mannered Joe, the hypocritical Pumblechook is closer in temperament and worldview to Mrs Joe than to his nephew, a sign that congeniality of outlook can produce greater resemblances than any direct blood connection. In the same way, the cold and haughty Estella is the daughter of Magwitch and a hot-tempered gypsy woman easily roused to homicidal jealousy. But despite a physical resemblance to her mother, Estella's personality has been formed by her guardian Miss Havisham, and that influence is so strong that it extends to her looks and gestures:

> In some of [Estella's] looks and gestures there was that tinge of resemblance to Miss Havisham which may often be noticed to have been acquired by children, from grown persons with whom they have been associated and secluded, and which, when childhood is passed, will produce a remarkable occasional likeness of expression between faces that are otherwise quite different.
>
> (GE, 259)

This is a description of resemblance resulting from influence, not heredity. In *Great Expectations* influence of this type replaces heredity as the formative factor in determining identity.

That Pip will be someone who will seek to define himself through the eyes of others is not immediately apparent from the start of the novel. On the contrary, one's first impression of Pip is that he is self-assertive. He has, after all, named himself: "So I called myself Pip, and came to be called Pip" (GE, 35). Pip's self-naming appears to be a sign, not only of his assertiveness, but also of his genealogical status and family connection. Pip's name is a childish corruption of Philip Pirrip, his father's name, and seems to define him as an extension of the line of descent. This opening gambit implies not only a strong sense of identity, but also an ability to make others take heed of one's claim to individuality – Pip comes to be called what he calls himself. But this initial impression of self-assertion turns out to be misleading: there is no aspect of Pip's young life which is his own creation, and eventually he will have to relinquish control even over his name.

One of the earliest and most formidable influences on Pip is that of his sister and its most obvious consequence is the boy's pervasive feeling of guilt.[12] Pip's upbringing has been made miserable by his sister's evangelical brand of Christianity, with its firm emphasis on the doctrine of Original Sin. This doctrine has been the guiding principle behind her philosophy of child-rearing, and Pip's being raised in this manner represents the theological conception of how personality is formed, a conception which the novel depicts as standing in opposition to a newer developmental model inspired by Darwinian ideas. According to his sister's religion – as filtered through Pip's eyes – the child is criminal by virtue of the fact that he is born:

> As to me, I think my sister must have had some general idea that I was a young offender whom an Accoucheur Policeman had taken up (on my birthday) and delivered over to her, to be dealt with according to the outraged majesty of the law. I was always treated as if I had insisted on being born, in opposition to the dictates of reason, religion and morality, and against the dissuading arguments of my best friends. Even, when I was taken to have a new suit of clothes, the tailor had orders to make

them like a kind of Reformatory, and on no account to let me
have the free use of my limbs.   (GE, 54)

Even the most ordinary events of childhood assume a criminal cast.

And then [she] entered on a fearful catalogue of all the illnesses
I had been guilty of, and of all the acts of sleeplessness I had
committed, and of all the high places I had fallen from, and all
the low places I had tumbled into, and all the injuries I had
done myself, and all the times she had wished me in my grave,
and I had contumaciously refused to go there.   (GE, 59)

His encounter with the convict endows Pip's feelings of sinful-
ness with human personification, and so supplies him with an
objective correlative for his sense of guilt. He begins to associate
the condemnable parts of himself with the convict. One consequence is that Pip's recollections betray an inclination towards
sententiousness that was entirely absent from the memoirs of David
Copperfield. David, after all, defined himself as innocent. Pip defines
himself as guilty. The result is that Pip's memoirs emphasize past
sins and errors, from which morals may be extracted and lessons
learned. This can best be demonstrated by his thoughts on his sister's
death:

... The times when I was a little helpless creature, and my sister
did not spare me, vividly returned. But they returned with a
gentler tone upon them that softened even the edge of Tickler.
For now, the very breath of the beans and the clover whispered
to my heart that the day must come when it would be well for
my memory that others walking in the sunshine should be softened as they thought of me.   (GE, 298)

This passage, with its suggestion of a common fate for all living
things and its implicit connection of death with the regenerative
functions of soil, sunshine, and growing things hints at the common sources of life as well as at their common ends. The allusion
to these natural processes sits side by side with the religious morality animating the restatement of the biblical maxim, "judge not,
lest ye be judged."

Here, in condensed form, are the antithetical concepts of the self
that the novel puts forth. The theological concept, to which may

be attributed the novel's persistent theme of guilt and criminality, conceives of the self as a unique creation deriving straight from the hand of God. The individual is born into the world in a fallen state, but at the same time, despite his degeneracy, he is the favourite child of Creation, standing separate and apart from the natural world. Against this is placed the theme of unifying natural forces, the self being connected in essence and destiny to the surrounding landscape and all the creatures in it.

Heredity in Dickens's fiction had used to stand as a mediating point between these two conceptions of individual derivation, translating the theological into the human sphere. Once it has been eliminated from consideration, the definition of selfhood begins to vacillate between the extremes of a rigid morality which defines identity as fixed and culpable, and the opposite pole of extreme fluidity. In the second case, the individual tries to fashion himself on any model which chance provides, being drawn particularly to those models bearing the stamp of social approbation. The second of these alternatives can be seen in Pip's relationship with the inhabitants of Satis House.

If Pip absorbs his sense of guilt from his sister and her moralizing hypocritical friends, he absorbs his sense of social inferiority from the inhabitants of Satis House. One of the consequences of Pip's need to define himself through others is that he is suggestible. He has only to hear Miss Havisham tell Estella to break his heart and his heart is as good as broken. As for Estella, "Her contempt for me was so strong, that it became infectious and I caught it" (GE, 90). He accepts without question the truth of Estella's scornful remark that he is nothing but a common labouring boy with coarse hands and thick boots who calls knaves jacks – the latter a particularly inspired hint at the arbitrariness of class distinctions – and feels ashamed. The extent to which Pip defines himself in terms of how others see him is underscored by his complaint to Biddy: "What would it signify to me, being coarse and common, if nobody had told me so!" (GE, 155). In other words, Estella's contempt is all that is needed to make Pip feel contemptible.

The extent to which *Great Expectations* defines the other as vital in supplying a sense of the self can be seen in Pip's frequent use of words like "influence," "contagion," "contamination," "coercion" to underline the importance of external forces on his attempts to create himself. Sometimes this terminology is given a slightly different context, as in Biddy's sarcastic reply to Pip when he expresses amazement that she manages to keep up with her studies, "I suppose I must just catch it [learning] – like a cough" (GE, 153). But in the main, these terms belong to Pip's vocabulary and form part of his conception of himself *vis-à-vis* others. So, in the example above, Estella's scorn is described as contagious, while of his brother-in-law Joe's beneficent affection, Pip writes: "It is not possible to know how far the influence of any amiable honest-hearted duty-doing man flies out into the world, but it is very possible to know how it has touched oneself in going by . . ." (GE, 135).

Pip attributes his positive qualities to the influence of Joe, and he attributes his timidity and sensitivity to "the capricious and violent coercion" of his sister's upbringing. Even more significant is Pip's use of the word "contaminated" to describe the "taint of prison and crime" which seems to haunt him wherever he goes and which he cannot seem to escape (GE, 284). All influences, both for the good and for the bad, are crucial to Pip, who has no other way to define himself. Since Pip has come into the world without any pre-determined or inherent sense of identity, he must try to forge his individuality out of an amalgam of such external factors. But it is not a happy amalgam. "Contagion," "contamination," "coercion," all have negative connotations. They suggest that Pip is too susceptible to outside authority and too little resistant or discerning when it comes to distinguishing harmful influences from beneficial ones.

The effect of external forces on the developing self constitutes Dickens's new post-Darwinian understanding of human nature. Darwin's theory attempts to explain evolution through a balancing of external forces and internal ones – that is, natural selection assumes that those individuals in any given species who adapt most successfully to their surroundings will be the most likely to pass on their hereditary material to their progeny, who will in turn have an advantage in adapting to their surroundings, which they will pass on to their progeny, and so forth. Thus the evolution of species is seen as encompassing a gradual response and reaction to external factors. In *Great Expectations*, the development of the individual is seen in similar terms. Estella, for instance, has been molded away from her "right nature" by the influence of Miss Havisham (GE, 411). Such an alteration of the essential self would never have been possible for an Oliver Twist, a Little Nell, or even a Paul Dombey.

The character who best illustrates this new developmental model is Pip. At every stage of his life, Pip has been influenced by someone else. But the paramount influence, the one around which the entire novel revolves, centers on his great expectations. This turning point in Pip's life and fortune is entirely dependent on the actions of another. Pip, who has understood himself only in the reflected light of other people's conceptions, now allows someone else's definition of what it means to be a gentleman to dictate the course of his life. In accepting the unexpected fortune that suddenly comes his way, Pip abdicates all say over his own destiny. He even abdicates the right to dispose of his own name, the one thing over which he had once had control. Now it is his anonymous benefactor who insists that he must never be called anything but Pip.

Pip's relationship to Magwitch forms the crux of the novel. From their first encounter, Magwitch functions as an alternate ego for Pip, and the identification between them is subtly suggested. Pip watches the famished convict eat the food which he has stolen for him and notices "a decided similarity between the dog's way of eating and the man's" (GE, 50). Later Pip is devastated by the thought that Estella feeds him "as insolently as if I were a dog in disgrace" (GE, 92). And later still, Magwitch will describe how he first came to self-consciousness in terms that are reminiscent of Pip's first instance of self-awareness. "I first become aware of myself, down in Essex, a thieving turnips for my living. Summun had run away from me ... and he'd took the fire with him, and left me wery cold" (GE, 360).

Contributing to the identification between Pip and Magwitch is the fact that Pip, in embarking on his privileged life, sacrifices his autonomy to become his patron's creature. He begins to play the part of a gentleman in instinctive and spontaneous accord with Magwitch's idea of what the concept entails, even before he knows that Magwitch is his benefactor. Magwitch – as becomes clear when he finally reveals himself – conceives of a gentleman as a being entirely defined by money, and therefore as a commodity to be bought. One of the cornerstones of Magwitch's belief is that the money which defines the gentleman and validates his existence should be money which he has not earned. The gentleman's existence must be one of leisure and idleness, graced by a smattering of learning.

Here again, Dickens is portraying a society in which the traditional defining power of heredity – in this case the original association of the concept of "gentleman" with the upper classes – has been undermined. One need no longer be the offspring of a gentleman to be called a "gentleman." If the appellation may be purchased, then it may apply to all, including such lower-class denizens as blacksmiths' apprentices. At the same time, the term's provenance among the elite and its aura of inherited privilege is the very thing that makes the idea of "gentleman" so appealing to such déclassé types as Magwitch and Pip, and so reaffirms their symbolic kinship.[13]

This symbolic kinship is, in effect, a relationship of father and son, achieved without any actual blood tie. The infusion of Magwitch's money into Pip's young life creates a relationship analogous to paternity. Jaggers' refers to Magwitch as the fountainhead, the source of Pip's money, and therefore the source of his rebirth as a gentleman. In case the point needs any more emphasis, Dickens has Magwitch himself exclaim: "Pip I'm your second father. You're my son . . . I've put money away only for you to spend" (GE, 337). In this father–son relationship, money substitutes for semen as the stuff out of which life is created.[14] In the same way, money stands for both the biological and the utilitarian aspects of Pip's love for Estella, when he writes that he cannot dissociate her presence from all of his hankerings after money and gentility, nor separate her from "the innermost life of my life" (GE, 257).

Pip's initial reaction to this new-found father is to recoil in horror, as if from the worst aspects of himself: "The abhorrence in which I held the man, the dread I had of him, the repugnance with which I shrank from him, could not have been exceeded if he had been some terrible beast" (GE, 337). But he gradually comes to accept and even to love Magwitch. Through this dance of repulsion and affection, Dickens presents the complexities of a father–son relationship which is based on circumstance rather than blood. It is also based on mutual identification. When, during his solitary life in the Australian bush, Magwitch drops a knife, the face he sees reflected in it is not his own, but Pip's. Similarly, Pip is haunted by the specter of Magwitch as another version of his own most detestable nature. When Magwitch asserts his ownership of Pip as a "brought up London gentleman" we are thrust into the arena of paternal power and boyish rebellion, and when Pip acknowledges that his rightful place is at Magwitch's side, we are meant to understand this as a sign of his maturity.

This is in keeping with the muddying of actual kinship ties throughout the novel. There is no hereditary thread to bind the two men, as Pip acknowledges when he writes: "I was not related to the out-law, or connected with him by any recognizable tie; he had put his hand to no writing or settlement in my favour . . . I had no claim . . ." (GE, 458). It is this lack of either a biological or a legal claim on either side that serves to underline and broaden the meaning of paternity here.

Pip constitutes Magwitch's claim to a place of equality and re-spect in the world. Magwitch can feel that he is equal to, if not better than the Australian colonists because, "If I ain't a gentle-man, nor yet ain't got no learning, I'm the owner of such" (GE, 339). In this assertion of ownership over another human being Magwitch the convict resembles no one so much as Dombey the capitalist. But in *Great Expectations* the corruptions of capitalism are mutual, affecting the giver and the recipient equally. Pip revels in the discomfiture of the Pumblechooks and Wopsles, in whose opinion he has so suddenly and unexpectedly risen. He allows his new-found wealth to lead him into dissipation. For both Magwitch and Pip, the making of a gentleman has a significance rooted in the insecurity and poverty of their origins. If Magwitch is the author of Pip's great expectations, Pip is no less the personification of Magwitch's.

But if the father–son relationship of Magwitch and Pip begins as a demonstration of the spoiling power of money, it ends on a far more affective and redemptive note. Magwitch had chosen Pip as the beneficiary of his largesse out of a sense of gratitude and loy-alty to the boy who once fed him when he was starving. As their relationship develops, Magwitch's belief that Pip has always acted out of the best motives begins to have an effect. Magwitch is con-vinced that even as a child Pip had recognized in him "some small redeeming touch," and this perception eventually becomes the truth. Pip does begin to see Magwitch's redeeming features and this in turn reinforces Magwitch's belief in Pip's goodness of heart. If Magwitch had presented for the child Pip the distorted image of his own guilty self-reflection, the image which he reflects back for the adult Pip tends in the opposite direction.

This demonstrates the positive side of Pip's suggestibility. Because Magwitch believes in Pip's better self, Pip becomes that better self and begins to feel for Magwitch the affection and gratitude which Magwitch has felt for him. Pip believes that the alteration in his feelings toward Magwitch is the result of a change in Magwitch rather than in himself. He believes that it is Magwitch who has softened, "indefinably, for I could not have said how" (GE, 390). Pip cannot say how, because the softening has occurred in himself and not in Magwitch. The transposing of one's emotions, thoughts and motives onto another – what in psychoanalysis is called projection – is the complement of absorption. Projection is an attempt to impose one's emotions onto another, while absorption is the attempt to take another into oneself. Both Magwitch and Pip attribute to each other qualities and feelings which do not initially exist, but these apparently mistaken attributions eventually become reality.

This shaping and reshaping of personal identity in answer to external factors further underscores Dickens's attempt to blot out hereditary determinism in this novel in favour of a more flexible model of human development. *Great Expectations* defines human nature as fluid and pliable with regard to the impressions left on each individual personality by its contact with others. The novel's principals impose their own beliefs, emotions, and prejudices on each other and are in turn imposed upon; they attempt to fashion others in their own images and are in turn fashioned by them. Viewed in these terms, the title "Great Expectations" takes on broader associations than merely the reference to Pip's sudden and ulti-mately elusive rise in fortune. It refers as well to the dynamic of interrelation in the novel, which conceives of human nature as attuned to the expectations of others, and of individual identity as forming itself in answer to those expectations – an idea not that far removed from the Darwinian precept of adaptation, which con-ceives of organisms evolving in response to their environments.

This new conception of human development is in keeping with the social concerns that animate Dickens's narrative. The fact that Pip becomes a gentleman through the infusion of Magwitch's money suggests that the susceptibility associated with individual develop-ment has ramifications which extend beyond the domain of the personal. Fluidity may extend also to class. For this reason, no-tions of descent and family line are irrelevant to the novel. If anyone with money can "make" a gentleman, then actual paternity be-comes meaningless, since class itself ceases to be a hereditary category and becomes subject to the pressures of the marketplace. What is more, if the formation of personal destiny is dependent on such uncontrollable factors as chance encounters with strangers, then heredity becomes worthless as a means of propagating the good.

The feeling of contamination which haunts Pip and which he associates with the netherworld of convicts and prisons is closely related to the feeling of guilt which permeates his conscience. But the criminal element in the novel functions not only as a metaphor for the corruption lying at the heart of society, but also as a reminder of the rudimentary connections linking all living things. *Great Expectations* is uncompromising in its assertion that the most respectable human institutions are shadowed by the least respectable, in much the same way as the dome of Saint Paul's can only be seen from behind the stone walls of Newgate Prison (GE, 189). *Great Expectations* defines the "underworld" as existing in symbiotic relation with the world "above" it.

The result of all this juxtaposition and intertwining of levels of society is to create an impression of a world in which everything is connected by invisible strings of complicity. This suggests another way in which *Great Expectations* constitutes a corrective to *Oliver Twist* – it overturns the plot of hidden identity. In *Great Expectations* Pip discovers that his wish to be a gentleman has allied him, not with the upper levels of society, but with the lower. The secret of his gentlemanly origin is not that he belongs to the aristocracy, but that he belongs to the underclass. His sudden wealth, which had seemed to catapult him into the social stratosphere, and which he had assumed to derive from the aristocratic Miss Havisham, in fact tied him ever more securely to the marginalized domain of convicts and low-lifes. What is more, the real secret of hidden identity which the novel reveals is that this apparently marginalized world exists at the core of society, interacting with the aristocracy, breeding with the middle class, turning all princes into potential felons under the skin.

The woman Pip loves, the one who mocks his working-class origins and to whom he is attracted because of her ladylike pretensions, turns out to be the natural daughter of Pip's convict-benefactor by a murderess. Not only is Estella a mirror-version of Pip, but she is, symbolically, his kin, since both she and Pip are, biologically and by adoption, children of Magwitch. Both have been "made" by their respective benefactors, for reasons which have as much, if not more, to do with their benefactors' private miseries as with their good intentions. Yet Pip and Estella learn their roles well. They become the creatures they were intended to become – thus totally undermining the prescriptive potential of heredity, and reversing, among other things, the optimistic thrust of *Oliver Twist*.

The absence of predetermined personality traits in *Great Expectations* would appear, at first glance, to confer greater autonomy on the novel's characters, hence a greater freedom to create their own sense of identity. In fact, this apparent liberty is obliterated by what Dickens depicts as a total reliance on others to supply a definition for the self – and by an unquestioning acceptance and subservience to the class system as a means of adjudicating values and determining desires.

Eliminating heredity as a primary factor in the formation of the self does not free the individual to create his or her own identity. Quite the contrary. Dickens portrays the lack of hereditary influence as potentially debilitating, because it allows external factors to play too large a role in personal development. The individual is left without a center, and is therefore subject to the will of others and to a form of weather-vane slavery imposed by the constant shifting of external conditions. There is no evidence that Dickens considered this definition of development as preferable to his earlier understanding of the self as an amalgam of inherited traits. Neither Pip nor Estella is presented as a contented being, free to create the self in accord with personal desire.

In *Great Expectations*, the definition of goodness is no longer what it was in *Oliver Twist*. It has ceased to be an inherited trait, and has acquired an aura of ambiguity and abstraction. This is a far cry from the concrete and distinct quality which goodness had in *Oliver Twist* and *The Old Curiosity Shop*, where it seemed to be simply a displacement of the theological concept of grace to the human sphere. In *Great Expectations*, goodness, virtue, beneficence have acquired such amorphous complexity that they are difficult to separate from their more negative cousins – narcissism, snobbery, condescension, self-righteousness. All are mixed together into one all-too-human whole.

4
Illegitimacy and Villainy: the Negative Aspects of Heredity

In 1851 alone, 42 000 illegitimate children were born in England and Wales, which meant that 1 in 12 unmarried women above the age of puberty had borne a child.[1] The result, for the Victorians, was a plethora of illegitimate children living on the margins of society, subject to strictures of various kinds, defined as eternal outcasts from the ideal of family life.

The distinction between legitimate and illegitimate children is rooted in the age-old dilemma of the male's uncertainty about the provenance of his offspring, and in the need, in patriarchal cultures, to ensure a stable inheritance from one generation of sons to the next. The Bible, which defines adultery as a sin punishable by death, gave a religious sanction to this need by hedging marriage with constraints – constraints which always applied more severely to women than to men.

Popular belief embellished these biblical constraints with a host of superstitions about bastards. Bastards were often thought to be differently endowed – more intelligent, braver, stupider, etc. – than legitimate children. An example of this can be found in Yiddish where the term for bastard, "mamzer," is often used as an endearment by a parent to a legitimate child, because bastards were thought to be unusually intelligent. English too reflects an ambivalence towards bastardy. The terms "love child" and "natural child" suggest that there is something unloved and unnatural about legitimate children.

The seventh-century prelate, St Isidore, accounted for illegitimacy by suggesting that, unlike the child born in wedlock who was formed from "one blood, that is from the same semen as the father," illegitimate children are called *spurius* because they spring from the mother alone.[2] The notion that women alone were implicated in the production of illegitimate children went through several elaborations over the course of time. Writing in 1687, Nicolas Venette took issue with the learned opinion of his day that children were legitimate if they resembled their fathers, and illegitimate if they took after their mothers. Venette argued that the imagination of women was so powerful that their minds could call up the faces of their husbands even while they were in the arms of their lovers. In this way, the child would resemble the mother's husband even when it was the product of an act of adultery.[3] This formulation neatly equated female imagination with female duplicity, and implicated both in the hereditary endowment of the child.

Nowhere is the effect of hereditary endowment more intensely emphasized and more ideologically charged in Dickens's fiction than on the question of illegitimacy. Dickens identified generally with the victimized child, and no child was so victimized, outcast, and marginalized in Victorian society as the one that was born on the wrong side of the sheets. Furthermore, an illegitimate child presupposes a hereditary drama, replete with the stuff of melodrama – secret origins, sexual misadventure, the quest for identity.

For the illegitimate child, the question of identity is especially crucial. In fact, identity becomes synonymous with heredity, since biological inheritance is the only link to family that such a child has. An illegitimate child stands outside the realm of man-made legality as a testament to the anarchy of natural impulse. In *Bleak House*, the illegitimate Esther Summerson is several times told that while she may exist in fact, she does not exist in law. Without the legal identity conferred by family connection, the illegitimate child must found its sense of self on bloodlines rather than on family ties.

Dickens's readiness to champion the rights of the dispossessed and marginalized child gives his early portraits of illegitimate children their idealized patina and ideological engagement. This ideological engagement can be seen in its purest form in *Oliver Twist*, which proposes a radical reassessment of the stigma of illegitimacy by insisting on the inherent purity of the bastard child.

Oliver Twist is the story of a child redeemed and vindicated by his bloodline. What is more, Oliver's inborn grace has consequences which extend beyond himself, since it retroactively obliterates the guilt of his parents, posthumously redeeming them. The virtue of the child presupposes the essential goodness of the parents from whom he sprang, and so absolves them of sin, at the same time as the middle-class virtues which Oliver has inherited from his parents make such a redemption possible. Oliver and his parents justify and absolve each other. Or, as Steven Marcus puts it, "the immaculateness of Oliver's character suggests as immaculate as possible a conception."[4]

Marcus takes his analogy to the Virgin Mary no further, but I believe that the comparison is apt. *Oliver Twist* closes with a reference to Oliver's mother. The setting is the village church, which contains a memorial slab in honor of Agnes, the mother who had been "weak and erring." The context is significant. Oliver has effectively disappeared from the last section of the novel, which concentrates instead on the perfidious scheming of Monks and Bumble, as well as on Sikes's murder of Nancy and its aftermath. The penultimate chapter features Fagin in his death cell on the night before his execution. Thus the spotlight for the last third of *Oliver Twist* focuses on the criminal and the depraved. This stress on criminality is briefly interrupted in the last chapter as Dickens ties up the loose ends of his plot and delivers the requisite happy ending. But then, unexpectedly, the text returns to transgression – this time that of Oliver's mother. The murder and larceny of Sikes and Fagin is thus ludicrously juxtaposed to the sexual "fall" of Agnes, highlighting the insignificance of the latter. But Dickens goes further and insists, not only on the insignificance of Agnes's transgression, but on its essential sanctity.

> But, if the spirits of the Dead ever come back to earth, to visit spots hallowed by the love – the love beyond the grave – of those whom they knew in life, I believe that the shade of Agnes sometimes hovers round that solemn nook. I believe it none the less because that nook is in a Church, and she was weak and erring. (OT, 479–80)

The passage reprises Dickens's ideological position on illegitimacy, namely that illicit love is purged of taint if it is prompted by genuine emotion, and that the children of an illicit union are born innocent and should be treated accordingly. The passage reinforces this message in two ways. The first is the emphasis on mystical connection – the spirits of the dead who watch over the living, the love beyond the grave – which casts a supernatural aura over the relationship between the deceased mother and her living son. The second follows from the first in emphasizing the primary role of the mother. It is her fate which brackets the novel, since her death in childbirth begins the action and her invocation by the narrator closes it.

This closing passage plays upon the Victorian tendency to sentimentalize motherhood. Its attempt to hallow Oliver's mother despite her fall – and through her Oliver himself – invites comparison with the Mother and Son of Christian belief, a comparison which is reinforced by the fact that the setting is a church. Instances of illegitimacy in Dickens's fiction, featuring as they do a primary bond between mother and child, and a father, distant and insubstantial, who exists on the perimeter of the relationship, tend to be evocative of the traditional Christian pairing of Mary and Jesus. Illegitimacy may invert the doctrines of immaculate conception and virgin birth, but it highlights the relationship between mother and child in a way that marriage, which accorded all legal rights to the Victorian father, does not. The Christian doctrines which relate to Mary and her son shed a reflected light on the dilemma of unwed motherhood, and provide scope for the claims which Dickens makes on behalf of Oliver's mother and her essential sanctity.

There is another, more realistic dimension to Dickens's emphasis on the role of the mother in *Oliver Twist*. One of his intentions in writing *Oliver Twist* had been to excoriate the Poor Law of 1834. The 'bastardy clauses' of that law placed the entire blame and burden for illegitimacy at the door of the unwed mother. Where, previously, such mothers had had the right to prosecute the father and force him to either marry them or pay an allowance to help support the child – an allowance which the parish made up if the father defaulted – the 'bastardy clauses' took that right away in order not to encourage moral depravity among young women. The Poor Law thus put a legal stamp on the popular belief that an illegitimate child is primarily its mother's offspring, her burden to bear alone.[5]

In *Bleak House* Dickens offers another portrait of an illegitimate child, this time a girl. Here, however, he treats the problem within a middle-class context. Esther Summerson is brought up to believe that she is the emblem of her parents' – especially her mother's – sin, thereby emphasizing the innocent child's complicity in biological processes over which she has no control. "Your mother, Esther, is your disgrace, and you were hers ... Pray daily that the sins of others be not visited upon your head, according to what is written," her godmother admonishes her (BH, 65).

Esther is raised in the Puritan gloom of her godmother's house, a godmother who turns out to be her aunt, the sister of her erring mother. In *Little Dorrit*, the illegitimate Miss Wade is similarly raised by a "grandmother" who turns out not to be a relation at all. The implication in both cases is that illegitimate children are doomed from birth never to know their exact relationship to anyone and especially not to those who are closest to them. They live in a world of scrambled bloodlines and shadowy connections. In fact, as long as their actual parentage remains in doubt, they are potentially related to everyone they meet. This potential for infinite relation in its heroine dovetails with the thematic concerns of *Bleak House*, a novel which is obsessed with connections.

In *Bleak House*, Esther's illegitimacy is generalized to imply a taint at the heart of society, just as her equivocal position with regard to the law echoes the larger concerns of a narrative which is structured around a law suit. Issues of legality and legitimacy form the broader thematic backdrop of *Bleak House*, so that Dickens's choice of a bastard child as a co-narrator and central character creates reverberations throughout the text of his novel.

But if Esther's illegitimacy has broader thematic implications, it also constitutes a personal dilemma. Dickens characterizes Esther's reaction to the knowledge of inherent taint as her determination, "to repair the fault I had been born with (of which I confessedly felt guilty and yet innocent)" (BH, 65). Later, when the identity of her mother has been revealed, Esther begins to think of her parent as "her, against whom I was a witness" (BH, 569). This ambiguous stigma of simultaneous guilt and innocence is, of course, the hereditary burden of all those who are born afflicted, whether it be with a club foot or a moral stain. (One could take this further and suggest that it is the burden imposed on all living things by heredity itself. In hereditary terms we are all innocent of the traits passed on to us, yet guilty by virtue of having to bear their consequences.)

Dickens champions Esther in the same way as he had earlier championed Oliver, by insisting on her essential goodness. He deliberately calls up the biblical injunctions in order to reverse them:

" . . . If the sins of the father are sometimes visited upon the children . . . I knew that I was as innocent of my birth as a queen of hers," Esther declares (BH, 571). In place of the harshness of the biblical code, Dickens substitutes an alternative genealogical morality. Says Mr Jarndyce: "I think it must be somewhere written that the virtues of the mothers shall, occasionally, be visited on the children, as well as the sins of the father" (BH, 287).

This harks back to the portrait gallery of virtuous women in *The Old Curiosity Shop* and sets up a genealogical distinction based on gender. The dimensions of this distinction are enlarged with Esther's assertion that as a child, she did not wonder who her father was so much as she wondered about her mother (BH, 63), thereby emphasizing the extent to which illegitimate children belong to their mothers, both emotionally and symbolically. To underline this notion still further, Dickens confers on Esther's father the pseudonym Nemo – nobody.

The importance of Esther's father to the narrative of *Bleak House* lies, almost totally, in his death. Through dying, he becomes the source of an unspecified contagion – probably smallpox – that reaches out to infect the entire social world encompassed by the novel. Nemo's function, as his name suggests, is therefore highly symbolic. He allows Dickens to locate the idea of taint and contagion within one individual, at the same time as his insubstantiality highlights the Victorian assumption that sexual misadventure is primarily a woman's sin.

From society's point of view, Esther is cursed, not so much by her father's act, as by her mother's, thereby reinforcing St Isidore's dictum that when it comes to illegitimacy, the child is entirely its mother's issue. In fact the father's lack of substance as a living being in the novel, compared to the pivotal role he plays as a dead one, suggests that Dickens is again drawing an analogy to the virgin birth. Here is the description of Esther's father on his deathbed: " . . . The lonely figure on the bed, whose path in life has lain through five-and-forty years lies there, with no more track behind him, that any one can trace, than a deserted infant" (BH, 196).

This can be read in several ways. The most obvious meaning is that Nemo is as anonymous in death as he was in life. But another, more ironic interpretation is possible, one which suggests that he has indeed left a track behind – a deserted infant. This in fact proves to be the case. At the same time, the passage also casts a supernatural pall over the dead man, a suggestion of the ethereal, enhanced by the fact that he dies of an overdose of opium, a drug associated with visions. The impression of Nemo's otherworldliness is later reinforced when it is revealed that, as Captain Hawdon, he was thought to have drowned long before his actual death. This makes him a revenant, a spirit risen from the dead, who can move through life and leave no track behind.

While the figure of Esther's father is thus freighted with symbolic significance, the fact remains that he does not matter much in her life and she spends very little time thinking about him. In chapter 5, she even passes his lodging without experiencing the least intimation that someone important to her personal history lives inside. This may not seem odd, since Esther has no way of suspecting her father's presence above Krook's shop, but when compared to her first, equally unwitting, encounter with her mother, the lack of premonition which she displays with regard to her father is striking.

What David Grylls refers to as "the unerring mystical semaphores of the blood relationship" in Dickens is nowhere so well demonstrated as during the first encounter between Esther and her mother.[6] Neither woman has any inkling of the existence, to say nothing of the identity, of the other. Lady Dedlock has been told that her illegitimate child is dead, whereas Esther knows nothing whatever about her mother. They happen by chance to be in the same church – as in *Oliver Twist*, a significant location for the symbolic redemption of fallen mothers – when Esther first lays eyes on Lady Dedlock. Esther reacts as follows: "Shall I ever forget the rapid beating at my heart occasioned by the look I met as I stood up!" The recognition is mutual: "Shall I ever forget the manner in which those handsome proud eyes seemed to spring out of their languor and to hold mine!" (BH, 304).

This instinctive apprehension of clues to her own identity appears to be encoded into Esther's blood, bespeaking the mystical powers of generation, and negating the need for rational explanation. There are similar examples of intuitive recognition throughout Dickens's work. In *A Tale of Two Cities*, when Lucie Manette encounters her jail-broken father, whom she has not seen since childhood, she touches his arm: "A strange thrill struck him when she did so, and visibly passed over his frame" (TTC, 75). David Grylls writes that these frissons are plainly delightful to Dickens, but that the hackneyed and histrionic language betrays his real disbelief.[7] The language may be hackneyed, but the belief is real.

The idea that parents and children are bound by invisible, near-mystical bonds was common in the nineteenth century, and persists into our own time. Such instinctive recognitions illustrate the irrational element in Dickens's portrayal of heredity, the point at which biology shades into fantasy. It is heredity as magic, but magic contained within the human agency of parental endowment, and therefore brought down to earth and secularized.

In describing Esther's first accidental meeting with Lady Dedlock, Dickens also returns to his favourite trope for establishing hereditary connection – that of the portrait, or its near relative, the mirror. The sense which Esther has on first seeing Lady Dedlock, that she is viewing a face which looks "like a broken glass to me, in which I saw scraps of old remembrances" (BH, 304) suggests again Dickens's assumption about the fixity of hereditary resemblance: " . . . I had never seen the face, but it affected me in the same strange way . . . There arose before my mind innumerable pictures of myself" (BH, 309). This type of instant recognition based on similarity of feature is common in Dickens's work. In the same novel, Mr George recognizes at first glance a nephew he has never seen before, because the young man looks like himself and "likenesses run in families" (BH, 902).

Of course, the rhetoric of mystical relation which Dickens uses to describe Esther's encounters with Lady Dedlock is colored by the sentimentalism which the Victorians associated with the mother–child bond. Thus, when Esther finally has her tête-à-tête with Lady Dedlock, the text sounds again its note of portentous recognition: "I was rendered motionless . . . by a something in her face that I had pined for and dreamed of when I was a little child; something I had never seen in any face; something I had never seen in hers before" (BH, 563). That mysterious "something" is, of course, an expression of the forsaken child's need for a mother, a need enunciated through the language of mystical blood-tie. As for Lady Dedlock, her maternal instincts are similarly activated. She may have thought her child was dead, but the instant she laid eyes on the strange young woman in church, she sensed their bond: " . . . She had been startled; and had thought of what would have been like me, if it had ever lived; and had lived on" (BH, 569).

Here again it is physical appearance that provides the key to family relation. So intent is Dickens on stressing the absolute resemblance between parent and child as a metaphor for the blood-tie, that not only does Esther notice the resemblance between herself and her mother, so does everyone else – Mr George, the law clerk Guppy, and Jo, the crossing-sweep. When Esther finally realizes that Lady Dedlock is her mother, her first impulse is to feel relieved that owing to her disfiguration through smallpox, no one would any longer think to connect her to her mother – or in the text's harsher words – "I could never disgrace her by any trace of likeness" (BH, 565). In fact, it is the physical resemblance between mother and daughter which first causes Guppy to suspect the connection between Esther and Lady Dedlock when he sees the latter's portrait hanging in Chesney Wold (BH, 138). Thus, as Juliet McMaster points out, while Tulkinghorn painstakingly gathers the truth about Lady Dedlock's affair from documents and careful observation, Guppy gets beyond the affair to the offspring with far less trouble because he works from a picture rather than a document.[8]

The revelation of Esther's parentage is intimately tied to Dickens's overall scheme in the novel. In a narrative which continually interrupts itself to pose the question, "what is the connection?"[9] Esther's illegitimacy and the fact that she is the daughter of an aristocrat and a pauper named Nobody suggests the centrality of her story to Dickens's ultimate intention of contracting the entire web of society into a single entwining knot.

Several interlocking metaphors accomplish this end, the first and foremost being the suit in Chancery. Related to the suit is the theme of contagion, which is closely associated with Esther. The suit in Chancery is the novel's primary symbol of interconnection, since it condemns suitors from all classes to the identical fate of awaiting a judgement that never comes. In the same way contagion levels the distinctions between classes by defining all humans as equally vulnerable to infection. Both of these overarching metaphors are related to heredity. The suit in Chancery is concerned with the disposition of a will, with who does and who does not have a right to inherit, with the legitimacy of bloodlines and the adjudicating of hereditary claims.

As for contagion, scientific thought of the time emphasized the link between reproduction and disease through contact theory. This theory held that fertilization resulted from a chemical reaction brought about through the contact of egg and sperm. The popularity of this theory derived from the fact that it could be used to explain a host of other organic phenomena besides reproduction, including contagious diseases, which were thought to occur when poisons generated in the body were propagated through the air. Rudolph Leuckart writing in 1853 makes the connection explicit:

> The sperm operates by contact, the same as a contagion or decaying body acts. Not through intimate relations with the egg, but in this way: that it imparts a certain motion to the molecules of the egg which transmitted from atom to atom produce new arrangements, new forms and new qualities.[10]

The use of contagion in *Bleak House* thus parallels the theme of tainted heredity which is embodied in Esther's illegitimacy. Contagion constitutes a restatement of the anarchic impulse underlying illicit sexual activity, activity of which Esther herself is the fruit. It makes sense, therefore, that Esther should also attract to herself that other symbol of disastrous and degenerate propagation – disease.

The smallpox epidemic in *Bleak House* begins with the burial of Esther's father, thereby further collapsing sexual misadventure, social profligacy, and infection into a single source. The graveyard in which Nemo is put to rest is "pestiferous and obscene," communicating malignant diseases to the living as legacies from the discarded dead. The "corruption" which rises from Nemo's burial place will eventually infect his unacknowledged daughter, reaching her by passing from the lowest social level – Jo, the crossing-sweep – up to the servant class represented by the maid Charley, and finally attacking the middle class represented by Esther. The circle is complete when the aristocratic Lady Dedlock, Nemo's lover and Esther's mother, lies dead at the gate of that same graveyard. What kills her is never specified, although she too has been exposed to "contamination."

This occurs when Lady Dedlock, disguised as her own servant, visits the cemetery where Nemo lies buried: "The servant shrinks... into a corner of that hideous archway, with its deadly stains contaminating her dress; and putting out her two hands, and passionately telling him [Jo] to keep away from her, for he is loathsome to her, so remains for some moments" (BH, 278).

In his description of the graveyard as pestiferous, Dickens is alluding to the Victorian belief that disease was spread by miasmic hazes which arose from decaying matter.[11] But Lady Dedlock, while dressed as her own servant, appears to fear contamination not from the miasmas of the cemetery, but from contact with Jo.

The scene links contamination to class in a way that foretells the eventual spread of the infection upwards from the lowest orders to Esther. Smallpox has an interesting relationship to social station. During the seventeenth and eighteenth centuries, the most famous victims of the disease were members of the royal houses of Europe, including in 1660 the brother and sister of Charles II. But by the nineteenth century, inoculation and variolation had turned small-pox into a disease of the lower classes.[12]

As such, smallpox becomes in *Bleak House* an instrument of social revenge, carried in the blood of the despised and dispossessed, awaiting an opportunity to infect the well-off and comfortable. "Here's the fever coming up the street," remarks Inspector Bucket as a palanquin is carried past him, and the metonymy suggests that the contagion is everywhere present and everywhere imminent. The corruption of tainted blood is elaborated into a metaphor for un-checked propagation that leaves no level of society untouched.

> There is not a drop of Tom's corrupted blood but propagates infection and contagion somewhere. It shall pollute, this very night, the choice stream (in which chemists on analysis would find the genuine nobility) of a Norman house, and his Grace shall not be able to say Nay to the infamous alliance. There is not an atom of Tom's slime, not a cubic inch of any pestilential gas in which he lives, not one obscenity or degradation about him, not an ignorance, not a wickedness, not a brutality of his committing, but shall work its retribution through every order of society, up to the proudest of the proud, and to the highest of the high. (BH, 683)

The revenge of the poor on the rich is the spread of contagion carried by corrupted blood. And the contagion that is spread is not merely physical disease, but moral corruption as well. Victorian social commentators frequently equated the contagion of disease with the perception of a moral plague among the poor. Describing the living conditions of the London poor, Archibald Alison writes in *Principles of Population* (1840): "The progress of vice in such circumstances is almost as certain and often nearly as rapid as that of physical contagion."[13]

The smallpox which attacks Esther is a ghostly bequest from her father, an amorphous, invisible, deadly essence that is not far different from heredity itself as a determinant of human fate. By means of this contagion Dickens generalizes the personal taint of Esther's birth to society as a whole, suggesting that both have a common source. *Bleak House* links illegitimacy to disease through the notion of the unchecked reproduction of moral stain, symbolized by the decomposing body of the sinning father, passed on as the disease which afflicts and scars the innocent daughter. Smallpox translates the abstract dictum of the sins of the fathers being visited on the child into the physical terms of an actual disease.

That *Bleak House* is concerned with linking heredity to both corruption and death can be seen in the singular demise of Krook, who dies through spontaneous combustion. Krook's destruction stands at the opposite pole from death by contagion. His is a death without sequence, consequence, or aftermath. Unlike death by infection, Krook's is not a death which leads to more death. It is a one-of-a-kind event, and its very uniqueness suggests its purpose. Although Dickens insisted on the realistic possibility of such a demise, the fact remains that Krook's is a fairy-tale ending, a vanishing in a cloud of smoke.[14] And as such it stands in ironic counterpoint to the web of death uniting all the other characters. But Dickens describes Krook's death too in hereditary terms, this time as incestuous, " . . . inborn, inbred, engendered in the corrupted humours of the vicious body itself . . . Spontaneous Combustion, and none other of all the deaths that can be died" (BH, 512).

Dickens's description of Krook's magical demise ties Krook to Nemo, and both to the novel's underlying theme of interrelation between all living things. There is no difference in essence between Nemo's death, which begets more death, and Krook's death, which is unique. Both are the result of "the corrupted humours of the vicious body," both define the living as potential masses of corruption encased in dying flesh.

Esther has long been a problem for critics and readers of *Bleak House*. There is a general sense that she is too good, too self-effacing, too syrupy altogether, although counter-arguments have been made that, given her upbringing, her self-abnegation and coyness are psychologically apt. Whatever one may feel about her credibility as a character, however, it is clear that Dickens is ideologically committed to cleansing her of the taint of illegitimacy and towards this end he exaggerates her complacency and sentimentalizes her virtues. The moral contagion implied by the smallpox epidemic takes her as its innocent victim, but it scars only her body. Her essential goodness remains untouched despite the devastation which has been visited on her exterior self.

It is important to bear in mind Dickens's insistence on Esther's admirable qualities when turning to a later portrait of illegitimacy, that of Miss Wade in *Little Dorrit*. There is a change here, which seems to be related to a growing sense in Dickens's fiction that not all those who suffered ill-treatment in childhood grow up to deserve compassion. *Little Dorrit* is a later novel, and one gets the impression that Dickens's perception of the emotional costs of an upbringing on the outskirts of Victorian family life has grown more realistic. Like Esther, Miss Wade is illegitimate, and, like Esther, she tells her own story; but her situation is almost the reverse of Esther's. Far from suffering ill-treatment because of her illegitimacy, Miss Wade is cosseted and protected from the knowledge of her disgrace. People are kind to her and treat her with compassion, yet she resents their consideration and interprets it as condescension. She is certain that she is being pitied and patronized, and she reacts in ways which are harmful to herself.

Miss Wade has received a great deal of attention from critics because of the assumption – based really on just one enigmatic line – that Dickens intended her to be a lesbian.[15] Whether or not this is the case, it is clear that she is intended as "unnatural" in some way and her "unnaturalness" is related to her uncertain provenance. As an illegitimate child, she has no obvious connections to those around her and no sense of belonging. ". . . I learned that I had no grandmother and no recognised relation. I carried the light of that information both into my past and into my future," she writes of herself (LD, 728). From this we may understand that her illegitimacy is the defining fact of Miss Wade's life.

What Dickens does in the brief fragment of her autobiography which he awkwardly inserts into the narrative of *Little Dorrit*, is to suggest the very real cost of illegitimacy to the human psyche. Miss Wade is presented without symbolism; she is the victim of no diabolical cruelty and is associated with no biblical taint, nor is there any sentimentalizing of her nature. She is Dickens's portrait of Esther without the fairy-tale interference of a Mr Jarndyce. Miss Wade has no one to rescue her from the internalized fury of her own nature and carry her off to Bleak House. She carries her own bleak house around inside herself, where it forms the domicile of a self-confessed Self-Tormentor.

With his portrait of Miss Wade, Dickens seems to have moved

towards a more complex understanding of hereditary influence, namely that it constitutes a condition which is only partly deterministic. Miss Wade can do nothing about her illegitimacy, which she is born into, but she alone is responsible for the way in which it affects her. If she feels herself scorned because of her bastardy, the fact remains that the anger is her own, and if she harms others because of it, then she stands condemned as unnatural. In other words, Dickens here portrays a biological taint – illegitimacy – for which the victim is not responsible, as mediated by her reaction to it. That reaction is not a function of heredity but of free will.

The portrait of Miss Wade is thus in keeping with a progressive weakening of determinism in Dickens's portrayal of the formation of the self. Miss Wade, the very epitome of the forsaken child Dickens once championed, elicits in this later work very little sympathy from her creator. She is presented instead as incapable of subduing her own tormented nature, and being responsible for her failure to do so.

∗   ∗   ∗

In the genealogical spoof that begins *Martin Chuzzlewit*, Dickens writes that, "It is remarkable that as there was in the oldest family of which we have any record, a murderer and a vagabond, so we never fail to meet, in the records of all old families, with innumerable repetitions of the same phase of character" (MC, 51).

This seems to imply that Dickens believed criminal behavior to be hereditary. But the fact that the passage occurs within an extended satire on pedigrees should warn against such an assumption. In fact there is very little evidence in the novels that Dickens believed vice to be hereditary in the way that goodness was. Even the possible exception of *Martin Chuzzlewit* itself, in which selfishness is defined as the family vice of the Chuzzlewits, collapses under closer scrutiny, since both young Martin and his equally selfish grandfather eventually prove themselves to be kind at heart. Old Martin, in particular, plays the role of secret benefactor to the Pinches, hardly the act of a selfish individual. What is more, Dickens's description of the family vice suggests that it owes more to environment than it does to heredity:

> Martin's nature was a frank and generous one; but he had been bred up in his grandfather's house; and it will usually be found that the meaner domestic vices propagate themselves to be their

own antagonists. Selfishness does this especially; so do suspicion, cunning, stealth, and covetous propensities. Martin had unconsciously reasoned as a child, 'My guardian takes so much thought of himself, that unless I do the like *by myself*, I shall be forgotten.' So he had grown selfish. (MC, 596–7)

Selfishness is the Chuzzlewit veneer, good-heartedness is their essence. Even Anthony Chuzzlewit's villainous son Jonas seems to have absorbed his viciousness from the unsavoury example of his father, rather than having inherited it.

In fact, most of Dickens's villains – Bill Sikes, Quilp, Rigaud, and Bradley Headstone – have no documented hereditary antecedents, because Dickens tends to present his villains as being *sui generis*. They are embodiments of evil who are seldom portrayed against the softening effect of a hereditary background, firstly, because to provide a genealogy is to open an avenue for sympathy, and secondly, because Dickens modeled many of his villains on fairy-tale characters, which meant that they were evil because the conventions of the form required them to be so. When it came to evil, Dickens tended to draw on the pantheistic model of spontaneous generation rather than on the biblical one of hereditary descent.

In this he ran counter to the general scientific assumptions of his time, which held that morbid phenomena were particularly amenable to hereditary transmission, and that the bad was more easily passed on than the good. This emphasis on the hereditability of negative characteristics grew more pronounced as the nineteenth century progressed. Oscar Wilde's personification of heredity as "Nemesis without her mask" summed up the wariness and fatalism of late Victorian attitudes about heredity, a fatalism which was complicated by a profound confusion as to what was and what was not hereditable.[16]

This does not mean, however, that the Dickensian villain is divorced from family life. On the contrary, there is a class of villain in the fiction, especially prominent in the early novels, who direct their malevolence against members of their own family. Ralph Nickleby in *Nicholas Nickleby* falls into this category, as does Jonas Chuzzlewit in *Martin Chuzzlewit*. John Chester of *Barnaby Rudge*, who declines to save his son from the gallows, is probably the most reprehensible example of a man whose primary sin is against his own flesh and blood.

Monks of *Oliver Twist* sets the pattern for all of these characters.

He is Oliver Twist's half-brother and the melodramatic villain of
the novel in which he appears. Appropriately enough, given his
fraternal relationship to the novel's protagonist, he bears a mark of
Cain in the form of a birthmark (OT, 413).

There is an irony in designating Monks as the family villain, since
it is he and not Oliver who is the rightful heir and legitimate issue
of his father. Monks is said to inherit his nature from his mother,
who was ten years older than his father, a woman who after separation from her young husband gave herself up to "continental
frivolities" (OT, 435). In designating Monks as primarily his mother's
offspring, Dickens is attempting to mitigate the guilt of Oliver's
father who does, after all, beget his second son out of wedlock.
Dickens further attempts to soften the father's guilt by making him
very young at the time of his arranged marriage: he is only sixteen
years old when Monks is born (OT, 436).

In portraying Monks as degenerate despite the fact that he is the
legitimate heir, and in defining Oliver as deserving despite his bastardy, Dickens is manipulating a tradition of contemporary beliefs
about heredity for his own purposes. Just as Oliver is quite literally
a love child whose virtue is the manifestation of his parents' devotion to one another, so Monks embodies his parents' reciprocal
hatred; their failed and unhappy marriage is incorporated into his
disposition, into his vice, malice, and degeneracy. Just as Oliver is
immune to the evil effects of his environment, so Monks is infected
by his. He is diseased, literally biting himself in his torment, so
that his body is covered with wounds (OT, 413). The description of
his condition may allude to epilepsy or to syphilis, Dickens does
not specify which, but the distinction does not really matter, although syphilis, because it is a venereal disease, carries stronger
connotations of dissipation.[17]

The distinction between the half-brothers may be traced to the
medical literature of the nineteenth century which suggested that
the entire emotional history of the parents could be transmitted to
the child. The physical and mental condition of the parents at the
time of conception was of paramount importance, and following
conception the slightest shock or unpleasantness would affect the
fetus. Pregnant women were advised to refrain from sex altogether,
because if they engaged in the act excessively, the child might develop
some sexual anomaly; if they drank, the child might become an
alcoholic; if they experienced intense emotions, the child might be
demented.[18]

Thus Monks is the way he is for reasons diametrically opposite to those which applied to Oliver. He is the living symbol of his parents' bad marriage. Speaking of his mother, Monks says that on her deathbed she bequeathed to him "her unquenchable and deadly hatred . . . – though she need not have left me that, for I had inherited it long before" (OT, 459). The statement seems to indicate a confusion in Dickens's mind between what is inherited and what is acquired. To the extent that such a confusion was general throughout the nineteenth century, this is so. But the passage can also be understood in another way. The mother's physical legacy and her deathbed bequest are essentially identical. The latter is merely a public confirmation of a private reality, in much the same way as a will is a public declaration of family connection. Wills bequeath openly what heredity apportions invisibly, so that distinctions between the two forms of inheritance are erased, and each stands as the equivalent of the other.

Despite the fact that Dickens was drawing on popular beliefs and prejudices to create and motivate his villain, Monks is not credible as an evil force in *Oliver Twist*. To some extent this is because Dickens heightens the melodramatic atmosphere which surrounds him, so that he emerges as far more histrionic and stagy an evil-doer than either Fagin or Sikes. But it is also true that Monks's family history serves in some degree to exonerate him. He is the unloved son, the legitimate but despised owner of the birthright. And, like Oliver, he is a victim of his parents' misdeeds. Try as he might to darken the portrait of Monks's evil, Dickens cannot entirely erase the fact of his victimhood, even though he draws on every descriptive trick in the grab-bag of fictional villainy.

A similar problem arises in Dickens's portrayal of Uriah Heep, the villain of *David Copperfield*, although in this later novel, Dickens is far more aware of what he is doing, and deliberately walks a fine line between evoking sympathy and arousing antagonism. He does this by establishing Uriah as an alter ego to David, the protagonist. The biblical names of the two characters underline their symbolic complicity in a cycle of guilt and innocence. In the Bible, King David sends Uriah the Hittite off to war because he covets Uriah's wife Bathsheba. In *David Copperfield* both David and Uriah are interested in Agnes Wickfield. To make the analogy between David and Uriah stronger, Dickens even has Uriah sleep in David's old bed at the Wickfield home (DC, 571). Uriah is what David might have become without money, middle-class parents and Betsey Trotwood.

As noted in the previous chapter, *David Copperfield* is the first of his novels in which Dickens defines human nature as partially freed from the constraints of heredity, and thus amenable to the formative effects of environment. This not only applies to the development of David's personality, but to that of the other characters as well, including most particularly Uriah. Uriah, like his father and mother before him, was brought up at a charity establishment and educated at a foundation school. "They taught us all a deal of umbleness... I ate umble pie with an appetite... 'People like to be above you,' says father, 'keep yourself down'" (DC, 639). Uriah even wins the same monitor medals in humility as his father did, thus repeating in his own history the destiny of his parents.

In both cases, that of his parents and that of Uriah himself, we seem to be dealing with learned behaviour, since the point of the story is that an enforced education in humility leads to the repression and perversion of natural impulses. Yet David thinks to himself: "It was the first time it had ever occurred to me, that this detestable cant of false humility might have originated out of the Heep family. I had seen the harvest, but had never thought of the seed" (DC, 639).

In this way, David negates the point of Uriah's story, refusing to acknowledge its environmental component and stressing instead its hereditary one. After all, Uriah takes after his parents because his early experience in the foundation schools resembled theirs, not because he inherited false humility along with his red hair. David seems purposely to misunderstand the significance of Uriah's upbringing when he concludes that "this detestable cant of false humility might have originated out of the Heep family." It seems, in fact, to have originated out of the charity schools – a favourite target of Dickens's satire. David's confusion of hereditary influence with learned behavior becomes even more apparent with his next remark, which seems to credit psychological factors rather than hereditary ones: "... I fully comprehended now, for the first time, what a base, unrelenting, and revengeful spirit, must have been engendered by this early, and this long, suppression" (DC, 639).

For the reader, however, the effect of knowing Uriah's early history is to humanize him rather than to condemn him. It places Uriah within a family context, explains his conduct and his nature.

David's refusal to acknowledge the pathetic component in Uriah's tale, his wish to ground his dislike of his rival on the latter's innate nature rather than acknowledge the effect of injustice on his personality, suggests how the confusions of the nature/nurture debate of Dickens's time might be put to literary use.

David's interpretation of Uriah's story tells us more about David than about Uriah. Dickens exploits the contemporary confusion between cultural, physical, and emotional inheritance to signal that David hears in Uriah's tale only what he wants to hear. Since *David Copperfield* is narrated in the first person, we are put on notice that our understanding of the events and characters in this "autobiography" is filtered through the subjective consciousness of a single individual, and must be judged accordingly.

David often resorts to symbols in describing Uriah – he is compared to the devil with splayed feet, and to a snake creeping along the ground – but, once Uriah speaks in his own voice, his manipulative personality assumes a dimension which undercuts this symbolic presentation and mitigates his stature as a villain.

The humanizing of Uriah Heep may go some way in explaining Dickens's reluctance, which grows more pronounced after *David Copperfield*, to place his malefactors within a hereditary context. Giving villainy a genealogy of the type Dickens applies to Little Nell suggests that evil, like goodness, is an inherent, and ineradicable trait which may be transmitted from generation to generation to the end of time. This wipes out all hope of the future triumph of goodness and justice. Such a genealogy places evil on the same footing as good in terms of human agency, thereby wiping out its metaphysical attributes. A genealogy of evil locates the devil as forever within ourselves.

The other problem with placing villains within a hereditary context is that genealogy, ironically, cancels out guilt, since moral responsibility is no longer within conscious and willful control. Once evil is defined as a hereditary trait, individual accountability becomes irrelevant, since we cannot help the natures that we inherit. To insist too strongly on the hereditability of evil is to place all morality within a deterministic context where it ceases to be subject to conscious control. Certain fundamentalist Christian beliefs, which insist on the inherent wickedness of humankind, do the same thing, but with the abiding safety valve that change is possible through piety and good works. However, when evil is ascribed to heredity and not to the Fall, the fallen world takes up residence in the blood of generation. There can then be no appeal and no means of mitigating the sentence of heredity.

These drawbacks to a hereditary approach to the problem of evil may explain why later Dickensian villains grow in psychological depth at the same time as they are diminished in family line. Such is the case with Bradley Headstone. Headstone appears in *Our Mutual Friend* which was published in 1865 and is Dickens's last completed novel. Like Uriah Heep, Bradley Headstone is a man whose nature has been distorted and perverted by a too-long suppression. But we are never given a reason for the suppression, nor information about Headstone's early history, his parents, or his childhood. The only thing we know is that his profession of schoolteacher constitutes a rise in social status. In Bradley Headstone, Dickens draws the portrait of a self-made man who has worked his way up in the world and who is desperate to hang on to the respectability which his own efforts have earned. Headstone's social class is presented as far more significant an influence on his subsequent actions than any hereditary legacy he may have acquired from his ancestors.

Bradley Headstone is a man at war with himself – one side of his nature longs for respectability and is under constant control, the other side seethes with impulsiveness and passion. The tension between the two makes him one of Dickens's most psychologically complex villains. His instant attraction to Lizzie Hexam coupled with his murderous jealousy of Eugene Wrayburn, her preferred upper-class suitor, suggests a nature which Dickens describes as follows:

> Suppression of so much to make room for so much, had given him a constrained manner . . . Yet there was enough of what was animal, of what was fiery (though smouldering), still visible in him, to suggest that if young Bradley Headstone, when a pauper lad, had chanced to be told off for the sea, he would not have been the last man in a ship's crew. Regarding that origin of his, he was proud, moody, and sullen, desiring it to be forgotten. And few people knew of it. (OMF, 267)

Dickens has described this type of self-made man before, most satirically in *Hard Times*'s Mr Bounderby. Uriah Heep qualifies as another example. But Uriah Heep and Josiah Bounderby are placed within a familial context – in both cases their mothers play a significant role in the advancement of their careers. In these earlier portraits, the theme of the self-made man rising above his origins at the expense of his soul is coloured by Dickens's definition of those origins as rooted specifically in the family rather than in social class. In Bounderby's case, the presence of a mother serves to underline the son's perfidy, since it undermines his boast that he is entirely his own creation, a man who owes his rise in the world to no one.

In the case of Bradley Headstone, however, it is clear that Dickens has lost interest in portraying family connection as the source of complications in future life. Headstone is one of Dickens's most human villains. Few symbolic trappings embellish him, and no genealogy explains him. His vindictive, passionate nature is portrayed as peculiar to himself, yet potentially present in all "animals." There is no attempt, as there was with Uriah Heep, to associate him with the devil or the snake in the garden of Eden. Even the blood that spurts from his nose as he prepares to murder Eugene Wrayburn, while clearly an attempt at foreshadowing and described in portentous language (OMF, 704), nevertheless, remains a nose-bleed – a prosaic form of bloodletting. Headstone's tragedy is partly rooted in his social class, which encompasses his choice of profession, as well as in his homicidal hatred of Eugene Wrayburn. But Headstone's fall is also rooted in his nature, which consists of qualities which Dickens labels "animal." These include his sexual attraction to Lizzie, and his murderous rage at her rejection.

Philip Collins notes that *Our Mutual Friend* marks the first time in his fiction that Dickens ascribes a sexual motive to murder, and suggests that this is connected to Dickens's passion for Ellen Ternan, whom he had met ten years earlier in 1857.[19] But there may well be another reason, one which also encompasses Dickens's choice of the term "animal" to describe the atavistic elements in Bradley Headstone's emotional make-up – the lust, jealousy, and murderous impulse. As I will argue at greater length in my last chapter, Dickens's new-found interest in sexual conflict and his elaboration of the term "animal" constitute a nod in the direction of Darwin.

Bradley Headstone is an example of a human animal who has tried to evolve away from his primitive roots. He has managed to suppress these roots and contain them through sheer willpower. He has worked hard to acquire a respectable position. All is well until he falls in love with Lizzie, at which point everything that is most elemental in his nature rises up to undo the civilized facade he has worked so hard to create. Headstone can never successfully tamp down the "fiery" side of his nature precisely because it is his nature.

When Dickens labels the emotional side of his villain's psyche as "animal," he is aligning Headstone's personality with what is general among human beings rather than with what is peculiar to the Headstone lineage. Through the word "animal," Headstone's emotional make-up, with its barely suppressed aggression, is defined as being potential in living creatures as a whole. The villainy in this villain is no longer specific to him, but is now located within the natural world of instinct and inner drive.

Headstone's sexual struggle with Eugene for the love of Lizzie has Darwinian overtones in being about the contention of two males to win the female. At issue for the male in such a struggle is the ability to pass on his particular hereditary material to the next generation. At issue in evolutionary terms is the preservation of those traits carried by the stronger – the fitter – of the two antagonists. Eugene Wrayburn bests Bradley Headstone in being more thoroughly urbane and sophisticated. He has the advantage of class, an advantage which he uses mercilessly to humiliate Headstone. Wrayburn's higher social rank implies that the primitive is located further back in his ancestry. His family has had more time to evolve away from their elementary roots.

What is more surprising than the outcome of the struggle between the two men is its choice of object. Lizzie, despite her many personal qualities and her physical attractiveness, is an odd choice for both men. In marrying Lizzie, Eugene would be marrying beneath him – and the temptation to merely seduce the girl rather than marry her is his major dilemma throughout the novel. For Headstone, the choice of Lizzie is even more perplexing, since it means loving a girl from the very class which he has tried so hard to escape. Falling in love with Lizzie is a recidivist move for Headstone, the more so since an appropriate alternative from the social point of view exists in Miss Peecher, a fellow schoolteacher. Why then is Headstone so smitten with Lizzie that he is willing to jeopardize his hard-won respectability to marry her? He is even willing to kill for her.

The answer, I would suggest, lies in Lizzie's position at the bottom of the social scale. Lizzie, whose father fishes bodies from the Thames for a living, presents a return to his origins for Headstone, a return to his basic nature, to his primitive roots. She also represents the triumph of emotional claims over the veneer of rationality and civilization. Headstone's passion for Lizzie is a restatement of the animal qualities in human nature. That these qualities will drive him to attempt murder suggests a new Dickensian understanding of human evil, one influenced by Darwinian precepts, in which the seething emotions lie always in uneasy quiescence behind the civilized facade. In this model, evil is defined as the remnants of our most primitive emotions unsuccessfully kept in check.

PART II
The Public Face of Heredity

5
Heredity, Class, and Race

The repressive sexual morality of the Victorian era was primarily a middle-class phenomenon – and even then applied, most specifi- cally, to middle-class women. At the two extremes of the social scale – the aristocracy and the lower classes – morals were looser. This fact accounted not only for the large number of illegitimate children among the lower classes, but also for the fact that some of these children were the offspring of parents from divergent social classes, usually an upper-class father and a lower-class mother. In the first three sections of this chapter I will examine how Dickens relates issues of heredity to issues of class. In the fourth and final section I will be concerned with the hereditary implications of his portrayal of race and ethnicity.

Barnaby Rudge: unacknowledged heredity

In the person of Maypole Hugh, one of the leaders of the riots in *Barnaby Rudge*, Dickens explores the complex relationship between class injustice and the vagaries of biological inheritance. Hugh is the unacknowledged son of a villainous upper-class father and a gypsy mother who was hanged when Hugh was six years old. In his depiction of Hugh, and in the complications and convergences of Hugh's personal history, Dickens expands the implications of hereditary endowment from the private sphere of domestic tragedy to the public one of insurrection. Through Hugh, Dickens addresses the ambiguous relationship of heredity to class, and the impact which this relationship has on the social order.

Hugh is one of five characters in *Barnaby Rudge* to become involved in the riots. Each of these characters functions allegorically as well as realistically – from mindless malleability and idiocy (Barnaby Rudge) to political folly (Lord Gordon) to opportunism (Dennis the Hangman) to proletarian resentment (Simon Tapertit).[1] Hugh represents the claims of the outcast, the dispossessed, the marginalized. He stands for what was once called the lumpenproletariat. Even his fondness for sleeping carries allegorical weight, suggesting as it does the dormant power of the underclass, which when roused to a sense of its own oppression explodes in unrestrained violence and anarchic destruction.[2] In *Barnaby Rudge* this outraged energy, embodied in Hugh, expends its despairing, nihilistic force in pointless violence and destructive chaos aimed against the society which has excluded it. It is no accident that Hugh misconstrues Lord Gordon's anti-Catholic rallying cry of "no popery" as "no property" (BR, 359).

Northrop Frye has suggested that, in contrast to the modern whodunit, the mystery in a Dickens plot tends to revolve around a birth rather than a death.[3] This is certainly true of *Barnaby Rudge* where the secret of Hugh's parentage is withheld until the last chapters. In fact, Hugh's journey towards self-discovery in *Barnaby Rudge* resembles that of Oliver Twist. In this later version of the plot of hidden identity the abandoned, illegitimate child finds that his unknown parent does indeed belong to the princely class, but the discovery in no way benefits him; it signals no rise in his own social standing. Hugh's aristocratic father, John Chester, the novel's primary incarnation of evil, declines to save his bastard son from the gallows. In his denial of kinship and his rejection of paternal responsibility for the fruit of his loins, Chester embodies the wrongs of the society which Hugh would like to tear down.

Rejected by his father, whose identity he discovers just before his execution, Hugh is left to assert his filial claim upon the gallows.

> What ... should teach me – me, born as I was born, and reared as I have been reared – to hope for any mercy in this hardened, cruel, unrelenting place! Upon these human shambles, I, who never raised this hand in prayer till now, call down the wrath of God! On that black tree, of which I am the ripened fruit, I do invoke the curse of all its victims, past, present, and to come. On the head of that man, who, in his conscience, owns me for his son, I leave the wish that he may never sicken on his bed of down, but die a violent death as I do now, and have the night-wind for his only mourner. To this I say, Amen, amen!
>
> (BR, 695)

The speech betrays a confusion between the symbolic parentage of the gallows tree and the actual parentage of the condemned man – and the confusion is deliberate. Hugh has been sentenced to death for his part in the Gordon riots, but the complications of his personal history hint at the ambivalence which Dickens feels on the subject of insurrection.

It has been suggested by several commentators that Dickens's attitude towards Hugh is condemnatory, that Hugh is presented in *Barnaby Rudge* as "a savage, society-created man-beast."[4] But Hugh's language in the speech quoted above, and throughout the course of the novel, contradicts this. He consistently speaks standard, grammatically correct English, despite the fact that he is supposed to have brought himself up in the fields, earns his living as a stable hand, and is regularly described as a brute by those who are his social superiors. The fact that Hugh speaks so well, in compliance with the Victorian convention that positive characters should speak standard English, is an indication that Dickens – who always conformed to the speech convention, as, for instance, with Oliver Twist – intended him to be sympathetic and heroic. (By way of comparison with a character whom Dickens despises, see any sample of the speech of Dennis the Hangman.)

Whereas in *Barnaby Rudge* the rational part of Dickens is clearly on the side of authority and order, his sympathy and his imaginative engagement are not so easily accounted for. This is particularly evident in his portrayal of Hugh, who – along with the idiot Barnaby Rudge – is certainly the most sinned against of all the rioters. It is in his depiction of Hugh that Dickens's stance on the subject of rebellion becomes highly complex.[5]

That complexity is symbolized by the gallows, which plays an equivocal role in the novel. Although the gallows is the emblem of social regulation, the instrument of justice, order, and the law, its most ardent advocates are the novel's least sympathetic characters – Dennis the Hangman, John Chester, John Willet of the Maypole Inn. These are men who gloat about hanging people "in bunches every six weeks" as a way of maintaining order and showing "how wide awake our government is" (BR, 140). Thus Hugh's cursing of the gallows and his cursing of his father are essentially the same curse. The hanging tree is a phallic symbol completely congruent with the thing it symbolizes. It is the symbol of a paternalism which executes its own children.

The symbolic equation of the gallows with John Chester is first suggested in chapter 28. Hugh, who has been serving as Chester's minion and spy, comes to see him and falls asleep on the stairs while he waits for his "master" to appear. When he wakes he sees Chester standing where he had dreamt that the gallows would be (BR, 277). Thus the gallows of the dream materialize into the figure of Hugh's unknown father. Each equals the other. Hugh will turn out to be the fruit of both.

But if the son dreams of the father, the father is no less haunted by the son. At the end of that same chapter, John Chester imagines that he hears Hugh calling him through his sleep "in a strange voice" (BR, 280). Chester is so upset by this intrusion into his dreams that, despite his usual stance of cold-blooded composure, he rises from his bed, sword in hand, ready to attack the intruder. Chester is quite certain that the voice belongs to Hugh; he calls him by name and looks to the spot where Hugh had been sleeping. There is no one there, but Dickens has given us yet another image of the father as his son's potential executioner. The two dreams – that of the son who does not know his father and that of the father who will not recognize his son – are yet another manifestation of Dickens's belief in mystical heredity. Both father and son sense a connection to one another without being consciously aware of it.

But the symbolic implications of Chester's dream go beyond a subconsciously apprehended consanguinity. They also serve to tie the issue of paternity to that of rebellion. The impoverished, illiterate, brutish, and brutalized Hugh represents the nightmare of all those who lie on "beds of down" – to use Hugh's phrase – and whose consciences are made uneasy by those who must sleep on the ground. In fact, in this particular chapter, Hugh has been sleeping on the landing to Chester's bedroom – a location that is even more symbolically threatening. The interplay between the nervous consciences of the upper class and the unstated resentment of the lower is represented in the dual dreams of Hugh and Chester. The fact that the pair are also father and son adds an Oedipal dimension to the class conflict which they represent, a dimension further refined by their respective dreams of violence.

The Oedipal allusions in *Barnaby Rudge* are plentiful, because, as Steven Marcus demonstrated in his influential reading, the novel uses the relationship of fathers and sons to talk about authority and rebellion.[6] Marcus identifies five such father/son pairs in the cast of characters. All the sons are rejected in one form or another, and all are eventually embroiled in the riots, although not on the same side. Joe Willet and Edward Chester, after leaving their fathers, return to fight on the side of authority. Joe Willet has even joined the army. But the sons who do not belong to the middle or upper classes, who have no patrimony to inherit and no property to come into, those whose class grievances are greatest – Simon Tapertit, Barnaby Rudge, and Hugh the Bastard – fight on the side of the rioters. Thus the novel not only relates the private domain of filial rebellion to the public one of class grievance and insurrection, but it also parcels out the sides along class lines.

In this respect it is interesting that Joe Willet, whose father is the insufferably reactionary John Willet, owner of the inn where Hugh works as a hostler, leaves England. Goaded past endurance by his father, he goes off to fight in the American revolution, where he loses his arm. Joe's act of rebellion is triggered by the humiliations to which his father subjects him – another example of how private conflicts with authority may result in actions in the public domain. But once in America he fights on the side of Britain, the fatherland, against the American revolutionaries. The two-sided nature of Joe's rebelliousness is an accurate reflection of Dickens's own ambivalence towards the mobs participating in the Gordon riots. On the one hand he does not approve of the rioters; on the other he cannot prevent his own imaginative complicity in the events he narrates.

In Hugh's case, however, because he has no idea who his father is, his relationship with Chester becomes one in which every interchange carries a submerged as well as an overt meaning. The superficial contrast between the two men could not be greater. They belong to the two poles of society: Chester is a member of the nobility – he is knighted during the course of the novel – while Hugh is as close to the underclass as it is possible to be. In fact, he is often referred to as subhuman. Chester calls him a dog and a brute, while Hugh calls Chester "master." Hugh, the most convincingly virile of Dickens's male characters, a man of powerful build who fears no one, is nevertheless consistently unmanned in Chester's presence. He is like putty in the older man's hands, trying desperately to please and placate the superior being whom he instinctively fears. The power dynamic between the two men and its relationship to wealth and station is illustrated in the following exchange:

"Are you going to speak to me, master?" [Hugh] said, after a long silence.

"My worthy creature," returned Mr Chester, "you are a little ruffled and out of humour. I'll wait till you're quite yourself again. I am in no hurry."

This behaviour had its intended effect. It humbled and abashed [Hugh], and made him still more irresolute and uncertain. Hard words he could have returned, violence he would have repaid with interest; but this cool, complacent, contemptuous, self-possessed reception, caused him to feel his inferiority more completely than the most elaborate arguments. Everything contributed to this effect. His own rough speech, contrasted with the soft persuasive accents of the other; his rude bearing, and Mr Chester's polished manner; the disorder and negligence of his ragged dress, and the elegant attire he saw before him; with all the unaccustomed luxuries and comforts of the room, and the silence that gave him leisure to observe these things, and feel how ill at ease they made him; all these influences... quelled Hugh completely.   (BR, 235)

The passage is a study in contrasts, but they are the contrasts of apparent superficialities, of the polish, self-confidence, and self-possession which privilege can confer, and the roughness, self-doubt, and insecurity which destitution and inferior social position can foster. The fact that Chester and Hugh, belonging as they do to two such apparently distinct social spheres, are actually father and son suggests that, far from underlining the irreconcilable differences between the two, Dickens is in fact suggesting their inherent connection. It is in this unacknowledged blood tie that the sins of the fathers are most devastatingly exposed. Consanguinity may be hidden, it may even be denied, but it cannot finally be erased. The connection between Chester and Hugh is a biological fact. Every time that Chester is contemptuous of Hugh, his remarks rebound, with unconscious irony, onto himself, since whatever Hugh is, Chester must also be. At least, this is what Chester himself intimates in his unctuous compliment to Mrs Varden on the beauty of her daughter, "Humanity is indeed a happy lot, when we can repeat ourselves in others..." (BR, 267).

Even Hugh's sexuality expresses itself as an unconscious imitation of his father's. It assumes its most threatening aspect when he accosts Dolly Varden as she is walking alone. Hugh's yearning for Dolly is as much a yearning for higher status as it is for sexual release. Sexuality, for both Hugh and his father, is associated with

class difference, the turn-on lies in the gap in status. "Softly, dar-
ling – gently – would you fly from rough Hugh, that loves you as
well as any drawing-room gallant?" (BR, 220), says Hugh to Dolly,
as she struggles in his arms. Hugh tries to do with Dolly what his
father succeeded in doing with his mother. But his social status
being so much lower than Dolly's, he can only accomplish his desire
through force, and even in this he fails. What is more, his longing
to transcend his own class sexually if not socially is given a check
by Chester, who, when Hugh admits to having stolen a kiss from
Dolly, cautions him that this is a hanging offence (BR, 239). For all
his powerful physicality, Hugh is consistently presented as unmanned
– unmanned by his father, unmanned by the class to which he
belongs, unmanned by his destiny.

Consanguinity thus plays a dual role in this novel. It is a symbol
both of the ineradicable connection which exists submerged and
unacknowledged between the classes, and of that connection's social
irrelevance. This ambiguity is brought home at the novel's end,
when John Chester's legitimate son Edward attends the midnight
burial of the executed Hugh and acknowledges him as a brother.
(This muted allusion to the theme of "my brother's keeper" will
reappear in more pronounced form in the later novels.) Edward
had tried to see Hugh in prison, but Hugh, echoing his father's
rejection of himself, in turn rejects his half-brother. Edward too
has felt the bitterness of being John Chester's son, so that his claim
to fraternity is based on shared blood and shared experience. But
his legitimacy makes for a greater gulf between the half-brothers
than the claim of fraternity makes for a connection. *Barnaby Rudge*
suggests that man-made laws and distinctions take precedence over
natural ties; or, to put this another way – the claims of inheritance
outweigh those of heredity. Edward and Hugh may both equally
be sons of John Chester, but only Edward is the acknowledged heir.
Hugh's midnight burial in an unmarked coffin ensures his anonymity
even in death. He will inherit nothing but the earth.

On the subterranean level, where no one can see, heredity binds
and connects all strata of society, implicating each class in the fate
of the other. But in the visible world which contains upper-class
fathers and lower-class sons the meaning is different. When John
Chester and Hugh are contrasted, the outward forms of the contrast all emphasize the apparent superficialities of dress, money,
and manners. But those superficialities are emblematic of differences in power, and *Barnaby Rudge* defines such differences as

ultimately irreconcilable. In this novel, the younger generation can only wrest power from the older by force. Power is never passed on peacefully, in accord with the processes of nature, and for this reason the novel portrays rebellion as the ugly eruption of a social conflict which is an extension of the domestic friction between fathers and sons.

In *The Variation of Animals and Plants under Domestication* (1868) Darwin speculated that the wildness shown by the hybrids of domesticated species had the same cause as the wickedness of human half-breeds.[7] The remark is interesting for the light it sheds on Hugh's actions in *Barnaby Rudge*, and as an indication of popular and scientific assumptions about the nature of half-breeds. The mistrust of hybrids seems to have extended to those who are the result of unions between the different classes. In *Great Expectations*, there is a suggestion that Miss Havisham's half-brother goes bad because he is the offspring of her father – a gentleman – and the cook.

In hereditary terms, Hugh is a hybrid. As the son of John Chester and a gypsy woman, he is the offspring of two races and two classes. Yet he does not represent a synthesis of the two. Socially, physically, and in terms of his destiny, he is far more his mother's son than his father's. Hugh's physical beauty, his dark looks and swarthy complexion, as well as his sexual nature, are inherited from his gypsy mother. She is described as "handsome," with a "high free spirit." "This and her good looks, and her lofty manner, interested some gentlemen who were easily moved by dark eyes..." (BR, 677). There is a racial element at play here. Not only were sexual attraction and moral laxity commonly assumed to be characteristic of gypsies, but all of the gypsies mentioned in the novel lose their lives by hanging, as if this type of death were racially determined.

Although Hugh's last words connect the hanging tree to his father, the symbol is in fact representative of both his parents. His gypsy mother had been hanged for passing forged bills when Hugh was a small boy. As Hugh puts it, his mother "died the death in store for her son" (BR, 669). Hugh's proleptic construction of this thought, with its confusion of past and future, collapses the distinction between generations. The destiny of mother and son is identical and interconnected. Hugh's mother had been deserted by her lover John Chester when Hugh was a boy. This led to her passing false bills as a way of making money. Hugh inherits not only her looks, but also her fate. Like his mother, he is manipulated by John Chester; like her, he is rejected by Chester; and like his mother, again, rejection leads to lawlessness and finally to execution. Thus, as he was to do later in *David Copperfield*, Dickens here locates the hereditary relationship between mother and son in identical patterns of behaviour leading to a similar end. Their shared destiny links the two in a way which defines the father as both outsider and villain.

Both Hugh and his mother curse John Chester before they hang. The mother wishes that when Hugh grows up he will avenge her death – an Oedipal wish if ever there was one – and one destined not to come true. But although the mother's hope for revenge is never fulfilled, the particulars of Hugh's curse of his father are realized. Dickens was too enamored of magical retributions for this not to be the case. Hugh's curse stipulates that Chester should "never sicken on his bed of down, but die a violent death as I do now, and have the night-wind for his only mourner." This is, in fact, what happens. Chester dies in a duel at the hands of his old enemy, Haredale. His body is not found for two days, the night wind being his only mourner.

If Hugh's father and mother both in different ways represent his death by hanging, a third character – Dennis the Hangman – foreshadows Hugh's inevitable encounter with the noose as a form of macabre birth. The birth imagery is introduced during Dennis's first encounter with Hugh, which occurs when Hugh goes to sign up for the anti-popery cause. Proclaims Dennis, "Put him on the roll. I'd stand godfather to him, if he was to be christened in a bonfire, made of the ruins of the Bank of England" (BR, 359). In this way, Dennis assists at Hugh's baptism into insurrection, initiating him into his new identity.

But Dennis plays a still more significant role with regard to Hugh – he pieces together the secret of Hugh's paternity. In this sense Dennis is the midwife of Hugh's identity, since he is the only person in a position to discover the clues to Hugh's origins. What puts him in this singular position is his profession as hangman. In effect, Dennis's professional alliance with death allows Hugh to be born into the knowledge of his paternity. In his function as hangman Dennis is privy to the last words of those about to be executed

– he is not merely priest at Hugh's baptism into revolution, he is also the ghoulish confessor of the condemned – and in this way he comes to know the secret of Hugh's birth, because it is he who "works off" Hugh's mother, and later, the mother's gypsy friend, who supplies the end of the story. Thus the gallows bestows an identity on Hugh at the same time as it robs him of his life, adding again to the sense in which he is its "fruit."

But despite the inverse metaphors which Dickens employs, Dennis's work is not birth but death. He joins Lord Gordon's anti-popery crusade because he is afraid that should the Catholics ever come to power his "sound, Protestant, constitutional, English work" will be in jeopardy, Papists being notorious for preferring boiling and roasting to hanging (BR, 355). Dennis is a man in love with his job – so much so that he cannot stop talking about it even when the talk might get him into trouble. When he first lays eyes on Hugh, his reaction is indistinguishable from rapture. Here is Dennis talking about Hugh to Gashford, Lord Gordon's secretary and recruitment officer:

> "He's a fine-built chap, an't he?"
> "A powerful fellow indeed!"
> "Did you ever, Muster Gashford," whispered Dennis, with a horrible kind of admiration, such as that with which a cannibal might regard his intimate friend, when hungry, – "did you ever . . . see such a throat as his? Do but cast your eye upon it. There's a neck for stretching, Muster Gashford!" (BR, 360)

The intimation that Hugh's physical assets make him an ideal candidate for hanging reappears in different guises throughout *Barnaby Rudge*. (A similar macabre compliment is paid to Lucie Manette in *A Tale of Two Cities*: "'She has a fine head for [the guillotine],' croaked Jacques Three. 'I have seen blue eyes and golden hair there, and they looked charming when Samson [the executioner] held them up'" (TTC, 388).)

Like a figure from mythology, Hugh is beautiful. The narrator describes him as " . . . muscular and handsome . . . A young man of a hale athletic figure, and a giant's strength, whose sunburnt face and swarthy throat, overgrown with jet black hair, might have served a painter for a model" (BR, 138). The suggestion that Hugh's physical proportions would make him ideal as a painter's model foreshadows the later remark that Hugh's neck is perfect for hanging. These two uses for Hugh's physical perfection are not as distinct as one might assume. There is yet a third suggestion of a similar order when John Chester speculates that, once executed, Hugh's body "would make a very handsome preparation in Surgeons' Hall, and would benefit science extremely" (BR, 671). In all these instances, Hugh's beauty is defined as having no value unless it can be anatomized by others. He is all object and all body – a beautiful animal just waiting to be dissected, hanged, or reproduced on canvas.

All these activities are mirror-images of one another. In fact, the connection between art, generation, and execution is an old one, often linked, for instance, in the literature on maternal impressions, where pregnant women who have witnessed executions are said to give birth to children with the marks of hanging or torture on their bodies, in much the same way as pregnant women who viewed paintings were thought to pass on the characteristics of the paintings to their offspring. Huet suggests that language itself provides a link between the two, since one can execute both a painting and a human being.[8]

Dickens suggests a similar link. Through Dennis the Hangman's use of the word "art," the novel presents the two activities as equivalents. Says Dennis: "I may call myself a artist – a fancy workman – art improves natur' – that's my motto" (BR, 372). In fact, Dennis habitually uses the language of aesthetics. When he praises his own hand for the many jobs it has done with "a neatness and dexterity [*sic*], never known afore," when he remembers the "helegant bits of work it has turned off" (BR, 372), he might as easily be mistaken for a painter or a sculptor as for a hangman. In fact, one of his auditors does mistake him for an artist and assumes that the carved reproduction of Dennis's face on the knob of his walking stick is Dennis's own work, whereas it is actually the work of one of Dennis's victims – gruesomely described by Dennis as "one of the finest stand-up men, you ever see" (BR, 372).

Dickens portrays Dennis as an aesthete of the gallows throughout the novel, and Dennis has definite opinions as to what constitutes an aesthetic hanging. In fact, it is not much different from a stage performance: "I've heerd a eloquence on them boards – you know what boards I mean – and have heerd a degree of mouth given to them speeches, that they was as clear as a bell, and as good as a play" (BR, 591).

And here are his instructions for an aesthetic hanging:

Always, when a thing of this natur's to come off, what I stand up for, is, a proper frame of mind . . . Whatever you do . . . never snivel. I'd sooner by half, though I lose by it, see a man tear his clothes, a' purpose to spile 'em before they come to me, than find him snivelling. It's ten to one a better frame of mind, every way!   (BR, 591)

When Dennis claims that art improves nature he is alluding to an aesthetic philosophy which is not ordinarily associated with his profession. Dennis's "art," after all, consists of depriving the living of their lives. His job is to impose an artificial end on a natural process. His art consists of improving upon what has elsewhere been called "natural death" (BR, 239). What is more, his "art" exists at the service of the state, whose official representative he is. Execution, therefore, belongs to the world of the man-made, of craft and art, in much the same way as painting itself does – or novel-writing for that matter. It takes the natural as its raw material and converts it into something subject to human will. It is a gruesome and ironic juxtaposition. Dennis's claim to being an artist calls into question all the values traditionally associated with art, and defines the concept of both artistic and biological reproduction as just another door to death.

Dombey and Son: class division and integration

In all of Dickens's writing about class and heredity, there is a tension between distinction and integration. This tension corresponds to the dichotomies of outer and inner, superficial and profound, which accompany all narratives of hidden identity. What is on the surface – that is, the social world of class division and man-made demarcations – is contradicted and obliterated by the submerged and unacknowledged effects of heredity which homogenize social gradations into a single biological entity. In *Barnaby Rudge* the tension between social distinction and the integrity of nature is located primarily in the relationship between the stable-hand Hugh and his aristocratic father, whose overt interactions represent an unbridgeable gulf of class, education, and wealth, a gulf which is negated subcutaneously by the fact that they are father and son.

In *Dombey and Son* the same tensions are formulated in a different way. In this novel, the wealthy Mr Dombey is forced, through the death of his wife in childbirth, to seek a wet-nurse for his son.

His enforced reliance on the intimate services of a working-class woman to fulfill this function brings him into contact with the Toodle family. Dickens locates the class divide in Mr Dombey's dependence on Polly to nurse his son, a dependence which may be generalized to the interreliance of society as a whole. Each class must depend on the other: Mr Dombey depends on Polly to provide sustenance for Paul, and he depends on Polly's husband's "underground" labour to maintain his wealth and social position. The lower-class Toodle stokes the industrial machine which makes Dombey's social eminence possible. The Toodles in turn depend on Dombey, and capitalists like him, for employment and patronage.

This system of interconnection appears to suggest a relationship of mutual dependence, but in fact reveals a hierarchical structure in which the classes are so divided that the wealthy feel no responsibility for the poor. This is a society made up of the "two nations," described in Disraeli's *Sybil*, "who are as ignorant of each other's habits, thoughts and feelings as if they were . . . inhabitants of different planets, who are formed by a different breeding, are fed by a different food, are ordered by different manners, and are not governed by the same laws."[9]

The contemptuous attitude of Mr Dombey to the Toodles exemplifies the disdain and repugnance which the upper class feels for the classes below it. But *Dombey and Son* condemns this attitude as being against nature, because it contradicts the biological impulse towards integration and connection. To bring home this point, Dickens presents the Toodle family as a rebuke to Dombey – a rebuke that is centered in the natural sphere of reproduction. Not only are the Toodles fertile, but they breed sons, the kind of child Dombey so desperately wants. What is more, the Toodle family expands as the novel progresses, permitting the Toodles' wealth in children to be contrasted to Dombey's far less fruitful monetary accumulation. At the same time, by presenting the Toodles' fecundity as a positive contrast to the Dombey sterility, Dickens is inverting the popular prejudice against what Sheila Smith labels "the multiplying poor," who terrified Malthus and inspired the 1834 Poor Law.[10] Dickens's strategy here is to accede to the stereotype that the poor are prolific in nothing but children in order to establish this superabundance as a form of innate generosity, the natural product of human warmth and physical affection.

The Toodles are an example of what Henry Mayhew called "the honest poor who will work."[11] They are the novel's primary exponents of family values, the father strict but loving, the mother all heart, totally given over to affection for her offspring, with enough love left over to nurture her foster children. Again, this is intended as a contrast to the chill of the Dombey household. By locating all human warmth in the lower classes – the novel's other exponents of the doctrine of the heart are the working-class Captain Cuttle, Sol Gills, and the socially "insignificant" Miss Tox – Dickens attempts to reverse the middle-class stereotype of the poor as alien beings without morals or emotions.[12] His insistence on the wholesome qualities of the Toodle family can be seen in his persistent use of apple imagery to characterize them. Both parents and children are routinely described as "rosy," "apple-cheeked" and "apple-faced." What is more, this wholesome quality is defined as hereditable, for instance in the following description of Polly surrounded by her children: " . . . Her own honest apple face became immediately the centre of a bunch of smaller pippins, all laying their rosy cheeks close to it, and all evidently the growth of the same tree" (DS, 123). The poor may have many children, but if so, the human qualities which they propagate are not necessarily undesirable.

In addition, the apple allusions underline, not only the salubrious moral qualities of the Toodles, but their physical health as well. In this too Dickens is writing against the grain of contemporary middle-class prejudice, which associated poverty with disease and working-class life with ill health. In fact, a large part of Mr Dombey's reluctance to hire a wet-nurse stems from his fear of contagion, by which he means both physical and moral infection. When Polly is interviewed for the job of Paul's wet-nurse, her entire brood of five children is brought along to attest to the health of the mother. Even the blister on the nose of the eldest son comes in for scrutiny, its cause being safely ascribed to accidental not constitutional causes (DS, 66). (That blister is significant, since it will be this son who will go wrong through the "charitable" interference of Mr Dombey in his education.) Nevertheless, despite the evidence of Polly's health and suitability, Mr Dombey remains appalled that a "hired serving woman" should act as mother to his son, thus establishing what Dombey sees as a biological connection between his offspring and the progeny of the Toodle family, all of whom will have been nourished at the same source.[13]

That even so tenuous a connection might confer a kind of kinship between the classes leads to Dombey's other obsessive thoughts of unnatural mixing. He worries that Polly will exchange her own newly born son for Paul, so that Dombey will end up raising the pauper in place of the prince. It is partly to avoid such a catastrophe that he denies Polly permission to visit her own children for as long as she nurses Paul. He thus takes advantage of his position as her employer to interpose the power of money between Polly and her maternal instincts. In order to vitiate her potentially corrupting influence he insists that once her services are no longer required, she will go away and stay away. He consoles himself with the thought that the class divisions between Polly and her charge are so great that they will make the inevitable separation that much easier.

Since *Dombey and Son* is concerned to demonstrate the redemptive powers of natural affection, Mr Dombey's strictures are doomed to failure. Polly eventually succumbs to the impulse to see her own children and takes young Paul with her. She does in fact exchange him for her own son "in a twinkling" when she takes her child from her sister's arms and gives her Paul to hold in his stead. Thus Mr Dombey's worst fear is realized; but the momentary exchange of Paul for the youngest Toodle is merely another demonstration on Dickens's part of the interconnection, in fact the interchangeability of all human beings. When Mr Dombey dismisses Polly, the stated reason is for taking Paul "into haunts and into society which are not to be thought of without a shudder" (DS, 142). But the real reason is Mr Dombey's fear of acknowledging the power of human emotions – especially maternal emotions. The impulse which prompts Polly to put her job in jeopardy in order to see her children is dangerously irrational from the Dombey point of view, and if it is irrational it is also subversive, full of anarchic potential that could undermine the cold monetary edifice of Dombey and Son.

Dickens touches on this same theme in the scene at the railway station. Mr Dombey is about to leave for Leamington where he will meet his second wife, Edith. Walking up and down the train platform in the company of the blow-hard Major Bagstock, Dombey is completely oblivious to Toodle's attempt to catch his eye. It is as if Toodle does not exist until he literally places himself in front of Dombey so that the latter can no longer avert his eyes from the "vulgar herd." Forced to look at what he does not care to see, Dombey reacts to Toodle "as if a man like that would make his very eyesight dirty" (DS, 351). Toodle has stopped Dombey to offer his condolences on the death of little Paul, but it is precisely this assumption of common humanity from one of the Great Unwashed that Dombey finds "dirty."

As long as he remains in his house or in his office, Mr Dombey is the master of his world, with powers to regulate his contacts. But as soon as he ventures out into "the dangerous promiscuity of public space,"[14] he abdicates his hegemony and must endure being confronted by the likes of Toodle. Public spaces demonstrate the links between humans, rather than their divisions. Here Dombey is forced to confront the existence of other classes and their common claim to be heard. The point is brought home by the introduction of the train as the symbol of death, which follows immediately on Dombey's encounter with Toodle. "The power that forced itself upon its iron way ... dragging living creatures of all classes, ages, and degrees behind it, was a type of the triumphant monster, Death" (DS, 354).

In this railway scene, Dickens associates the death of Paul with the humiliation which Mr Dombey feels at being consoled by Toodle and so suggests the tensions between separation and cohesion in terms of the man-made divisions of class and the natural leveler Death. Mr Dombey can only allow himself to feel any emotion through "his sense of property in his child" (DS, 70), a sense which is disturbed when he is reminded of his reliance on the Toodles. Thus death, class, and property begin to stand for one another and to refer to one another, a trope which recurs throughout the novel, most notably in the death of Alice Marwood, whose body is referred to as "the ruin of the mortal house, on which the rain had beaten ..." (DS, 923). From this description of the death of a fallen woman, Dickens turns immediately to a description of the ruined house of a fallen merchant – Mr Dombey.

At the same time as he dramatizes the class divide in the relationship of Mr Dombey to the Toodles, Dickens locates his argument for social cohesion in his presentation of the look-alike cousins, Edith Dombey and Alice Marwood. Through them and through the various strands of narrative that are filtered through the fact of their consanguinity, Dickens demonstrates the hidden hereditary connections of all levels of society. The cousins' uncanny resemblance to one another serves as the outward sign of more intricate relationships which remain unseen. *Dombey and Son* is one of Dickens's first attempts to present in global terms the implications of the kind of blood-tie which in *Barnaby Rudge* was particular only to Hugh and his upper-class sire. This theme of hidden consanguinity allying all levels of society and reducing the human world to a single complicitous mass becomes more insistent in Dickens's fiction as his career progresses, finding more extensive expression in such novels as *Bleak House* and *Great Expectations*.

In *Dombey and Son*, Edith Dombey and Alice Marwood represent the link between the themes of heredity, class, and money. The two women belong to two different classes, yet they are related, their fathers having been brothers. The two brothers were gentlemen, but Edith's father was married to her mother, while Alice's father toyed with Alice's mother and then deserted her. That the sexual history of these two women – and, significantly, the histories of their mothers – is identical in all respects except for the crucial fact of marriage is demonstrated through their physical resemblance. Alice and Edith look so much alike that a portrait of one could pass for a portrait of the other – and does.

Portraiture, Dickens's favourite trope for reproduction, is once again in *Dombey and Son* the medium through which a blood-tie is demonstrated, the portrait in question being a painting that Carker had had made of his former mistress, Alice. Dickens funnels the destinies of the cousins through the one man who will be the seducer of both, as a way of demonstrating that the two women's physical resemblance is emblematic of their shared essence. They are alter egos, linked through the villain Carker, who stands as the masculine crucible through which the upper-class woman dissolves into her lower-class counterpart, and vice versa. The medium which effects this dissolution is sex, which, like death, is a natural equalizer.

Dickens cleverly weaves Alice's portrait into his thematic scheme. The first time the portrait is mentioned, we are told that the woman depicted in it is "like Edith." Since Alice's relationship to Carker has not yet been established, the reader is left to suppose a former illicit relationship with Mr Dombey's newly made wife. That relationship, however, lies in the future, while the one with Alice belongs to the past. Thus the two look-alike women coalesce into a portrait of Carker's sexual history. He may be the male link between high- and low-class women, the despoiler who reduces all females to one – and that one a whore. But he is simultaneously the victim of this same composite woman, and is ultimately undone by the women whom he has victimized. Alice reveals to Dombey the location of Carker's assignation with Edith, while Edith denies him the satisfaction of consummating his desires.

Alice's portrait is also the occasion for another of Dickens's dem-
onstrations of the blindness of Mr Dombey. When Dombey goes to
Carker's rooms to complain about his wife, his eye falls on the
portrait of the woman who looks so much like Edith. Yet he does
not seem to remark the resemblance, does not express surprise, nor
wonder at the identity of the woman in the painting. His eyes rest
on the portrait and then move on. Dombey's obtuseness lies in his
inability to see connections, not merely between himself and Toodle,
but also between himself and Carker, who, we are told in the same
paragraph, has the habit of mimicking his employer's mannerisms.
Carker reproduces Dombey's mannerisms, the painting reproduces
the features of Dombey's wife, but Dombey notices none of this,
reproduction of any kind not being one of his strong points.

In 1846, just after he began *Dombey and Son*, Dickens was forced to
break off his work on the novel and turn his attention to writing
another Christmas Book. That book, "The Battle of Life," features
two sisters, who are both in love with the same man. The younger
sister renounces her claim to the suitor, so that her older sister
might marry him. That some residue of this theme may have carried over into Dickens's conception of Edith Dombey and Alice
Marwood seems likely. (The theme of the self-sacrificing sibling recurs
in *A Tale of Two Cities*, between two men who are alter egos but
not brothers.)

Edith and Alice are similar in more than just their looks; their
natures too are identical. Both women are proud, high-strung, and
passionate; both have been exploited by their mothers. In effect,
both mothers are panderers, and both daughters sell themselves –
although Edith's form of prostitution is not recognized as such because
she marries the men who are rich enough to make her their wife.
Both Alice and Edith are treated like commodities by their mothers,
and by society at large. In the mercantile world of *Dombey and Son*,
female beauty is merely another counter in the social economy,
and is woven into the fabric of capitalist exchange.

Dickens is not subtle in his insistence on the similarity of Edith
and Alice and what he expects us to understand by it. Here he is
describing Alice Marwood and her mother:

Were this miserable mother, and this miserable daughter, only
the reduction to their lowest grade, of certain social vices some-

times prevailing higher up? In this round world of many circles within circles, do we make a weary journey from the high grade to the low, to find at last that they lie close together, that the two extremes touch, and that our journey's end is but our starting place? Allowing for great difference of stuff and texture, was the pattern of this woof repeated among gentle blood at all?

(DS, 579)

Alice Marwood and Edith Dombey's shared heredity links upper and lower classes through a blood tie. Sexual activity is the great leveler, creating the link between the classes – Alice's mother was seduced by the brother of the man who married Edith's mother. The connection is underscored still further through the suggestion that Alice's unsanctioned liaison with Carker is no different in essence from Edith's legitimized union with Dombey. Both involve the barter of female flesh for wealth, position, and security. The difference in the two relationships is purely a matter of legal convention – and social hypocrisy – which sanctions one form of sexual exchange and stigmatizes the other. In his insistence on the physical, familial, and moral similarity between Edith and Alice, Dickens comes close to suggesting that marriage is nothing more than legalized prostitution.

Had Edith actually committed adultery with Carker – as Dickens originally intended – then the identification with Alice, her lower-class twin, would have been complete, both women having been mistresses of the same man. Even without this consummation, the implications of Dickens's narrative are clear: sex erases class differences by blurring hereditary lines, turning prince and pauper into kin, and creating a fluidity between seemingly rigid divisions of society.

Yet there are differences. In a crucial scene, the two mother–daughter pairs come together on the beach at Brighton. It is a public arena, reminiscent of the scene at the railway station where Dombey encounters Toodle. The classes mix freely in the open air, rubbing democratically against one another, and partaking equally of the natural scene. Nevertheless they are not equal. Dickens stresses the similarities between the two mothers and daughters, but he does so over an exchange of money. Mrs Brown – Alice's mother – begs money of Mrs Skewton – Edith's mother. Mrs Skewton recognizes in Mrs Brown another "good mother," just like herself, and is inclined to be generous. Thus the essential similarity between the mothers and daughters is simultaneously stressed and undermined. Nature and blood may unite these mother–daughter pairs, but money and class divide them. For all the leveling effects inherent in consanguinity, man-made social distinctions still differentiate between those who dispense largesse and those who must beg for it. The injustice of this is articulated by Good Mrs Brown when her daughter Alice falls ill with the wasting disease that is the frequent fate of fallen women in Victorian fiction:

> "... If you could have seen my gal, as I have seen her once, side by side with the other's daughter, you'd have seen, for all the difference of dress and life, that they were like each other. Oh! is the likeness gone, and is it my gal – only my gal – that's to change so!
> "... What have I done, I, what have I done worse than her, that only my gal is to lie there fading!" (DS, 921)

Alice is a fallen woman and this marks her as no different in essence from a prostitute, although the novel never shows her in any illicit dealings with men. As far as the plot of *Dombey and Son* is concerned, Alice seems to be guilty of nothing more than the sexual lapse with Carker. She is transported for robbery, not prostitution. The ambiguity of Alice's position reflects the fact that middle-class Victorians did not distinguish between the niceties of sexual lapse and sexual sale – although among prostitutes themselves there was a rigid hierarchy which mimicked the social distinctions of the larger society.[15] The loss of chastity alone was considered sufficient to label a woman a prostitute. The Victorian statistician Hemyng had no compunction about decreeing that, "literally every woman who yields to her passions and loses her virtue is a prostitute."[16] Women who ventured out on the streets had to move briskly, as if they were about their business. Loitering without obvious errand was seen as unnatural, since female activity was centered indoors. Wandering about came to be perceived as a sign of doubtful morality.[17]

The lack of gradation encompassed by the Victorian term "fallen woman" suits Dickens admirably in this novel, since it permits his equation of the marriage market with the morality of sex for sale. Nineteenth-century European writers seem to have been fascinated with the figure of the prostitute. The thematic territory she occupies tends to vacillate between notions of degradation and redemption on the one hand, and a kind of reductionist leveling on the other, in which all men of all classes are implicated in her activities. Peter Brooks writes that the prostitute speculates on the *libido universalis*, "on the capacity to make every man succumb to his erotic needs."[18] In this speculation all men are reduced to their sexual essence and all women to manipulators and exploiters of that essence.

It is this leveling tendency in prostitution which interests Dickens in *Dombey and Son*. (In *Oliver Twist*, on the other hand, it is Nancy's potential as a figure of redemption that he stresses.) In *Dombey and Son*, the figure of the prostitute is split in two between the low-class Alice and the aristocratic Edith. By suggesting that Alice, the fallen woman, is a prostitute, and that Edith, the married woman, is prostituted through her marriages, Dickens comes close to implying that all women sell themselves and that prostitution itself is not merely a female business but a female family business, passed on from mother to daughter, and not much different from the mercantile dynasty of a Dombey and Son. This impression is reinforced by the fact that Alice's putative customers are nowhere to be seen. We must take her dealings with them on faith. But we do see her mother in action, just as we see Edith's. Prostitution, as it is presented in *Dombey and Son*, means not only that women's bodies are for sale, but that it is their mothers who do the selling. Little wonder that Dickens refers to the two mothers as "distorted shadows" of one another, even though they are not blood relations (DS, 662).

The personal histories of Alice and Edith's mothers suggest that in their youths they were similar to their daughters – beautiful, proud, and the playthings of men. Mrs Skewton exploited her looks and married well – albeit into a family with more blood than money. Mrs Brown, being a "fresh country wench" was the inamorata of Mrs Skewton's brother-in-law. The sexual pattern is repeated with the daughters. It is the pattern of exact repetition from one generation to the next, which is so typical of Dickens's presentation of hereditary relationships, especially those of women.

In *Dombey and Son*, this female genealogy occurs in two opposing patterns: firstly, in the form of the degenerate seed which passes from panderer mothers to prostituted daughters; and secondly, in the negation of that pattern, when the angelic Florence inherits her virtuous nature from her mother and then passes it on to her daughter. The fact that Polly and Florence are fertile underscores Dickens's redemptive message: the maternal solicitude of a Polly

Toodle and the inherited grace of a Florence Dombey will be passed on to future generations. On the other hand, the bad seed which was passed on to Alice and Edith will die with them. The fact that both Edith and Alice are barren is another indication of their linked association to prostitution, since the Victorians believed that prostitutes were infertile – a belief which dates back to the Middle Ages.[19]

A Tale of Two Cities: the sins of the fathers

A Tale of Two Cities represents Dickens's most extensive fictional portrayal of the "sins of the fathers" as a genealogical motif. Like all models based on the biblical notion of hereditary taint, *A Tale of Two Cities* is vitally concerned with the manner in which the past infringes on the present. This is made most explicit in the novel's "embedded narrative," i.e. the seminal episode out of which grow the complications of the plot.[20] There we learn for the first time the extent to which the *Tale*'s several thematic strands are interwoven.

The genesis for the novel's present action occurred some thirty years earlier, when the young Dr Manette was called to treat a young peasant woman who had been abused and assaulted by the St Evrémonde brothers. The brothers had also killed her husband and mortally wounded her brother, with the result that by the time Dr Manette arrives, the peasant woman has become half-crazed and repeats compulsively, "my husband, my father, and my brother," then counts up to twelve. This mad scene symbolizes in highly melodramatic form the fate of France itself as a country violated and despoiled, for which time is rapidly running out. A similar analogy between private acts and public consequences is made more explicitly earlier in the novel when Dickens draws the parallel between the Marquis de St Evrémonde's swallowing his chocolate and swallowing France (TTC, 134).

The young peasant woman's repeated evocation of her husband, her father, and her brother echoes Lucie Manette's appeal at the height of the Terror to Mme Defarge: "O sister-woman, think of me. As a wife and mother!" (TTC, 297). These recurring allusions to the bonds of kinship are linked to the theme of dismemberment in the novel, which constitutes a subtext to the revolutionary motif. Evil in the *Tale* is defined as an assault on the integrity of hereditary bonds. The same diabolical impulse which decapitates the aristocracy during the revolution, and tears the peasantry limb from limb before the revolution, accosts as well the ties of kinship, dismembering human families as well as human bodies. The abuses of power in *A Tale of Two Cities* are therefore portrayed as violations against the notion of integrity – the integrity of the family and the integrity of the body.

This theme is first sounded in "The Shoemaker" chapter of the novel, when Lucie Manette – who has not seen her father for many years – cradles his head against her breast. Dickens describes the scene as follows: "... She now stood looking at him ... trembling with eagerness to lay the spectral face upon her warm young breast, and love it back to life and hope ..." (TTC, 73–4). What Dickens is suggesting here is an overturning of the normal nurturing relationship between parent and child. The incestuous reverberations he sets in motion are connected to the hereditary bond between the principals. Immediately after the reference to Lucie's warm young breast, we get the following statement of hereditary association: "... So exactly was the [old man's] expression repeated (though in stronger characters) on her fair young face, that it looked as though it had passed like a moving light, from him to her" (TTC, 74). The link here between heredity and role-reversal is too blatant to be coincidental. That Dickens is deliberately reversing the roles of father and daughter is clear, but that he does so within the context of hereditary description implies a stopping of time, which suddenly seems to run backward.

This is in keeping with the thematic position of this recognition scene within the framework of the novel. For Dr Manette, maddened through many years of unjust confinement in the Bastille, time has indeed stood still, and whenever he subsequently relapses into his former delusive state, time may be said to move backwards. *A Tale of Two Cities* is, in fact, a novel in which time plays a major role, the revolutionary chaos of the present having been planted and predicted by the legalistic injustices of the past. When Dickens writes that the light of heredity moves from father to daughter, he is describing an orderly succession, a chronological relationship where everything is as it should be, but when he describes the daughter's nurturing actions, he reverses chronology and so hints at anarchy as the daughter becomes mother to her own father.

While we are clearly intended to understand the nurturing and restoring role of Lucie, whose physicality is here presented as instinctive and at the service of an intense sympathy for a feeble father whom she has not seen since girlhood, the fact remains that

Dickens's description is highly sexual, even to the point of depicting father and daughter lying together in the dark:

> Then, as the darkness closed in, the daughter laid her head down on the hard ground close at her father's side, and watched him. The darkness deepened and deepened, and they both lay quiet, until a light gleamed through the chinks in the wall. (TTC, 79)

As he did earlier in *Little Dorrit*, where Amy Dorrit's nursing of her father in prison was compared to the classical story of Euphrasia breast-feeding her imprisoned father, King Evander of Syracuse, Dickens here stresses a blood-tie that partakes of the sexual while yet being beyond sex, precisely because it involves a father and child.[21] The sexual atmosphere which hovers over such parent–child pairings in Dickens's work – and this includes David Copperfield's attachment to his mother, Steerforth's love–hate relationship with his mother, and Amy Dorrit's nursing of her father – is usually a metaphor for exploitation, for the unjustified pressure applied to the young by weak and incompetent parents. But in *A Tale of Two Cities*, the scene between Lucie Manette and her father serves instead as a foreshadowing of revolutionary chaos. It is an emblem of the world turned upside-down.

The "unnatural" associations which hover over Lucie's recognition scene with her father, and which Dickens simultaneously evokes and dismisses, foreshadow the role of women in the novel. *A Tale of Two Cities* is full of "unnatural" women, mothers of death rather than life. The novel describes how "the crowd of ladies of quality and fashion" watched with lustful avidity the horrendous public execution of the traitor Damiens (TTC, 200). The reigning symbol of the revolution is female – Sainte Guillotine. Her minions and votaries are female, in particular Mme Defarge and La Vengeance. These female harpies, who are repeatedly described as more vicious and bloodthirsty than the men, constitute the vengeful female response to the crime against women that is central to the narrative – the rape of the young peasant woman by the aristocratic St Evrémonde brothers. Thus the ambiguity inherent in Lucie's loving behaviour towards her father – whose own personal history is intimately connected to the rape – demonstrates the sophistication with which the mature Dickens manipulates hereditary issues to suit the symbolic needs of his narrative.

Dr Manette had been imprisoned by the St Evrémonde brothers when he denounced them in a letter to the minister. While in the Bastille, he writes another letter detailing the brothers' crimes and cursing "their descendants to the last of their race" (TTC, 361). This same prison letter, produced nearly thirty years later during the height of the revolution, will serve to condemn Charles Darnay, the descendant of the St Evrémondes, who has since become Dr Manette's son-in-law, husband of his daughter Lucie and father of his grandchild, also called Lucie. Thus Dr Manette's curse of the descendants of the St Evrémondes to the last of their race rebounds onto his own family, implicating the innocent in the fate of the guilty.

This is not the only consequence of the imbedded narrative: Mme Defarge, the woman who personifies the bloodlust of the revolution, turns out to be the younger sister of the same raped peasant woman who was treated by Dr Manette. There is thus an ambiguity injected into our perception of Mme Defarge, who is otherwise presented as a figure of mindless evil and raving savagery. Knowledge of her kinship to the young brother and sister who were so cruelly victimized by the aristocratic St Evrémondes softens our perception of her. Her vengefulness is explained if not excused, and our full-hearted condemnation of her receives a check. This kind of ambiguity – in this case, an ambiguity tied directly to our own perceptions of the obligations of kinship – exists everywhere in the plot of *A Tale of Two Cities*, complicating our perceptions of the revolutionary masses and arresting any impulse we may have to commiserate with one class or the other.

Dickens's use of embedded narrative in this novel owes a debt to the biological theory of preformation. Preformation argued that all future generations were present at the creation, and that each individual carried within him or herself the germs of all future descendants. These descendants already existed fully formed, but miniaturized, in the germ, waiting only for a trigger to make them grow. Preformation therefore attributes inevitability to the processes of nature; it is the hereditary equivalent of fate. Dickens alludes to this form of embedded destiny throughout *A Tale of Two Cities*. The most startling example occurs in the introductory chapter, which describes the execution of a youth sentenced to have his hands cut off, his tongue torn out with pincers, and his body burned alive, for failing to kneel in the rain before a procession of monks. The narrator then goes on to tie this act of legalized savagery to future events:

> It is likely enough that, rooted in the woods of France and Norway, there were growing trees, when that sufferer was put to death, already marked by the Woodman, Fate, to come down and be sawn into boards, to make a certain movable framework with a sack and a knife in it, terrible in history. It is likely enough that in the rough outhouses of some tillers of the heavy lands adjacent to Paris, there were sheltered from the weather that very day, rude carts, bespattered with rustic mire... which the Farmer, Death, had already set apart to be his tumbrils of the Revolution.
> (TTC, 36)

The seeming dissociation between the execution of the youth and the pastoral innocence of trees growing in the forest or farm carts sheltering from the weather is shown to be illusory. The forces of history link them all. The trees that grow today will turn into the instruments of torture and retribution tomorrow, avenging the death of the youth, whose dismemberment is an affront against the integrity of Nature. The passage is a perfect example of embedded destiny – the invisible workings of fate, obscured by the apparently random events of history, will eventually make clear their design. The future exists in the womb of the past and only awaits the fullness of time to bring it to fruition. Or, as Dickens puts it, "that Woodman [Fate] and that Farmer [Death]... work silently, and no one heard them as they went about with muffled tread" (TTC, 36).

This emphasis on the future encapsulated in the past is closely allied to the theme of resurrection, which is one of the novel's major motifs. Dickens himself calls attention to the importance of this theme when he entitles the first section of the novel "Recalled to Life." Subsequent allusions to resurrection are scattered throughout the text. These include such disparate narrative strands as Dr Manette's return to life after eighteen years of imprisonment, and the occupation of the Crunchers, father and son, who work as resurrectionists, or grave-robbers, unearthing the dead to sell their bodies to science. Several characters in the novel try to present themselves as dead when they are in fact very much alive – Roger Cly, for instance, the spy Barsad, and the aristocrat Foulon. Sydney Carton intones "I am the Resurrection and the Life," just before his execution. More significantly, he has a vision in his last moments of Lucie's as-yet-unconceived son, who will bear Carton's name and make it "illustrious." Through his namesake, Sydney Carton will live again.

The notion of resurrection is tied to that of preformation because both concepts deny the finality of death. Resurrection suggests that the dead may live again, preformation confers immortality through the repetitiveness of generation, with its suggestion that the future is always the same as the past and awaits only the fullness of time to reproduce a copy of what has gone before. This notion of the replication of creation, of things never ending because they never change, is connected to that other great motif of the novel – the double. Within this motif of doubleness lies Dickens's conception of the historical relationship of the past to the present as one of revolutionary overthrow in which nothing has changed but the relative positions of the powerful and the powerless.

The most important pair of doubles in *A Tale of Two Cities* are Sydney Carton and Charles Darnay. Darnay himself is the offspring of doubles, being the son and nephew of twin brothers. But Darnay is tainted by his descent from the St Evrémonde twins, who represent the decadence and degeneration of the French aristocracy squared. Speaking of his father to his uncle, Charles Darnay says: "Can I separate my father's twin brother, joint inheritor, and next successor, from himself?" (TTC, 154). In other words, the twins are interchangeable, each stands for the other, and Darnay, in being related to both as son and nephew, is doubly stained by the family taint.

Darnay's nature is clearly different from that of his father and uncle – he takes after neither one. However, the reason for this hereditary disjunction has nothing to do with self-actualization or free will. Darnay's rejection of his father and uncle's way of life, his condemnation of their treatment of the peasantry, is not based on any principled philosophical dissent. Dickens is not yet ready to discard heredity as a determining force in human conduct. Darnay's disapproval of his father and uncle stems from the moral traits which he has inherited from his mother.

In what is a fairly common pattern for Dickens, the child evades the consequences of the father's evil through his or her descent from a saintly mother. In *Dombey and Son*, both Florence and her brother inherit from their mother with the result that their natures differ significantly from that of their father. Little Nell and Little Dorrit also evade the corrupting influence of flawed fathers and grandfathers through having inherited from a good mother who is conveniently dead when the novel's action starts. In *A Tale of Two Cities*, Darnay's mother appears in only one scene, but it is enough to establish her as a "good, compassionate lady," who is unhappy in her marriage to the Marquis of St Evrémonde. Since she plays no part in the plot, it is clear that the mother is brought on stage merely to establish her beneficent effect on the emerging personality of her young son. In fact, it is in order that her son may "prosper in his inheritance" that this kind wife of the cruel marquis wishes to make restitution to the remaining sister of the peasant family whom the marquis and his twin brother have destroyed. We must therefore understand that Charles Darnay's self-sacrificing heroic stand *vis-à-vis* his aristocratic patrimony is the result of his moral inheritance from his mother. It is another instance, albeit a late one, of Dickens's belief in the inheritance of goodness.

But if Charles Darnay is the nominal hero of *A Tale of Two Cities*, he is nevertheless a hero under constant judicial threat. He is presented as a man of upstanding moral character, forever acting on the best of motives; he is both altruistic and brave. Yet he is constantly being accused of transgression and brought before the courts of two countries. Darnay is accused of treason in England, and he is accused of treason in France. All told, he is brought before tribunals three times during the course of the novel, once in England, twice in France. And in both England and France, his father-in-law is the primary witness against him.

Darnay's guilt is typical of inherited taint, which has no reference to individual actions, but defines the transgressor as a member of a particular bloodline and the guilt which attaches to him as the collective guilt of his tribe and therefore indicative of primordial sin. The concept of the sins of the fathers draws attention to notions of genealogy, and equates birthright with moral stain. Inherited guilt thus plays itself out as the guilt of a race – in the case of *A Tale of Two Cities*, that race is the aristocracy. (The application of the word "race" to the aristocracy is Dickens's.)

Because inherited taint defines guilt collectively, it turns innocence on its head, fudging all moral distinctions and undermining the concept of justice. This upside-down effect extends even to those who testify against the accused. Thus, no matter how unwilling a witness Darnay's father-in-law is, he is nevertheless forced into the position of a vindictive father figure condemning the son for faults which are not his.[22] Dickens's handling of the guilt motif in *A Tale of Two Cities* anticipates his preoccupation with the same theme in his next novel, *Great Expectations*. It also anticipates Kafka's rendering of the all-pervasive guilt of the innocent in *The Trial*. Kafka's Joseph K. is defined as culpable by virtue of having been accused. Darnay's guilt in *A Tale of Two Cities* is exactly of this metaphysical type; it is tied to no deed, it is all-pervasive, it cannot be disproved. Darnay is tainted by what he is, not what he does – he is tainted by his essence.

Unlike Joseph K., however, Darnay has a savior. His guilt by inheritance finds its counterpart in Sydney Carton's guilt by action. Carton is a debauched lawyer who has squandered his promise. He drinks too much, is morally lax, careless of his own betterment, and generally full of self-hatred. It must be said, however, that Dickens is so unconvincing in his delineation of Carton's moral flaws that it is not easy to know how exactly he has sinned beyond the minor vices listed above. We must take his guilt on faith. What is important is that these lapses are his own doing and not attributable to any suspect inheritance.

Carton is Darnay's alter ego. In *A Tale of Two Cities* Dickens reverses the negative connotations which attached to the alter ego cousins Alice and Edith in *Dombey and Son*, who parceled out the degeneracy of the upper and lower classes between them. In the *Tale*, the relationship of the doubles is redemptive – doubling disarms the contagion of genealogical taint. Only the existence of his alter ego can rescue Charles Darnay from the doom of his inheritance. The man whose actions have defined him as guilty takes the place of the man whose blood has defined him so. In this way, the moral universe is righted again – the guilty are punished, the innocent set free. Or is it the opposite? By sacrificing his life, a Christ-like act, Carton proves both his nobility and his superiority to the ordinary run of men. Perhaps, then, it is the innocent who die under the knife and the guilty who are set free? The conundrum cannot be resolved because the two men, Carton and Darnay, are really two halves of the same individual. They are essentially substitutes for one another.

Carton and Darnay are physically so much alike that they may be mistaken for one another. In fact, they look like twins, even though they are not related – the resemblance is a coincidence. Thus, in the *Tale*, Dickens takes his universalizing metaphor a step beyond consanguinity. It is not remarkable that brothers should resemble each other, but when two men who are not brothers look as if they were, then the notion of consanguinity is lifted clear from the constraints of heredity and the definition of brotherhood is no longer limited to blood kin. Darnay and Carton's uncanny physical resemblance alludes to what is common in the human condition. What is more, the fact that the two men's physical resemblance suggests consanguinity where none actually exists expands the fraternal metaphor to include other sets of doubles in the novel, including the two cities of the title.

Universal brotherhood – one of the rallying cries of the French Revolution – is not the only thing Dickens is alluding to in portraying Carton and Darnay as doubles. The two men also represent opposites. Here, for instance, is Sydney Carton pondering his attitude towards Charles Darnay, just after the first trial in London when Darnay has been acquitted of treason because of his resemblance to Carton. Significantly, Carton is looking in the mirror while he ruminates:

> "Do you particularly like the man?" he muttered, at his own image; "why should you particularly like a man who resembles you? There is nothing in you to like, you know that . . . A good reason for taking to a man, that he shows you what you have fallen away from, and what you might have been! Change places with him, and would you have been looked at by those blue eyes as he was, and commiserated by that agitated face as he was? Come on, and have it out in plain words! You hate the fellow."
> (TTC, 116)

Technically, the purpose of this scene is to prepare the ground for the eventual substitution of one double for the other, which will mark the climax of the plot. Carton is in love with Lucie who is in love with Darnay. It is for Lucie's sake that Carton will take Darnay's place on the guillotine – thereby committing the ultimate sacrifice. But there is more going on here than this. While the passage foreshadows future events, it also delineates the thematic relationship between the doubles. Carton and Darnay are simultaneously alike and different. Carton's vacillating between love and hatred for his look-alike suggests the kind of polarization which

Dickens uses to define most of the dualities in this novel – the relationship of twinship is presented as one of opposites which are essentially the same. The differences between Darnay and Carton are given the same weight as the resemblances, and this form of oppositional balance between doubles is reflected in the construction of the novel as a whole.

In fact, the concept of doubling infects every level of the narrative, from its structure, to its theme, to its language.[23] The famous opening passage introduces the antipodal motif: "It was the best of times, it was the worst of times, it was the age of wisdom, it was the age of foolishness . . ." (TTC, 35), and so on through an entire paragraph full of similar polarities. The doubling continues into the political sphere described by the next paragraph: the monarchs of England and France both have large jaws, but the complexions of their wives differ. More ominously, the year is 1775 and revolution is about to shake both countries, which are personified as "sisters." England will get its taste of violent upheaval from the American colonists; France from its own citizens. From this opening of implied consanguinity between the countries of England and France, Dickens proceeds to develop his dualities in terms of their respective capital cities.

London could easily stand for Paris. The two cities exist in the same kind of relationship to one another as do Carton and Darnay, their representatives. The differences only serve to underline the resemblance. The appalling punishment meted out to a traitor in London is the exact counterpart of that meted out to a parricide in France. (See Book 2, chapters 2 and 15 for a comparison of the gory details.) There is no distinction between the barbarity of one country's laws and that of the other. The description of the crowd watching Darnay's trial in London and mentally picturing him being hanged, beheaded and quartered is the exact counterpart of the crowd lusting for his blood in Paris. *A Tale of Two Cities* presents the alter ego as a trope for the essential similarity of all things, even those which appear as contrasts.

And this in turn has ramifications for the presentation of class in the novel. The viciousness of the French aristocrats was no different, finally, from the viciousness of the revolutionaries. When it comes to violence and barbarity, each group may stand for the other. The point is underscored when Carton thinks of "the long ranks of the new oppressors who have risen on the destruction of the old" (TTC, 404). The only difference between the aristocracy and the lower classes lies in the dynamics of power, who wields it and against whom.

This reversal extends as well to the role of women in the novel. The revolution not only upends the roles of the upper and lower classes, but also reverses the sexual dynamics implied by the rape of the young peasant woman. Female subservience becomes the murderous dominance of women. Thus the assumed passivity of Victorian women is equated with the subservience of the lower classes, and reversed during the upheaval of revolution.[24]

What the revolution accomplishes is merely a substitution, a rollover, an exchange of places. Dickens sees the new revolutionary elite as no different in essence from their predecessors. The substitution of one dominant class for another has had about as much impact on the ways of the world as the substitution of a Carton for a Darnay.

In fact, the novel's insistence on the similarities inherent in doubleness undercuts what Dickens clearly intended as a moving act of redemption and self-sacrifice. Carton's martyrdom is no more than a noble gesture stripped of consequence; it does not matter, either historically or in terms of the novel. It has no resonance beyond itself, because the thematic thrust of the narrative suggests that even sacrifices such as Carton's will not stop the hand of the executioner, quell the frenzy of the crowd, or wipe human folly off the face of the earth. And it does not matter because Charles Darnay, who is another form of Carton himself, will go on living, and Darnay's son and grandson will be named after Carton and therefore, in a sense, be Carton – as if any more evidence were needed that the two men are substitutes for one another – and in this way Carton will go on living.[25] The use Dickens makes of doubles in this novel, the emphasis on the motif of resurrection, deprives individual actions of meaning and effect.

If Dickens's conservatism shows itself in anything, it shows itself in this – that his method of extracting comfort from the horrors of the revolution is to insist on the underlying immutability of change, anchoring his belief in the repetitive nature of generation. The one thing which Dickens is loath to acknowledge in this novel is that change can make a difference. When the issue is class struggle, the comforting philosophy of preformation – which encompasses the idea that history repeats itself – stands in opposition to the notion that each historical event is unique and therefore capable of affecting the future in such a way that it will never resemble the past.

Heredity and race

The complicated pattern of descent from twin brothers in *A Tale of Two Cities* causes a curse to fall on the aristocratic descendants of the St Evrémondes. This begets a plot that confounds genealogy with class, and appears to justify Dickens in his persistent reference to the aristocracy as a race. (See especially Book 3, chapter 10.) Nevertheless, the classification is startling to twentieth-century eyes. We would designate the aristocracy as a class, and define both upper- and lower-class Frenchmen as members of the same race. The difference, to us, is crucial. Race is a hereditary classification, class is a social one.

But Dickens's use of the term "race" reverts to its older meaning of a limited group of people descended from a common ancestor (OED), thus a hereditary aristocracy may be a race.[26] And, in keeping with the generalizing tendency of the *Tale*, the curse of the St Evrémondes is the curse of an entire class as represented by one family. Nevertheless, the confusion of the terms in this novel suggests that for the Victorians the distinction between race and class was not cut and dried, and that the categories tended to spill over one another.[27] In a society where the class structure was rigid and movement up the ladder difficult, it is not surprising that class too might be deemed a hereditary category. Certainly Oliver Twist belongs to the middle class by virtue of his heredity rather than by virtue of his upbringing. At the same time, a fall below one's station was fraught with implications of deracination – witness the young Dickens's traumatized reaction to being sent to work in Warren's blacking factory among those whom he considered his social inferiors.

Dickens's early novels tend to assume a hereditary basis to social station, and this is reinforced by the fact that his characters usually marry within their own class. Sexual congress between different classes in the novels may result in illegitimate offspring, but not in matrimonial alliances. *Dombey and Son* presents the first exception to this rule, when the dimwitted upper-class Mr Toots marries Florence Dombey's sharp-tongued lady's maid, Susan Nipper. A still more striking example of social miscegenation occurs in *Our Mutual Friend*, when Eugene Wrayburn marries Lizzie Hexam.

Given this confusion between race and class, how does Dickens treat actual racial issues in his novels, and how is this expressed in hereditary terms? Here it is necessary to draw a distinction. Dickens's racial types fall into two categories. The first of these consists of the dark-skinned peoples of India and Africa, those who have been colonized and those who have been enslaved. The second category comprises the ethnic and national groups of Europe – the French, the gypsies, the Jews.

Indians and Africans tend to be linked in the novels as essentially representing the same kind of people and the same kind of problem. The extent of their interchangeability can be seen in *Our Mutual Friend* when Mr Venus, the taxidermist, while showing off his collection of specimens, points to "Preserved Indian baby. African ditto" (OMF, 126). Indians and Africans occupy a sphere of significance in the novels which lies outside the domain of heredity. They are ideological constructs designed to transmit Dickens's feelings about slavery or about the abuses of imperialism. Dickens does not define them in racial terms so much as he defines them in political terms – that is, the importance of dark-skinned people to his narratives lies in the extent to which they throw into relief the actions of whites. The best example of this is Major Bagstock's servant, known generically as the Native, who lives in a constant "rainy season" of blows and is the unceasing butt of the Major's abuse. Yet the miseries of the Native are presented comically. Dickens is more intent on eliciting our contempt for the major than he is in arousing our sympathy for his servant.[28]

Dickens's attitude towards issues of race is extremely complex. On the one hand, he consistently attacked slavery throughout his career and his portrait of the Native in *Dombey and Son* suggests that he had an imaginative grasp of the sufferings of subject people under colonialism. On the other hand, he was capable of the most extreme responses to oppressed peoples who did not know their place. His reaction to the Indian Mutiny of 1857 was to call for the extermination of the entire Indian race.[29] Angus Wilson suggests that this event marked the turning point in Dickens's thinking on the subject, and that he afterwards came to believe that the white race must dominate and order the world of the blacks and the browns.[30]

But four years before the Indian Mutiny, in 1853, Dickens had published an essay in *Household Words* called "The Noble Savage" in which he ridiculed black Africans: "I call him a savage, and a savage is something highly desirable to be civilised off the face of this earth ... He is a savage – cruel, false, thievish, murderous; addicted more or less to grease, entrails, and beastly customs ..."[31] This, taken in conjunction with Dickens's support of Governor Eyre's vicious suppression of a black riot in Jamaica in 1865 seems to justify Lillian Nayder's charge of racism.[32]

Dickens's most consistent ideological position on the subject of colonized races in the novels is his insistence that conditions among the poor and disenfranchised at home warrant more attention than romanticized do-gooding among the wretched abroad. He sounds this theme very early in his career, taking aim in *The Pickwick Papers* at the God-fearing citizens of the borough of Muggleton who present "no fewer than one thousand four hundred and twenty petitions against the continuance of negro slavery abroad, and an equal number against any interference with the factory system at home" (PP, 161).

The same point is made forcefully in *Bleak House*, where Mrs Jellyby, who can see "nothing nearer than Africa," neglects her own children while worrying about the blacks in Borrioboola-Gha. The equation of the two follies – that of protesting the conditions of subject races, and that of neglecting the conditions of subject classes, illustrates again the extent to which issues of class and race were linked in Dickens's mind.

The primary target of Dickens's satire in these instances is an attitude of woolly romanticism which attaches itself without much comprehension or genuine emotion to the exotic malaises of far-away peoples. In *Bleak House* Skimpole ruminates on the fate of the black slaves on American plantations: "I dare say theirs is an unpleasant experience on the whole; but, they people the land-scape for me, they give it a poetry for me, and perhaps that is one of the pleasanter objects of their existence" (BH, 307). Similarly, in *Martin Chuzzlewit*, Mrs Lupin sorrows over Mark Tapley's departure for America, where she is certain that he languishes in jail for having helped "some miserable black" to escape. Cries Mrs Lupin, "Why didn't he go to some of those countries where the savages eat each other fairly, and give an equal chance to every one?" (MC, 731). The sting of this particular barb is aimed as much at America and its democratic ideals as it is at the well-intentioned confusions of the speaker. At the same time it makes sport of one of Dickens's favourite fantasies of horror – the idea of cannibalism.[33] For the Victorians, a horrified fascination with cannibalism served as a trope for the dangers of imperialism, illustrating the dark fears of those who would subdue the Dark Continent.

In *David Copperfield*, Dickens presents the highly romantic Julia Mills, who at the advanced age of 20 compares her life to the Desert of Sahara, because she has suffered a disappointment in love. Julia goes off to India and when she returns it is as a married woman with a black man to carry cards and letters to her on a golden salver, and a copper-coloured woman to wait on her in her dressing-room. Julia, we are informed, has now become the Desert of Sahara (DC, 948), her earlier romanticism having given way to the worship of money. Money underscores the real value of exotic countries and their inhabitants – they exist to be exploited. Whether that exploitation takes the form of the romantic fantasies of young girls or the crass commercialism of imperial powers makes very little difference.

Julia's black man and copper-coloured woman represent the importation of colonial resources to England. In *David Copperfield* this importation is balanced by another scene which depicts the export of English emigrants to Australia. The emigrants are depicted as "bodily carrying out soil of England on their boots... taking away samples of its soot and smoke upon their skins" (DC, 882). In this way England becomes the center of the world, importing other races to work as its servants, exporting its underclass of plough-men, smiths, and prostitutes to people the colonies and continue the work of exploitation. It is another link between class and race.

With the exception of the Native in *Dombey and Son*, colonized peoples make only the briefest appearances in Dickens's fiction. His depiction of European ethnic minorities, on the other hand, is far more extensive, and far more liable to mix issues of race with those of heredity. The most prominent minority group in the novels are the Jews, and towards them Dickens's approach is frankly racial. He makes this explicit in his reply to Mrs Eliza Davis, a Jewish woman, who had written to complain that Dickens's portrayal of Fagin encouraged "a vile prejudice against the despised Hebrew":

> ... [Fagin] is called "The Jew," not because of his religion, but because of his race. If I were to write a story in which I pursued a Frenchman or a Spaniard as "the Roman Catholic," I should do a very indecent and unjustifiable thing; but I make mention of Fagin as the Jew because he is one of the Jewish people, and because it conveys that kind of idea of him, which I should give my readers of a Chinaman by calling him a Chinese.[34]

Dickens's response is interesting for its formulation of what was undoubtedly the correct liberal attitude of the time, namely that it is acceptable to caricature racial and national types, but not their religions. Dickens's attitude towards the Jews may be summed up by a quote from one of Flora Finching's many unpunctuated monologues in *Little Dorrit*.

> "... If you don't like either cold fowl or hot boiled ham which many people don't I dare say besides Jews and theirs are scruples of conscience which we must all respect though I must say I wish they had them equally strong when they sell us false articles for real that certainly ain't worth the money I shall be quite vexed ..." (LD, 328)

In other words, the religious habits of the Jews must be respected, but that does not mean that their racial shortcomings should be excused.

Since Dickens's method of characterization was always inclined towards typing, it is clear that he could not resist appropriating the qualities of the villainous stage Jew for his portrayal of Fagin.[35] His answer to Mrs Davis is, in effect, a justification of this practice, as well as a reminder that he has treated the Jewish religion with respect, and should therefore be absolved from blame.

It is possible to read into *Oliver Twist* the suggestion that Fagin's villainy is the result of his having fallen away from his faith. This would make him an example of a godless Jew unrestrained by religious scruples. Certainly Fagin is shown as being contemptuous of Jewish tradition: he pays no heed to the dietary laws and is first seen toasting sausages; he turns away with curses the "venerable men of his own persuasion" who come to pray with him on the night before his execution (OT, 469). However, the theme of the lapsed Jew is very faint in the novel, and does not quite detract from Dickens's poison-pen delight in Fagin's wickedness.

Throughout the novel Fagin is referred to as the Jew, which makes it difficult to avoid the conclusion that his villainy and his Jewishness go hand in hand. But while this designation is clearly racial – and, one might argue, racist – it is nowhere placed within a hereditary context. This may seem like a contradiction in terms, since what is racial is perforce hereditary. But in emphasizing Fagin's race, Dickens is primarily intent on exploiting the symbolic ramifications of his Jewishness, rather than his line of descent. In common with Dickens's other villains, Fagin is presented as *sui generis*.

Of Fagin's various symbolic functions within the novel, one of the most interesting lies in the fact that he holds up a kind of distorting mirror to some of the key events in the narrative. His membership in the underworld combined with his racial origin allows him to stand as a representative of an alternative society, a world turned inside-out, which reflects back ironically on the doings and undoings of the "normal" world. For instance, Fagin's school for thieves, with its roasting sausages, boys' games, camaraderie, and laughter suggests another – warmer – version of the cold-blooded orphanage where Oliver was beaten and starved. Fagin is determined that Oliver should earn his keep and so trains him to steal hand-kerchiefs, but this is no different from the workhouse system which saw the boy farmed out, first as a chimney-sweep, then as an under-taker's apprentice. The underworld and the "upright" world echo one another, and it is an open question as to which is worse.

Fagin himself calls everyone "my dear," a mock genteel form of address – and, one might add, a feminine form of endearment.[36] But while the "my dear" may be intended ironically, it is neverthe-less suggestive of affection; it is the sort of thing a parent might say to a child. Fagin, in fact, stands as the alternate version of two other father-figures in the novel, the bumptious and reprehensible Mr Bumble, and Oliver's genteel middle-class benefactor Mr Brownlow.

Terry Eagleton identifies Fagin as one of a long line of "false fathers" in Dickens's fiction, who are attractive in their roguish irresponsibility yet dangerous in their fickle desertion of true pater-nal duty. Eagleton writes that while Fagin is predatory, he is also "curiously warm, comic and paternal," and notes that when first seen by Oliver, Fagin is frying sausages, and food is always a sign of festive companionship in Dickens.[37] What is more, Fagin is often referred to as "the old gentleman," thus casting a jaundiced shadow over Oliver's own aspirations for middle-class status, and suggesting that Fagin is the good Mr Brownlow turned inside-out.

When Fagin walks past the fences' shops along the alley leading to Saffron Hill, we are treated to a description of the neighbourhood which reflects ironically on more ordinary venues of trade:

It is a commercial colony of itself: the emporium of petty lar-ceny: visited at early morning, and setting-in of dusk, by silent merchants, who traffic in dark back-parlours, and who go as strangely as they come. Here, the clothesman, the shoe-vamper, and the rag-merchant, display their goods, as sign-boards to the petty thief; here, stores of old iron and bones, and heaps of mildewy fragments of woollen-stuff and linen, rust and rot in the grimy cellars. (OT, 235)

Trade is here defined as merely another form of criminal activity. That most of the inhabitants of this upside-down world are Jews is made clear by the next sentence which informs us that Fagin "was well known to the sallow denizens of the lane." The complexion of Jews in Victorian fiction is always either "sallow" or "swarthy." In fact, a sallow complexion seems to stand as an indication of Jewishness even when other signs are lacking.[38]

In Saffron Hill, Fagin is conscious that "he was now in his proper element" (OT, 235). The association of Jews with underworld activity, especially with the fencing of stolen goods, had been cemented in the public mind by the trial of Ikey Solomon, on whom it has generally been assumed that Dickens modeled Fagin.[39] Thus, though Dickens attempted to suppress the designation of "The Jew" in later editions of *Oliver Twist* and completely eliminated it from his stage readings, the fact remains that in writing his novel Dickens exploited the popular association of Jewishness with criminal activity as a way of portraying a twice marginalized society in which villainy lurks behind the mask of normality.

More than either of the novel's two other villains – the brutish Sikes and the degenerate Monks – Fagin represents the force of evil as a metaphysical construct. In this novel, which features as its hero an orphaned, illegitimate boy who is the embodiment of grace, Fagin is equated with the devil, an equation in which his Jewish origin certainly plays a part: he is repulsively ugly, has the red hair of a Judas, as well as the requisite hooked nose. When Noah Claypole tries to imitate Fagin's habit of striking the side of his own nose, he cannot manage the feat, because Noah's gentile nose is not large enough (OT, 382).

Not content with letting Fagin's physiognomy bespeak his villainy, Dickens underlines Fagin's repulsiveness metaphorically. Fagin is compared to "some loathsome reptile, engendered in the slime and darkness through which he moved: crawling forth, by night, in search of some rich offal for a meal" (OT, 186). In this way, Fagin's very nature is associated with the forces of darkness; and the forces of darkness are associated with his Jewishness: "It seemed just the night when it befitted such a being as the Jew to be abroad" (OT, 186), is how the reptilian passage begins.

At several points in the narrative Fagin is directly identified with the devil. "Don't you know the devil when he's got a great-coat on?" Sikes rhetorically asks his dog (OT, 187). Fagin's being called "the old gentleman" may suggest Oliver's hidden middle-class inheritance on the one hand, but on the other, it euphemistically evokes Satan. So do Fagin's other attributes: he brandishes a toasting fork, steals innocent children, and leads them into corruption. Sikes even supplies Fagin with a devilish genealogy:

> "Reminds me of being nabbed by the devil," returned Sikes. "There never was another man with a face such as yours, unless it was your father, and I suppose *he* is singeing his grizzled red beard by this time, unless you came straight from the old 'un without any father at all betwixt you; which I shouldn't wonder at, a bit." (OT, 398)

This is the closest we get to Fagin's family tree, and it is a spurious tree at that, since it is the product of Bill Sikes's coarse mind. Nevertheless, the passage does reinforce the notion that Jew and devil are so similar that they may stand for one another – or be descended from one another. But while the portrait of Fagin in *Oliver Twist* is anti-Semitic in many of its details, there is a curious omission of genealogical context which would tie Fagin to his people in such a way as to tar all Jews with the same brush. The reason for this omission is that, as I suggested in my earlier chapters, Dickens tends to see heredity as a positive force. He does not place his villains within a hereditary framework unless he is trying to evoke sympathy for them.

By way of comparison, and as an example of just how closely Dickens associated goodness with heredity, I would like to turn to Dickens's other extended portrait of a Jew – that of Riah in *Our Mutual Friend*.

Riah is meant to right the wrong which Mrs Davis accused Dickens of committing when he created Fagin. Towards this end, Riah is established as a saintly Jew, the unwilling stooge of a Christian money-lender for whom he must work as a front. Riah is the only character in *Our Mutual Friend* whose manner and personality are dictated by his physical and racial inheritance, a fact which is all the more striking in that he inhabits a novel in which heredity has been largely discarded as a determining force in human conduct. Juliet McMaster has called *Our Mutual Friend* "a novel of and about fragments,"[40] and it is accordingly peopled by characters whose link to their genealogical past is fragmentary, or – more often – non-existent. Riah is unique in being the only one of the novel's dramatis personae who is consistently tied to a pedigree, so that unlike Fagin, Riah's racial characteristics are set within a hereditary framework.[41]

For example, when Lizzie Hexam and Jenny Wren come to visit Riah, the narrator informs us that, for them, "perhaps with some old instinct of his race, the gentle Jew had spread a carpet" (OMF, 332). The urge to spread a carpet can hardly be described as a racial instinct. It is in Dickens's use of such terms as "race" and "instinct" that we sense the desire to place Riah within a context where his Jewishness may be given a positive spin. In this case, Riah's gesture betokens a form of oriental generosity which we are to understand as so endemic to his race that it has become second nature, or instinctive. Dickens determinedly emphasizes the "eastern" quality of Riah's actions, even though there is no hint anywhere in the text that Riah is anything other than an English Jew. It must therefore be understood that Riah's oriental traits are part of his racial inheritance, passed down to him in an unbroken line from the ancient Hebrews.

In fact, when Riah is first introduced he is described as "a man who with a graceful Eastern action of homage bent his head, and stretched out his hands with the palms downward, as if to deprecate the wrath of a superior" (OMF, 328). Riah then proceeds to address his boss, Fascination Fledgeby, as "generous Christian master."[42] In fact, Riah addresses all non-Jews as "Christian gentleman," as if Dickens were anxious to establish religion as constituting the chief difference between Jew and non-Jew in this novel. A late scene depicts a Protestant reverend and his wife being reassured that not only are Jews kind people, but they do not, as a rule, try to convert unsuspecting Christians to their religion (OMF, 579, 585). And despite the fact that Riah seems to be intended as a pious individual, he is never depicted as practicing his religion, and Dickens seems not to know that an observant Jew would never appear in public bare-headed, as he has Riah do in the chapter called "Mercury Prompting."

Dickens's insistence on the exoticism of Riah and on his orientalism are aspects of the Jewish personality that were totally absent from his portrait of Fagin. Here, too, however, Dickens is drawing on the conventions of Victorian melodrama. In those nineteenth-century plays where Jews were shown in a positive light and depicted as adopting positions of moral rectitude, the Jewish type tended to be construed as picturesque rather than repellent.[43] The same goes for the following passage, which betrays its theatrical roots in the stylized description of a gesture: "[Mr Riah] made a gesture as though he kissed the hem of an imaginary garment worn by the noble youth before him. It was humbly done but picturesquely, and was not abasing to the doer" (OMF, 329). The "excitable" Jew supplicating Mr Jaggers in *Great Expectations* similarly raises Jaggers' coat to his lips several times (GE, 192).[44]

This form of submissiveness, which is "not abasing to the doer," belies another Victorian assumption concerning conquering and conquered peoples: Riah is described as habitually submissive, a trait encoded in his blood, and passed down through the generations as a badge of suffering: "It was characteristic of [Riah's] habitual submission, that he sat down on the raw dark staircase, as many of his ancestors had probably sat down in dungeons, taking what befell him as it might befall" (OMF, 480).

Riah's submissiveness fits in with the broader racial ideology of the nineteenth century, which characterized "conquering and ruling races" as fair-skinned, while "vanquished and submissive races have been dark." The phrases are from John Beddoe's *Races of Britain*. Beddoe goes on to write:

> If anything can be confidently predicated as to the two principle complexions, it is that the fair goes more usually with active courage and a roving adventurous disposition, the dark with patient industry and attachment to local and family ties – the one with the sanguine, the other with the melancholic temperament.[45]

In accordance with this theory, it was claimed by race theorists that the swarthy Jewish complexion could be construed as African. The criminologist Cesare Lombroso suggested that climatic changes might alter racial characteristics with the result that Caucasian Jews would possess Negroid features in hot climates.[46]

Riah's submission is linked as well to the history of his people as a vanquished race – vanquished politically and vanquished religiously – and this sense of inferiority is further underlined by his feminization. Although he plays the part of protector to two of the novel's heroines, Riah's role is nevertheless defined as feminine.

Jenny Wren repeatedly refers to him as "godmother." When searching for comfort after her father's death, she hides her face in the "Jewish skirts." Riah's habit of submissiveness adds to the effect of his feminization, which coupled with his advanced age, is intended to defang the monster, conjuring up associations of nurture at the same time as it reinforces the impression of Riah's beneficence. Since, throughout his fiction, Dickens persistently allocates the qualities of loyalty, kindness, gentleness, goodness, and modesty to his heroines, often defining these as hereditable characteristics passed down from mother to daughter, it is no surprise that he seeks to locate Riah symbolically within just such a sphere of feminine virtue. At the same time, the feminine aspect of his personality reinforces Riah's "otherness," just as his "otherness" allows Dickens to ascribe feminine qualities to Riah without appearing to emasculate him. (In this respect, it is interesting that Daniel Deronda, the eponymous Jewish protagonist of George Eliot's novel, is similarly portrayed as harboring certain feminine qualities which, nevertheless, do not detract from his masculinity.)

Racial stereotypes, construed now as positives and attributed to heredity, are everywhere apparent in Dickens's portrayal of Riah. For instance in the following: "[Fledgeby's] grateful servant [Riah] – in whose race gratitude is deep, strong, and enduring – bowed his head . . ." (OMF, 335). Dickens is here designating gratitude as a racial characteristic in much the same way as earlier in his career he had characterized goodness as hereditary.

The qualities which describe Riah's essence – gratitude, goodness, kindness, gentleness – not only locate him within a feminine sphere, but are made synonymous with his foreignness. Riah's inherent and inherited orientalism serves the purpose of establishing him as a descendent of the patriarchs in the Hebrew Bible, thus tapping into the Christian tradition of typology which exalted the Old Testament as a preparation for the New. The association is consciously made several times throughout the course of *Our Mutual Friend*. Riah carries himself with the air of a biblical patriarch; he carries no walking-stick, but "a veritable staff." He steals through the streets "in his ancient dress, like the ghost of a departed Time" (OMF, 465). In fact, he is the embodiment of this departed Time. Even the cynical Eugene Wrayburn cannot resist the biblical parallel, calling Riah – whom he dubs with the biblical name Aaron – "quite a Shylock, and quite a Patriarch" (OMF, 598). The double sense here evokes nicely the polarized stereotypes of the Jew which Dickens himself perpetuated in his creation of the bad Jew Fagin and the good Jew Riah.

Gillian Beer notes that in the nineteenth-century debate about races the Jews posed a particular difficulty, because they did not comply with all the characteristics which were ascribed to "Homo asiaticus." Most anomalous of all was the fact that, despite being a wandering people, the Jews represented a stable racial group.[47] Paul Broca, writing in 1864 – five years after the publication of *The Origin of Species* – claimed that the Jewish race "scattered for more than eighteen centuries in the most difficult climates, is everywhere the same now as it was in Egypt at the time of the Pharaohs."[48] This sweeping statement attributes to the Jews a position outside history, ascribing to them the magical property of being immune to change. In this formulation nineteenth-century Jews are essentially the same as their biblical forebears, and so carry the dust of the desert with them wherever they go, even if they happen to be raised in England.

This attempt to suggest the immutable racial characteristics of the Jew was made possible through an equation of religion, culture, and race. The Hebrew Bible provided a portrait of a people at a particular point in its history. To the extent that the Jews remained loyal to the observances outlined in that book, they might be said not to have changed. In this way, religious beliefs were equated with culture, which in turn was equated with race. The popular imagination then blended all three categories together into an undifferentiated knot to form the basis of both the negative and the positive Jewish stereotypes current in nineteenth-century England. Since the patriarchs and prophets of the Hebrew Bible tended to be regarded positively by Protestant tradition, it was possible to shine some of that reflected light on a character like Riah by associating him with the traditions of the patriarchs. And this in turn made acceptable the anomaly of an English Jew behaving in so determinedly foreign and archaic a manner.

Dickens significantly locates the negative attitudes towards Jews in the persons of his villain Fledgeby and of his anti-hero, Eugene Wrayburn. The latter's habit of genteel contempt betrays the ingrained prejudice of the English upper classes. When he speaks to Riah, Eugene is insulting and dismissive: "If Mr Aaron . . . will be good enough to relinquish his charge to me, he will be quite free for any engagement he may have at the Synagogue" (OMF, 464). He insists on calling Riah by the wrong name " . . . because it appears to me Hebraic, expressive, appropriate, and complimentary. Notwithstanding which strong reasons for its being his name, it may not be his name" (OMF, 598). But Eugene is sarcastic and dismissive towards everyone – this is, in fact, his character flaw, and he is at his most obnoxious in the interview with the unstable Bradley Headstone, whom he goads about his class origins. Thus Eugene's prejudiced contempt is in keeping with his personality and reflects not so much on Riah as it does on himself. The same holds true for the despicable Fledgeby whose inherent nastiness is reason enough to discount his opinions.

Nevertheless, despite such obvious attempts to educate his readers away from their anti-Jewish biases, Dickens's narrative method with regard to Riah plays on both sides of the street at once. Riah embodies his creator's fascination with doubles. He appears to play the part of ruthless money-lender and hard-hearted exploiter of those who default on their debts. He is, in fact, only acting on behalf of his employer, Fascination Fledgeby, into whose debt he has himself fallen. Thus Riah is outwardly a Shylock, inwardly a saint, the reverse of the treacherous Victorian stage Jew whose outward pretense of poverty concealed vast wealth. Riah's actions have a double meaning, and he plays a double role.

In this he resembles his non-Jewish counterpart, Mr Boffin, who simultaneously plays the part of hard-hearted miser and kindly benefactor. Yet because he is Jewish, Riah's doubleness verges on duplicity, suggesting an ambivalence in Dickens's presentation. Although the conscious intention is to absolve the Jewish money-lender by making him the stooge for the Christian, the fact remains that Riah's two parts undermine one another, with the result that Dickens reinforces the stereotype at the same time as he appears to contradict it.

The anomalous position of the Jew, whether his actions are intended for good or ill, is in fact expressed by Riah himself:

> I reflected that evening ... that I was doing dishonour to my ancient faith and race ... In bending my neck to the yoke I was willing to wear, I bent the unwilling necks of the whole Jewish people. For it is not, in Christian countries, with the Jews as with other peoples ... They take the worst of us as samples of the best; they take the lowest of us as presentations of the highest; and they say "All Jews are alike." If, doing what I was content to do here ... I had been a Christian, I could have done it

compromising no one but my individual self. But doing it as a Jew, I could not choose but compromise the Jews of all conditions and all countries. It is a little hard upon us, but it is the truth. I would that all our people remember it!   (OMF, 795)

This is a statement of collective responsibility, and it contains unpleasant echoes of the collective guilt traditionally ascribed to the Jews as the killers of Christ. While Dickens's overt intention here is to present the difficulties of being Jewish in a Christian world, Riah's words imply that the actions of each individual Jew taint the Jews as a whole. This defines the individual as being secondary to the group, and the group itself as being subject to the prejudicial whims of others for its sense of identity. Riah's speech here establishes the Jews as tribally and racially all of a piece, the ill-repute of one Jew affecting the fate of the others.

This declaration by Riah is a good example of how difficult it was for even well-meaning nineteenth-century thinkers to conceive of race as anything but a monolithic category which erased individuality. The designation of the Jews as "tribal" was a nineteenth-century commonplace, suggesting as it did the primitive quality of the Jewish religion and furthering the association of Jews with the dark-skinned tribes of Africa.[49] Dickens refers to gypsies too as tribal. In *Barnaby Rudge*, he even speaks of the gypsies as trusting to "the God of their tribe" (BR, 678), which underlines how closely allied to the Jews they were in his mind.

Such collective designations suggest that heredity, when applied to race in the nineteenth century, had a homogenizing effect, highlighting the qualities of permanence and uniformity while scanting those of change and diversity. As Dickens presents them in both their negative and positive incarnations, the Jews are not only unchanging, they are also interchangeable, so that the qualities of one may be generalized to all. Dickens cannot conceive of Jews as individuals. They exist in his mind merely as particles of one collective stereotyped whole.

6
After *The Origin*: the Last Three Novels

It has been my contention that Dickens's conception of how personality is formed changed throughout his career, evolving from the strict determinism of the early novels to a looser model of development in his middle period, until finally in the last three novels he discards heredity entirely as a factor in the formation of the self. In this chapter, I would like to examine the three novels which Dickens wrote after 1859 – the year in which Darwin's *The Origin of Species* appeared – to see what effect Darwin's book had on Dickens's understanding of heredity.

Dickens's declining interest in heredity as a way of explaining personality is an anomaly. In general, the effect of Darwin's theory on European and American fiction of the late nineteenth century was to intensify interest in heredity as a literary theme. In fact, one might easily argue that hereditary determinism becomes the major philosophical motif of the latter part of the century. For writers of the Naturalist School, for Hardy, Wilde, Zola, Ibsen, Strindberg, Dreiser, and others, hereditary issues become a central and nearly obsessive concern. It is clear that this new emphasis was in large part a response to Darwin's theory of evolution. It is therefore ironic that Dickens's initial reaction to Darwin is to blot out heredity altogether from his conception of human development and to replace it with the formative effects of environment. Those aspects of evolutionary theory which Dickens does extract from the *Origin* reflect a new concern on his part to accommodate external factors within the developmental pattern of the individual. It is as if Darwin's theory allowed Dickens to shake off his earlier adherence to heredity as a way of explaining personality, and in this way to escape the determinism of his own earlier portrayals.

One reason for Dickens's slighting of the hereditary aspects of Darwin's theory may well be that Darwin himself was so vague about how heredity worked. In the *Origin*, Darwin admitted that "the laws governing heredity are for the most part unknown."[1] Despite this, hereditary transmission is the sine qua non of evolutionary theory, representing the mechanism by which successful variations are integrated into the developmental pattern of a species over time. Yet neither Darwin nor his contemporaries had any clear idea of how hereditary transmission worked. At first, Darwin was content to account for the causes of variation by ascribing them to chance, or to unknown factors. Then in 1868 he published *The Variation of Animals and Plants under Domestication* in which he tried to fill the gap by reviving the ancient Greek idea of pangenesis.

Hippocrates had been the primary exponent of this theory in classical times, arguing that each part of the body of each parent sheds some aspect of itself into the blood. When these "pangenes" are collected together, they form a kind of reproductive fluid or seed, blending the characteristics of the parents to construct the child.[2] (This is the theory which Aristotle rejected, when he argued instead for a "single seed" model, in which the male provided the blueprint for the embryo, while the female provided the raw matter.)

Darwin's early writing had betrayed a willingness to accept "soft" heredity. Soft heredity is the belief that what a parent transmits to his or her offspring is subject to modification by external causes. But soft heredity posed certain problems for Darwin's evolutionary theory, since if environment can affect heredity, there would be little variation, all individuals in a given population having absorbed and reacted to similar influences. To make selection a viable theory, Darwin had to abandon soft heredity in favour of hard heredity – the belief that what each individual inherits from his or her parents is inviolable, and not subject to modification by external factors.[3]

Pangenesis, Darwin's version of hard heredity, is essentially another form of blending, where the offspring represent a fusion or average of the parents' characteristics. Blending was the most commonly accepted explanation for hereditary transmission among Darwin's contemporaries. Darwin's version of this theory was to posit that physical traits were carried by "gemmules," defined as granules or atoms, which issued from the cells of the body and mingled during sexual union. According to this theory all parts of the body manufacture and throw off particles, which then move through the bloodstream and conglomerate in the reproductive organs where they become the components of heredity in egg or sperm. Fertilization occurs when the gemmules of both sexes mix. Because each parent contributes gemmules for every physical characteristic, the result of their coming together is a blend of the characteristics of both parents, although there may be exceptions where the traits of one parent will predominate.

Darwin did not believe that the gemmules themselves were cells, but merely capable of turning into cells. He also imagined that the actual quantity of gemmules produced by each organ of the body was controlled by the activity of that organ or by the intensity of environmental pressures upon it. And he accepted another common misconception of his time, namely that the entire mass of sperm constituted the fertilizing agent and that the sex of the embryo and its resemblance to its father depended on the amount of sperm released.[4]

To substantiate this theory, Darwin pointed to telegony – the belief that the hereditary characteristics of a woman's first sexual partner are transmitted to the offspring of all her subsequent partners – citing the case of Lord Morton's mare to support his claim. Telegony is an ancient concept, going back to biblical times. The levirate marriages described in Deuteronomy 25: 5–6, in which a man's brother or father is required to marry his widow if the man dies without issue, is an example of this belief. The first-born of such a marriage is considered to be the child of the deceased husband.

Lord Morton's mare represented the most credible – and the most cited – evidence for the existence of telegony in the nineteenth century, the more so since it had been accepted as a verified instance of the phenomenon by the Royal College of Surgeons. In 1815, the mare had been bred with a quagga – a zebra-like African animal, now extinct – and had given birth to a hybrid. The mare was then sold and mated by her new owner to an Arabian stallion. The offspring that she bore in 1817, 1818, and 1823 all resembled the quagga rather than the mare, thereby seeming to substantiate the belief that her first partner, the quagga, had played a decisive role in the physical inheritance of all the mare's subsequent offspring.[5] Basing himself on this example, Darwin theorized that some of the gemmules from the original partner remained dormant within the mother, thus affecting the hereditary make-up of all her future children, regardless of their subsequent paternity.

Darwin's theory of pangenesis was similar not only to Greek theories of the classical age but also to theories of generation which had circulated in the eighteenth century. Pangenesis allows for a form of Lamarckism – especially Lamarck's assumption of the inheritance of acquired characteristics – because when the parts of the body manufacture their own hereditary material, they become subject to changes in the structure of the organs from which they derive. These changes would be reflected in the gemmules budding off the individual body parts and would therefore become the stuff of heredity.[6]

The difference between Darwin's theory and those of such earlier theorists as Lamarck lay in the fact that Darwin's espousal of pangenesis was an attempt to account for evolution, so that the emphasis was on the transmission of variation and not on the preservation of type. The emphasis on variation in Darwin's theory and the attempts to account for its existence suggest why most nineteenth-century inquiries into the nature of heredity fell so wide of the mark – they were an attempt to explain the exception without having determined the rule. This was also the reason that Mendel's discovery of the mathematical laws for hereditary transmission – published in 1866 – was so completely ignored. Unlike Darwin, Mendel had set out to determine not the laws of variation but the laws of resemblance. In other words, Mendel was looking for something which no one else at the time was interested in finding.

This, then, gives some idea of the confused state of knowledge about heredity during Dickens's last decade. Darwin's imperfect grasp of the mechanics of descent made it difficult for him to defend certain aspects of his theory. Peter Morton suggests that in the years following the publication of *The Origin of Species* no other biological issue – with the exception of evolution itself – was more fiercely debated, or caused the scales of informed opinion to swing more drastically, or took longer to reach equilibrium than the one concerning the mechanics of heredity.[7] It is little wonder, then, that Dickens absented himself from the fray, and looked to *The Origin of Species* for other sorts of inspirational ideas.

There seems little doubt that Dickens was well acquainted with Darwin's book, which was favourably reviewed in Dickens's journal

All the Year Round only a few months after it appeared. Not only was *The Origin of Species* the subject of intense discussion and debate in the year following its publication in November 1859, but Dickens, who had many friends in scientific circles, was especially close to Richard Owen, an anti-Darwinist and key figure in the controversy which followed on *The Origin*'s publication.[8] A copy of Darwin's book was found in Dickens's library after his death.

Dickens tended to assimilate scientific discoveries into his fiction as a matter of course, and references to the latest findings and theories may be found in all the novels.[9] Darwin's evolutionary theory intersects with Dickensian concerns and themes at several points. And this influence worked both ways. Dickens was one of Darwin's favourite authors. In fact, Gillian Beer has argued that the organization of Darwin's *Origin* owed much to his reading of Dickens, especially the notion of an apparent overabundance and disorder of material which gradually and retrospectively reveals its design.

Superabundance represents for both Darwin and Dickens a metaphor for fecundity. Darwin saw fecundity as a liberating and creative force which led to increased variability. It was closely allied in his thinking to what he called the "appetite for joy" in living things.[10] Darwin believed that happiness had a survival value and joked in his autobiography that novels should be legislated to end happily, because then statute law would reflect natural law and the problem of literary realism would be solved.[11] Dickens's insistence on the pleasures and benefits of fecundity – an insistence which won him the reputation as a champion of domestic life – is certainly a manifestation of "this appetite for joy." The early novels, which end so blissfully with happy adults surrounded by happy children equate human pleasure and human duty with reproduction. But the pleasures of the hearth weaken in Dickens's fiction as he grows older. The later novels end with fewer children and betray a much darker vision.

Nevertheless, it is the idea of family as a hereditary web encompassing all living things which most ties Dickens to Darwin. In *The Origin*, Darwin had written that all true classification was genealogical, that the community of descent was the hidden bond. Dickens's fiction may be read as a literal demonstration of this proposition. George Levine has noted that Darwinism took one of the great metaphors of Christian belief – the family of Man – and turned it into a literal and biological fact. Evolution turns all living things into kin.[12] Dickens's translation of this same idea is to turn all human beings into family through the various complications and revelations of his plots. What is more, he is just as concerned as Darwin with descent and therefore with issues of time. The repetitive naming of children with which so many of the novels end is clearly an attempt to extend the past into the future. But it also indicates that in his conception of time, Dickens differs from Darwin. For Darwin time projects into the future without alluding to the past. It is analogous to biblical time – it moves forward but never back. Dickens's conception of time is cyclical. The repetitive naming of children alludes to the reanimation of personality from one generation to the next.

And this in turn suggests another difference between Darwin's theory and Dickens's philosophy. Darwin insisted on the finality of death – that is, he accepted that extinction exists, that both individuals and species die and are not revived. Thus, while there is no closure to the system of nature, evolutionary theory emphasizes extinction and annihilation equally with variation. Darwin admitted the idea of paedomorphosis – that is, attributes which die out before adulthood but recur in future generations, and he admitted the reappearance of long-dormant characteristics, but the idea of return, "of supping at a feast forever fresh" – to use Gillian Beer's formulation – was a mythological construct alien to evolution.[13] Darwin wrote that natural selection entailed extinction. Death is therefore part and parcel of evolutionary theory; it is inherent in nature, and it is final. The individual is both vehicle and dead end.[14] This is in keeping with a conception of time as moving in one direction only, and it is a thoroughly secular idea. The comfort of most religions lies in their insistence that death is merely a step into an alternate reality, that there is an afterlife, or that the soul lives on in another state of being.

For Dickens, the notion of the finality of death is anathema. It is significant that those few occasions when he straightforwardly – and, one might argue, sentimentally – evokes Christianity as a positive in the novels occur at a death. Christian notions of an afterlife accord well with the theme of resurrection, a favourite Dickensian motif, often depicted literally, as when a character who has been presumed dead turns out to be alive. In fact, Dickens's propensity for this motif is what makes his intentions in *The Mystery of Edwin Drood* such a mystery. Did he intend that the vanished Edwin be murdered, or was he planning to have him return? Dickens's own death has assured that we will never know the answer.

Closely allied to the theme of resurrection is Dickens's fascination with hereditary resemblance, with doubling, and with the recycling of names from one generation to the next. All of these suggest an apprehension of time as repetitive and essentially unchanging. As I argued in my discussion of *A Tale of Two Cities*, this understanding of the nature of time encompasses a view of history as constant and immutable in its essence, no matter what the superficial variations.

Even the form by which Dickens first introduced his novels to the public – serialization – may be seen as an attempt to deny the finality of an ending by spinning out a plot from one installment to the next. The reader of a serial will never have the entire novel in hand at any one time, will never be able to consult the beginning and end simultaneously, and so is not confronted with a finite entity in the form of a book, but rather with an ongoing narrative and the illusion of an ending constantly postponed.

Great Expectations (1860–1): a meditation on the low

Great Expectations lends itself easily to a Darwinian reading. This is not surprising, since it is the novel closest in time to the *Origin*, hence the novel most likely to have been affected by Darwin's book and by the remarkable public reaction to the theory of evolution, which was at its most intense in the year after the *Origin*'s publication. Dickens began *Great Expectations* in October 1860, 11 months after the publication of *The Origin of Species*.

In Chapter 3, I argued that *Great Expectations* represents the first time that Dickens jettisons heredity entirely as a factor in the formation of the self, and replaces it with the influence of environment. I further suggested that this denial of hereditary impact on the make-up of the individual was a result of Dickens's reading of Darwin. In this chapter I would like to return to a discussion of *Great Expectations*, but this time focusing on ancillary issues which connect the novel both to Darwinism and to some of the broader motifs raised by heredity, such as the nature of descent, and the problematics of time.

Great Expectations is, among other things, a meditation on the low, basing its demonstration of the inherent connection between human beings on the interrelationship between the criminal world and its more genteel counterparts. The attitude of those above to those below becomes the defining criterion of a novel in which the criminal class is more important for the base position it occupies in society than for its antisocial behaviour. In a sense, *Great Expectations* neutralizes the moral dimension of crime. To be a convict in this novel is to occupy a position of shame, a shame which is primarily associated with being outcast and reviled rather than with being a villain. Evil, which has been a major preoccupation in all of Dickens's fiction, is no longer simply black in this novel, nor is it exclusively associated with crime. In fact, the concept of criminality has here been generalized to a very broad category, which includes such flawed beings as Pip himself, who sin in their hearts rather than in their deeds. The world of *Great Expectations* is not totally amoral, as is the natural world in *The Origin of Species*, but neither is it manichaean to quite the same extent as in the earlier novels. Instead, the moral distinctions between categories of behaviour have become blurred and overlapping.

One effect of the novel's attitude towards criminality is to overturn the plot of hidden identity. Traditionally, this plot depicts the lower-class hero as belonging biologically to a higher station than the one to which circumstances have assigned him. In this sense, as Gillian Beer points out, secret identity is opposed to Darwinism, which insists on the opposite – that all human beings, no matter how advanced they may take themselves to be, share the same lowly animal origins.[15]

As I noted in Chapter 2, by overturning the plot of hidden identity, *Great Expectations* constitutes a reassessment of *Oliver Twist*. But this reassessment goes beyond Pip's discovery that his sudden wealth allies him to the underworld rather than to the aristocracy. There is a concomitant reassessment of the very nature of that underworld and its relation to the rest of society. Where the early novel defines the genteel and criminal spheres as contrary and antithetical, *Great Expectations* maintains that the upper-class world of the gentleman is implicated in the criminal domain of the underclass, and that the relationship between the two, far from being mutually exclusive, is redolent of complicity and inter-dependence.

Because it generalizes criminality by universalizing the concept of guilt, the stress in *Great Expectations* is on punishment rather than on crime. For this reason, the novel is replete with the symbols of chastisement. These run the gamut from Tickler, which represents the corporal punishment meted out to children, to instruments of physical restraint and confinement: the gibbet, the Hulks, leg irons, Newgate Prison, Molly's incarceration in Jaggers's house, Miss Havisham's self-immurement in her own house. Other methods of exacting retribution are also amply presented, from expulsion (Magwitch's transportation to the "underworld" of Australia) to execution (the death masks in Jaggers's office, Magwitch's death sentence). Thus the inner landscape of Pip's mind with its constant load of guilt is reflected in the larger landscape through which he moves.

So completely woven into the fabric of the novel is the underworld motif that the two poles of society – the gentleman and the convict – are consistently presented as linked. Compeyson and Magwitch – the first being the gentleman, the second the convict – are always portrayed together. On the marshes, Pip first runs into Magwitch and then into Compeyson. Similarly, on the night of Magwitch's return from Australia, he is shadowed by his aristocratic double. Dickens broadens the doppelganger effect by giving Magwitch the first name of Abel. An Abel requires a Cain and Dickens takes care that these two – the dirt-poor, orphaned Magwitch and the well-educated, privileged Compeyson – are always juxtaposed. Magwitch's first name hints at his fraternal relation to those above him, at the same time as it evokes the human species' ceaseless depredations against its own kind.

The twinning of Magwitch and Compeyson is the most obvious example of the ways in which the novel blurs the distinctions between the criminal underclass and the genteel upper crust, implicating each in the life of the other. Other examples abound: the wealthy and genteel Miss Havisham was once engaged to the criminal Compeyson, who jilted her, and so sowed the seeds of her obsessive hatred of men. Estella – cold, arrogant, and disdainful though she may be – is in fact the daughter of the convict Magwitch and the murderess Molly. The lawyer Jaggers – who makes his living off the criminal class – serves as a link between these two poles of society, acting simultaneously on behalf of Miss Havisham and on behalf of Magwitch, providing the proud chatelaine of Satis House with the offspring of a convicted felon to raise as a grand lady. In this way the threads of two apparently irreconcilable worlds are systematically woven together.

Dickens suggests that what is true of the connection between Miss Havisham and the criminal class, and between Compeyson and Magwitch, is true as well for society as a whole. He does this symbolically in the court scene when he describes a shaft of sunlight falling with "absolute equality" on those who have just been condemned to death and on the judge who condemned them (GE, 467). The shaft of light wipes out distinctions between judge and judged, between the criminal and the righteous, the guilty and the innocent. It is a reminder that Nature is indifferent to moral categories, and functions instead according to its own imperatives. The shaft of light constitutes a reassertion of the Darwinian belief in the interdependence of all living things occurring in the midst of the apparent triumph of man-made restrictions and legalities. The courtroom is, after all, the perfect venue for demonstrating the superiority of Man over Nature, because it defines human beings as seekers of justice, adjudicators of law, dispensers of retribution – moral concepts alien to the natural world. Dickens's equalizing shaft of light calls into question that smug distinction.

The connection between the underclass and the upper world is further reinforced by the use of coincidence to constrict the parameters of the novel. In *Great Expectations*, coincidence functions like synecdoche, suggesting that the small part of society presented by the narrative stands for the whole. Dickens has often been accused of overusing coincidence in his novels. Sylvère Monod complained of *Great Expectations*: "The use of coincidence in the novel is . . . excessive. It would seem, for instance, that there can be in the whole of England only three convicts: Magwitch, Compeyson, and Magwitch's mysterious messenger."[16]

There are even more glaring coincidences than this – that the convict who terrifies Pip as a boy and later becomes his benefactor should turn out to be Estella's father; that Magwitch's nemesis Compeyson should be the same man who jilted Miss Havisham. It is true that such unlikely congruences strain credibility, but they also give the impression of a society that is integrated and comprehensive, where the upper and lower classes exist in unacknowledged symbiosis, and where corruption of one sort or another lies at the root of all wealth, like a worm in a bud.

In *Great Expectations* the criminal element is eventually discovered to stand in some form of relation to every character, a discovery which implies that criminality stands for whatever is universal in the elemental nature of Man. The criminal represents the primitive in human nature, the base, the fundamental material out of which – and away from which – all civilized behaviour must evolve. Once the novel's design is revealed, it becomes clear that the only common denominator is the lowest.

In fact, the convicts in *Great Expectations* are literally compared to "lower animals" (GE, 249). Magwitch is described as eating his food like a hungry old dog with fangs (GE, 346). Pip himself, before he comes into his expectations, feels that Estella feeds him as insolently as if he were a dog. To further underline the degeneracy of the criminal class, we have the description of Jaggers who feels compelled to wash his clients off, "as if he were a surgeon or a dentist" and uses for this purpose a scented soap (GE, 233). The image is wonderful in its doubleness: on the literal level, it reinforces the view of the criminal world as scummy, pestilent, and infectious, so filthy that it requires constant cleansing. But there is also a covert allusion to Pontius Pilate who washed his hands of the fate of Jesus. Jesus himself, after all, had suffered the fate of a criminal – execution at the hands of the authorities. While the image of the criminal as Christ figure is not stressed in *Great Expectations*, it nonetheless hovers in the background, serving Dickens well as a symbolic backdrop against which to locate Magwitch. (In Christian typology, Abel was one of the several Old Testament figures who were thought to represent the type of Christ, and to predict his advent.)

Despite such biblical allusions, however, the stress in *Great Expectations* is not on the exalted and spiritual but on the primitive and material. This highlighting of the elemental qualities in human nature constitutes a new departure for Dickens, who had previously insisted on the essential godliness of the good-hearted. What is more, he had defined their transcendence as amenable to hereditary transmission from one generation to the next. In *Great Expectations*, the emphasis on the ideal has given way to a demonstration of the omnipresence of the base. When Pip says of Magwitch, "convict was in the very grain of the man" (GE, 352), the remark resonates beyond the individual to whom it is applied. The equation of essential nature with criminality applies to Pip himself:

> I consumed the whole time in thinking how strange it was that I should be encompassed by all this taint of prison and crime; that, in my childhood out on our lonely marshes on a winter evening I should have first encountered it; that, it should have appeared on two occasions, starting out like a stain that was faded but not gone; that it should . . . pervade my fortune and

advancement ... I beat the prison dust off my feet as I saun-
tered to and fro, and I shook it out of my dress, and I exhaled
it from my lungs. So contaminated did I feel...   (GE, 284)

Pip's feeling of self-hatred is built on the assumption that "convict" is as much a part of his grain as it is of Magwitch's, that it is
born into him, arising out of the marshes of his childhood – the
primordial slime – and pervading every aspect of his life, so that
no amount of shaking and exhaling and beating will ever cleanse
him of the despised, primitive, degenerate part of himself.

In *The Origin of Species*, Darwin had deliberately eliminated Man
from the argument, thereby implying the subservient stature of the
human species when placed against the vast forces of nature. It is
possible to argue, however, as Harriet Ritvo does in *The Animal
Estate*, that what is really displaced in Darwin's book is God, not
Man. Divine sanction for human superiority has been eliminated,
but now the source of Man's pre-eminence is located within human nature itself. The result of dethroning God has been to put
Man in His place.[17]

Dickens the novelist cannot relegate Man to second place, any
more than any novelist could. Human beings are at the center of
creation in *Great Expectations*, they dominate the landscape, but
they do so by imposing a retributive dimension on nature's non-
judgemental way. The environment of Pip's boyhood contains the
primordial marshes, on which the only things that stand upright
are a beacon and a gibbet, symbolic of human attainment at both
its highest and its lowest.

Nature in *Great Expectations* has had the Romantic light bleached
out of it. For instance, while Pip defines himself as the victim of
his surroundings, the opposite is also true – that he imposes his
own interpretation on what he sees around him. So much so that
he even extends his own feelings of class consciousness to such
natural phenomena as the stars: "The very stars to which I then
raised my eyes, I am afraid I took to be but poor and humble stars
for glittering on the rustic objects among which I had passed my
life" (GE, 171). When he comes into his expectations, the young
Pip thinks that even the grazing cows have a more respectful air
when they look at him, that they "face round, in order that they
might stare as long as possible at the possessor of such great expectations" (GE, 174).

These, of course, are instances of pathetic fallacy, but they are presented as instances to be mocked; they are located firmly within the deluded mind of Pip, and are not offered up uncritically by an omniscient narrator. There is, in such passages, a determined intention of diminishing Nature to a figment of the mind of man, who is himself no more than another manifestation of Nature's amoral neutrality. By way of contrast with Dickens's earlier treatments of Nature, see the description of the tempest in *David Copperfield*, where the storm outside is made directly analogous to the turmoil in David's mind, in addition to functioning within the narrative as a natural instrument of divine retribution directed against the sinning Steerforth.

Dickens's new-found distrust of the Romantic approach to nature echoes the intellectual development of Darwin himself. As a young man, Darwin had been much influenced by his reading of the Romantic poets, and consequently had perceived nature through their eyes, but after viewing the wilderness of South America, he had come to accept that disharmony and disequilibrium rather than their opposites were the rule, that there was no supernatural design to the natural world, that no pantheistic spiritualizing impulse animated the processes of nature. Darwin's theory stripped nature of all mystical intention or externally imposed design.[18]

In *Great Expectations*, Dickens too strips nature of inherent mystery by redefining it as a tabula rasa on which the human imagination paints fantastic images all of which echo human concerns. By choosing guilt as one of the major motifs of *Great Expectations*, Dickens dramatizes the extent to which human hubris consistently places Man at the center of creation. Nothing is so self-centered, nor so self-involved as guilt. When the boy Pip brings Magwitch the stolen pork pie, all of nature seems to accuse him. " . . . Instead of my running at everything, everything ran at me . . . The gates and dykes and banks came bursting at me through the mist . . ." (GE, 48). The landscape of the novel with its natural scenes consistently disturbed and dominated by the symbols of human chastisement echo this sense of a neutral nature reinterpreted according to human concerns. As Harriet Ritvo suggests, Darwin may have redefined human beings as animals, but they are top animals, and have in this way appropriated to themselves some of the attributes previously reserved for the deity.[19]

Religious notions are in fact evoked in this novel only to be recategorized according to secular principles. Pip's encounters with

Estella take place within a "rank garden," a degenerate echo of that other garden in which the first man was undone by the first woman. (The novel even sports a snakey individual in the person of a Mrs Coiler.) The garden is adjacent to the brewery behind Miss Havisham's house. It is in this garden, "overgrown with tangled weeds," – recalling the metaphor of the tangled bank with which Darwin ends *The Origin of Species* – that Pip has his hallucinations. One of the first of these concerns Estella, whose figure appears wherever he looks, until finally he sees her "go out by a gallery high overhead, as if she were going out into the sky" (GE, 93). It is while standing in this garden that Pip twice has the vision of Miss Havisham hanging from the beam of an adjacent building. Given the fact of these apparitions, the garden appears to be magical, but its visionary quality is firmly located within the mind of Pip; it is he who creates the vision and generates the magic.

It is in this same garden that Dickens sets the novel's final scene of the meeting between Pip and Estella. Around the garden now all the buildings have been torn down, as if the land were reclaiming its own, an image reinforced by the description of old ivy which has struck root anew and is growing on "low quiet mounds of ruin" (GE, 491). It is Estella, however, who makes the point: "The ground belongs to me. It is the only possession I have not relinquished. Everything else has gone from me, little by little, but I have kept this" (GE, 492).

The notion of ground, its function as the natural repository of both life and death, and the extent to which it may with justice be deemed a human possession is a theme which becomes increasingly insistent in Dickens's final novels. The first note is sounded quite faintly in *Great Expectations*, but becomes more prominent in *Our Mutual Friend* and *The Mystery of Edwin Drood*.

In another echo of Darwinism, Dickens introduces the notion of fitness as applied to nature.[20] Miss Havisham's crime, we are told, lies in her being against nature, in her trying to shut out the sun, and secluding herself "from a thousand natural and healing influences." What is natural is then confounded with the supernatural and God's appointed order of the world. Miss Havisham's brooding solitary mind has grown diseased, "as all minds do and must and will that reverse the appointed order of their Maker" (GE, 411), which leads to the conclusion that she has been punished by her "profound unfitness for this earth on which she was placed..." (GE, 411).

There is an assumption in this passage that what is natural is in perfect accord with God's design, and what is unnatural is also antireligious, and hence condemnable. The natural and the godlike have become synonymous. But the notion that Miss Havisham is unfit for this world is not truly theological – since all of God's creations are by definition part of God's world and therefore, whether saint or sinner, must be part of His design. The idea of not fitting, of not having adapted to one's environment, and therefore cheating and distorting the next generation – as Miss Havisham does to Estella – this appears to be a Darwinian, not a theological construct.

Miss Havisham is not the only character in *Great Expectations* who is not well adapted to her surroundings. The same is also true of Joe, although in his case, it depends on the surroundings. Joe is a natural in the sense that any form of behaviour which forces him away from his essential nature is uncomfortable to him, and this includes all the conventions associated with "polite" society. Clothes afford the most obvious example of Joe's inability to cope with civilization. He is uncomfortable in anything but his work clothes. And he is uncomfortable anywhere out of his natural element – the country and the forge. His boots are too big; he is clumsy on stairs; he learns to read only with difficulty. The city – that ultimate symbol of human civilization – is his nemesis. "I'm wrong in these clothes. I'm wrong out of the forge, the kitchen, or off th' meshes" (GE, 246), he says. In fact, he is so incapable of adapting to the dictates of society that the text implies they literally unman him: "Joe changed his clothes so far as to make a compromise between his Sunday dress and working dress; in which the dear fellow looked natural, and like the Man he was" (GE, 301).

Yet Joe is not merely the novel's symbol of the natural man, he is also its embodiment of the affective ideal in human nature. It is he who recognizes Magwitch as a "poor miserable fellow-creatur" (GE, 71). In fact Joe and Magwitch may legitimately be viewed as substitutes for one another, the more so since both are surrogate fathers to Pip. At the same time, Pip is ashamed to be connected to both of them. Both Joe and Magwitch are men who act with their hearts; and while this is generally defined as good, there is also something to be said against such behaviour. With Magwitch the ambivalence is built into the ambiguities of the plot – the man is a thief and a convict. Even the altruism of Magwitch's love for Pip is complicated by his wish to "own" a gentleman. Joe's love for Pip is more truly selfless, but it is also inept. It cannot save Pip from the harshness of his sister's upbringing, and it cannot serve Pip as a model for getting along in a world which is more complicated than mere goodness will allow for.

Thus while Pip feels constant guilt for his neglect of Joe, and expiates that guilt through his reconciliation with Magwitch, there is also a sense in which his return to his former boyhood relationship with Joe would be regressive. Pip represents the evolution of the human species away from its primitive origins, whether the primitive be defined as the degenerate or the spontaneously good-hearted. For better or for worse, Pip – and the rest of humanity with him – has been civilized. He has learned to adapt to the city, and eventually he learns to enjoy the benefits of civilization without succumbing to its corruptions.

Pip can never go home again. In its insistence on the finality of that proposition, *Great Expectations* breaks most dramatically with Dickens's earlier novels. Unlike David Copperfield, Pip does not get a second chance at life; he cannot make good on earlier mistakes. In fact, chapter 45 of *Great Expectations* is devoted to Pip's reaction to the injunction, "don't go home," a message which he receives from Wemmick on his return to London. The phrasing of this interdiction is subject to several constructions during the course of the chapter. For instance, there is Wemmick's query to Pip and Pip's response – significantly styled a "return":

> "Halloa, Mr Pip!" said Wemmick. "You did come home then?"
> "Yes," I returned, "but I didn't go home."   (GE, 381)

The subtle distinction of nuance between "come home" and "go home" and the added confusion of "returned" to mean "replied" when the issue has to do with an actual return has been earlier adumbrated by Pip obsessively turning the injunction "don't go home" into an exercise in grammatical tenses, as if he were conjugating a Latin phrase. "Do not thou go home, let him not go home, let us not go home, do not ye or you go home ... I may not and I cannot go home; and I might not, could not, would not, and should not go home ..." (GE, 381).

This playing with the tense of the message – to say nothing of the punning on "return" and the distinguishing between "go home" and "come home" – carries implications beyond the overt, since

both the literal meaning of the message and Pip's mental manipu-
lations address issues of time. Where once time in a Dickens novel
was cyclical, in *Great Expectations* it is historical. The extent to which
this is so can be seen by a brief comparison to Dickens's other
first-person narrative, *David Copperfield*. *David Copperfield*'s attitude
towards the past is consistently nostalgic. It is based on memory
and on the ability of memory to recreate and relive the past in the
present. *David Copperfield* ends with the naming of David's children, among whom there is another Betsey Trotwood and another
Dora. The repetition of names suggests the cyclical nature of time,
and is one of Dickens's favourite devices for concluding his fictions on a positive note. Nor is it a coincidence that the memorializing
aspect of this cyclical naming has the appearance of wish-fulfillment.
Betsey Trotwood's dearest wish throughout the novel has been to
have a niece named after her. This wish is now fulfilled. And this
same quality of wish-fulfillment applies to the name of the other
daughter, Dora, who stands as a consolation for the loss of the
first Dora. David's daughter Dora even wears the same ring that
David had once ordered for his wife Dora (DC, 550).[21]

Name recycling occurs as well in *Great Expectations*, but only once,
and this time the meaning of the repeated name is far more ambiguous, since the name's originator, Pip himself, is still very much
alive. The new Pip – infant son of Joe and Biddy – stands as a form
of reproach to the old Pip, whose guilt-ridden heart can never re-
gain the purity and unspotted innocence of his namesake. And this
new Pip serves equally as a reminder to the original of all that he
does not have, most especially the satisfaction of married life with
Biddy and children of his own. In *Great Expectations*, such negative
implications balance the memorializing positives associated with
having a child carry one's name into the next generation.

The profusion of recycled names in the earlier work suggests that
Dickens had conceived of the past as being repeatable in the present.
But *Great Expectations* views the past as a continuous march for-
ward, not a constant repetition of what has gone before. Pip praises
Magwitch for never yielding to the temptation "to bend the past
out of its eternal shape" (GE, 465).

The past has an eternal shape because it cannot be altered nor
repeated in the present. Not only is the nostalgic element of *David
Copperfield* missing from *Great Expectations*, but the value of nostalgia itself is put in doubt. The smell of a blackcurrant bush may
always remind Pip of a conversation he had with Biddy, but the

memory is hardly sweet, since it evokes an instance of Biddy putting Pip in his place for snobbishness (GE, 175). And when Pip returns to see Miss Havisham and once again pushes her chair, he announces it was like pushing her chair back into the past, but that past was not a pleasant place. Nevertheless, if memory is not pleasant, its opposite – forgetfulness, the enemy of nostalgia – is no better. Estella does not remember that she made Pip cry as a boy, and this makes him cry all the more inside, because it means that he has left no impression on her mind, not even a negative impression.

Pip cannot go home again. He cannot return to the time before he came into his expectations. He can never reestablish the easy camaraderie and affection that marked his earlier relationship with Joe. Once Joe has learned to address Pip as "sir," the chill of formality between the two men can never again be erased. Nor does Pip marry Biddy. He cannot even expect to find her waiting for him as Agnes did for David. The past as it is presented in *Great Expectations* is past and must remain so.

To illustrate this new attitude towards time, Dickens evokes the metaphor of a chain:

> That was a memorable day for me, for it made great changes in me. But it is the same with any life. Imagine one selected day struck out of it, and think how different its course would have been. Pause you who read this, and think for a moment of the long chain of iron or gold, of thorns or flowers, that would never have bound you, but for the formation of the first link on one memorable day. (GE, 101)

This is a statement of both randomness and inevitability. Here the past is equated with fate. A single chance day may unavoidably alter the course of a lifetime, and what occurs after that day will never resemble what went before. This is a decidedly different conception of time than that which pertained in *A Tale of Two Cities* in which so momentous an event as the French Revolution was described as essentially a reiteration in other terms of previous injustices, without consequences for change in the future. What we have here is Darwinian time – the ceaseless moving into the future without recourse to what has gone before.

Our Mutual Friend: disintegration, articulation and dust

All hereditary issues lie within the metaphoric domain of cohesion, connection, and integrity. They are concerned with conservation and recreation through the transmission of characteristics from one generation to the next. In this sense, hereditary concerns mirror Darwinian ones in alluding to the underlying similarities and connections which bind all living things through the processes of evolution and descent. This being the case, it is hardly surprising that when Dickens jettisons heredity, what he replaces it with are metaphors of disintegration and dispersal. Nowhere is this more apparent than in *Our Mutual Friend*, whose major thematic preoccupation is with refuse and decomposition, with the waste of both biology and civilization.

Hereditary relationships hardly exist in this novel. The exception is Mr Riah, who is consistently placed within a hereditary context because he is Jewish. Heredity is occasionally exploited for satirical purposes as well: we are told, for instance, that Mrs Boffin descends from good Anglo-Saxon stock, her ancestors having been bowmen who fought at Agincourt and Cressy. This is evidently a dig at the upper-class habit of substantiating social superiority with pedigree. Mrs Boffin's lineage demonstrates that even the common folk have genealogies and therefore a claim on the pageantry of history.

On a more personal level, Pleasant Riderhood inherits her swivel eye from her father, but her personality does not resemble his, a point which is underlined when John Harmon compliments her for a sympathetic remark: "The sentiment does you credit . . . the more so, as I believe it's not your father's . . ." (OMF, 411). Pleasant and her father are one of several father–daughter pairs in the novel, but the stress here is on the inversion of the normal dynamic between parent and child, with the daughters mothering their fathers. The relationship between parent and child is thus defined more by psychological than biological factors.

Furthermore, although the plot is set in motion by a will, and therefore alludes to issues of inheritance, the symbolic ramifications of this will tend more towards the temporal than they do towards the biological. In *Our Mutual Friend*, the will of the dead John Harmon stipulates that his son can only inherit if he marries Bella Wilfer, the girl whom his father has picked out for him.[22] In other words, the will represents the future as being in hock to the past, thereby testifying to the tyranny of the past over the present.

The ruses employed by the younger John Harmon to secretly test the moral quality of his future bride – a young woman whom he has never previously met – suggest an attempt by the living present to assimilate, mitigate, and adapt to the impositions of the dead past – a very Darwinian idea.

The will, of which several alternate versions exist, stands as a statement of the power of parents to exert influence even beyond the grave – an influence that, in this case, appears capricious and potentially harmful. It also amounts to an attempt to regulate nature by assuring the future hereditary composition of the family, mimicking Darwin's "eminent breeders [who] try by methodical selection with a distinct object in view to make a new strain... superior to anything of the kind in the country."[23] Dickens was always drawn to wills as a plot device, but this "breeding stock" stipulation occurs only in the last two novels. The provisions of the will in *The Mystery of Edwin Drood* are similar to those in *Our Mutual Friend*. In both novels, the wills are concerned with ensuring the future marriages of children to partners picked out by their fathers, as if the older generation wished to control the hereditary make-up of the family's future.

While these wills often result in awkward and hard-to-believe narrative contrivances, their thematic purpose is obvious: they represent an obstruction to the present imposed by the past, played out as an attempt to regulate the course of biological destiny. In this sense, wills are analogous to physical inheritance in that they represent fate. They are an analogue for the way in which the hereditary endowment of parents may influence the destiny of offspring. It is not surprising then that when Dickens loses interest in biological heredity as a means of expressing the constraints of determinism on the individual, he should turn to wills as a more malleable alternative. In *Our Mutual Friend* and *The Mystery of Edwin Drood*, the will expresses its dictatorial impulse through an attempt to regulate the hereditary endowment of future generations by stipulating the intended mate of the legatee. In *Our Mutual Friend*, Dickens surprisingly rewards this form of biological hubris by depicting the successful, fertile union of the two people involved, thus retrospectively turning old John Harmon into a wiser and more prescient man than his earlier reputation had led us to expect. In *The Mystery of Edwin Drood*, however, the prescribed union falls apart.

But if heredity as a determinant of personality is scarcely present in *Our Mutual Friend*, the broader issues implied by heredity do exist in the novel.

Dust, dirt, refuse, waste are the major recurrent symbols of *Our Mutual Friend*, which opens with the fishing of dead bodies from the Thames. These symbols overpower the faint-hearted attempt at balance embodied in the John Harmon resurrection motif. Examples of dissolution and corruption – both literal and metaphoric – are everywhere, occurring in finer as well as in grander details. Sometimes they occur as whimsy. "Come up and be dead," is Jenny Wren's invitation to Riah to join her on the roof. Sometimes they occur as Darwinian evocations, like the chapter titles alluding to birds of prey (chapters 13 and 14) and dismal swamps (chapter 17). Notions of corruption in its moral sense hover over the Veneering table, site of endless feasting. Mostly, however, the abstract concepts of disintegration and dissolution are anchored in the concrete all-encompassing symbol of dust. "Coal-dust, vegetable-dust, bone-dust, crockery dust, rough dust and sifted dust – all manner of Dust" (OMF, 56).

The organizing metaphor in *Our Mutual Friend* no longer encompasses all classes and levels of society, as did the court of Chancery in *Bleak House*, or the prison in *Little Dorrit* or the criminal underworld in *Great Expectations*. The organizing principle in *Our Mutual Friend* is decomposition, dispersal, decay, and dissolution – the disintegration of all unities. This death-haunted novel speculates on the relationship of death to life, and does so, in part, by continuing the Dickensian rumination on the meaning of ground. In *Dombey and Son*, Dickens wrote of "the warm ground . . . where the ugly little seeds turn into beautiful flowers, and into grass, and corn . . . Where good people turn into bright angels, and fly away to heaven" (DS, 78). In *Great Expectations*, Pip meditates on the beans and the clover, juxtaposing their growth with the memory of his sister's death, whose grave he describes as opening a gap in the smooth ground of his life (GE, 297). That same novel contains Estella's claim that the ground is her only possession. In *Our Mutual Friend*, the notion of ground expands to cover many things – dirt, dust, death, waste, excrement, money, as well as the Darwinian concepts of extinction and regeneration. The preoccupation with ground as a repository for life and death segues into a fascination with the fertility of death as embodied in the money-making potential of dust and refuse. In this novel there is gold in dung heaps, and meat and drink derive from corpses.

The dust in *Our Mutual Friend* is associated not only with the decomposition of the human body after death – as evoked by the funerary phrase "dust to dust" – but also with the decomposition of food as it passes through the body towards elimination. The living are therefore as much involved in the process of decomposition as the dead. The dust hills, which have made the fortune of old John Harmon, are full of excrement, offal and other waste matter. Humphry House in *The Dickens World* was the first to point out that human excrement was an important and financially viable component of Victorian dust heaps.[24] In case we miss the point, Dickens even provides an illustrative example in an interpolated story called "The Treasures of a Dunghill," in which a miser by the name of Dancer hides a substantial amount of money in a dungheap in the cowhouse (OMF, 543). Excrement, dust, and money here enter into an indivisible metaphoric alliance, each referring to and equated with the other. Excrement and dust allude to the transformations to which flesh is heir; money alludes to the economic value of such transformations, a relationship which is elsewhere made manifest in Mr Venus's living off stuffed animals and reconstructed skeletons and in Gaffer Hexam's fishing for bodies in the Thames. When his daughter Lizzie complains to Gaffer that she dislikes this occupation, he angrily retorts: "As if it wasn't your living! As if it wasn't meat and drink to you!" (OMF, 45).

Dickens seems to have been fascinated by all manner of regenerative processes, as can be seen by some of the articles he published in *Household Words*. These dealt with such subjects as the transmuting of gaseous refuse into perfume, or how to transform the shavings of horses hooves into gelatin; they explored how old bones and old rags could be turned into cosmetics, while the refuse of the smithy, the gas-works, and the slaughterhouse might be made to yield the most useful commodities. There was even an article in the July 1850 edition entitled "Dust; or Ugliness Redeemed."[25]

Given this evident interest on Dickens's part in the physical transformation of one thing into another, it is not surprising that in *Our Mutual Friend* scientific metaphors are applied to everyday physical processes, such as eating. "Lady Tippin has made a series of experiments upon her digestive functions, so extremely complicated and daring, that if they could be published with their results it might benefit the human race" (OMF, 53). Not coincidentally, Lady Tippin's meal is presided over by a character dubbed the Analytical Chemist, who is in fact the Veneering's butler. Similarly, the feasting that occurs in one part of the novel is balanced by excretive activities in the other, which in turn supply "meat and drink" to those who live by reclaiming waste.

This stress on the transformative characteristics of bodily processes is a restatement in scientific and physical terms of the metamorphoses inherent in myths and fairy tales. It represents a coalescence between the supernatural and the earthly, the spiritual and the carnal. Throughout his life Dickens was attracted by the world of fairy tales, fantasy and magic, so it seems only natural that he should translate the metamorphic parts of that world into the scientific domain. In fact, Dickens tends to exploit science in much the same way as he exploits fairy tales. Both provide him with metaphoric material which push his fiction away from pure realism and into the realm of the magical and the surreal. In the Dickensian universe, the improbabilities of fantasy occupy the same place as the "miracles" of science, each enhancing the other, and each to a large extent equal to the other.

There is another scientific dimension to the dust heaps in *Our Mutual Friend*: Howard Fulweiler suggests that Dickens took his imagery of the mounds from Lyell's *The Geological Evidence of the Antiquity of Man*, which was reviewed in *All the Year Round* in 1863, a year before Dickens began his novel. The review spoke of prehistoric kitchen-middens found on Danish islands. These were mounds of refuse, three to ten feet high, and a thousand feet long, wherein were unearthed musical instruments, fragments of pottery, tools, shells, bones and other waste matter. Howard Fulweiler suggests that the description of these middens may have given Dickens the idea for the dustheaps of *Our Mutual Friend*.[26] There is certainly evidence for a geological interpretation in the text of the novel itself. There we are told that John Harmon senior, the original dustman, "threw up his own mountain range, like an old volcano, and its geological foundation was Dust" (OMF, 56).

The mounds in the novel resemble the Danish refuse heaps in being composed of the detritus of the living, a jumbling together of things both worthless and valuable. Viewed from this geological perspective, the mounds become a reification of the history of the earth, and a demonstration of the manner in which life quite literally lives upon death. What lies beneath our feet is the history of the Earth, a history made up, not of the grand and the gorgeous, but of the accumulated waste of generations.

There is another character in the novel who lives upon death – Mr Venus, the taxidermist. If one strand of the motif of disintegration takes the form of corporeal transformation – food into excrement, flesh into dust – another concerns the disjuncture of body parts. This motif is centered around Mr Venus and his extraordinary shop. In this shop life feeds on death, while death masquerades as life. A dead robin lies on the counter with its head resting on Mr Venus's tea saucer. Mr Venus removes the wire piercing the robin's breast and uses it to toast a muffin. Body parts lie scattered about; teeth get into everything including the coffee pot and the money till where they are in danger of being confused with coins. Babies of all nationalities float in bottles, the English baby on a par with the Hindoo and African specimens. Mr Venus's occupation recalls the obsession with body parts in *A Tale of Two Cities*, where execution by dismemberment or decapitation stood as a symbol for the disintegration of society.

In *Our Mutual Friend* the theme of disintegration is part of a larger concern which encompasses decomposition and dispersal. The rascally Wegg has sold his leg to Mr Venus to be incorporated into a skeleton which will eventually be sold to a medical college or an art school. But Wegg's leg cannot be made to fit into any other "miscellaneous" skeleton. Finally, Wegg, who has in the meantime replaced his amputated leg with a wooden one, decides to buy back the original. He objects, he tells Venus, to being dispersed, "a part of me here, a part of me there" and wishes to collect himself like a genteel person (OMF, 127).

Little does Wegg realize that even the genteel may be made up of parts not their own. Lady Tippin, for instance, wears on her head a mixture of dyed hair and false hair, and has a glass eye. "You could easily buy all you see of her, in Bond Street" (OMF, 164), asserts the narrator. As for Mrs Podsnap, she appears to be nothing more than a "quantity of bone" (OMF, 52), and would make an ideal subject for an articulator of bones such as Mr Venus. In fact, the text suggests another use for her – as a fine specimen for Dr Richard Owen, head of the Natural History Section of the British Museum, and a specialist in the study of extinct animals. Human beings in *Our Mutual Friend* tend to be defined as anatomical conglomerates, their physiology is in constant danger of dissolution, because they are so precariously put together, while their various parts are not necessarily their own.

Mr Venus is an articulator by profession – someone who puts things together by the joints. He fashions skeletons out of miscellaneous bones, assembling the nations of the earth into a harmony they might never otherwise enjoy. "One leg Belgian, one leg English, and the pickings of eight other people in it," is how he describes his latest "Beauty," recently sold to an art school (OMF, 124). But Venus's skill extends beyond reassembly: he has the art to make the dead seem alive. His calling card describes him as a "Preserver of Animals and Birds" as well as an "Articulator of human bones" (OMF, 128). Of a stuffed canary, he boasts: "There's animation! On a twig making up his mind to hop!" (OMF, 125).

Not surprisingly, Mr Venus considers himself an artist; he is a "workman without equal." This odd juxtaposition between art and dismemberment, that is between art and death, has occurred before in Dickens's work, notably in *Barnaby Rudge*, where we were treated to a disquisition on the fine art of hanging. In *Our Mutual Friend* the juxtapositions go further – here we are dealing with art, death, dispersal, and reassembly. By placing two such apparently unrelated concepts as art and death side by side, Dickens suggests a kind of cannibalistic relationship between aesthetics and the processes of existence. The remodeling, reassembling, and reanimating of inert materials into a new reality is the domain of the artist, who dissects the actual material of life in order to create a semblance of life. The connection to cannibalism is reinforced by the fact that Mr Venus is continually partaking of tea while surrounded by the gruesome objects of his trade – bones, skulls, bottled babies, glass eyes, etc. Like Dennis the Hangman, Mr Venus makes an art of death. The added touch of tea-drinking and muffin-eating underlines the intimate association between art, death, and food, and locates us within the realm of cannibalistic absorption. Death is meat and drink to Mr Venus – and death is his art.

The fact that tea is Mr Venus's favourite beverage adds a dimension of imperialistic exploitation to the brew, which throws a faint colonialist light over the Hindoo and African babies floating in bottles. The light is faint because Mr Venus's shop also sports an articulated English baby, to say nothing of the bits and pieces of other European nationalities, which seems to neutralize the implication. If Mr Venus is an imperialist, then the human body is the colony which he ransacks for his riches.

Mr Venus plays an ambiguous role in the plot of *Our Mutual Friend*. His occupation makes him appear sinister, and his association with the villain Wegg confirms that impression. But he is eventually revealed to be on the side of the just when he betrays his erstwhile partner and is rewarded with marriage to the woman he loves. The duality inherent in Mr Venus can be found in the very terms which describe him. His name is a wonderfully ironic allusion to the goddess of beauty and love, and so evokes both the aesthetical sublime and the emotional sublime. And the name of his profession – "articulator" – lies on the cusp of grotesquerie and fluency.

Mr Venus's tragedy is the tragedy of the artist – he is not understood; or more precisely, the woman he loves does not appreciate his art. Instead she is repulsed by it and refuses to marry him, not wishing to be regarded in "that boney light" (OMF, 128). This seems to cast aspersions on the nature of Mr Venus's desire, whether it be for the woman in the flesh, or for the skeleton beneath the flesh. Mr Venus reacts badly to this characterization of his motives. He broods, sitting alone amid "the lovely trophies of my art," feeling that his profession has ruined him. But so intimately is the very essence of his being connected to his profession that it has become a part of every emotion. Even the sorrow of rejection is expressed in terms of bones: "My very bones is rendered flabby by brooding over it. If they could be brought to me loose, to sort, I should hardly have the face to claim 'em as mine" (OMF, 563). Mr Venus is that rare being – the true artist – whose every thought and emotion are at the service of his craft.

Pleasant Riderhood, the woman he loves, runs a pawnshop – a commercial establishment not so different from that of Mr Venus in that it too deals in scraps and remnants, in those objects which people feel obliged to sacrifice in return for money, on much the same principle as Wegg sacrifices his leg. A pawnshop makes money out of the discarded and extraneous – it makes money out of the need for money.

But despite being in almost the same line of work as her suitor – and having, in addition, a father who retrieves dead bodies from the river – Pleasant is discriminating. The material in her shop is more respectable than what can be found in Venus's. Nevertheless, it is she who sells Venus the sailor's parrots which he will eventually stuff. She deals in the raw living material, he in the processing. In her fastidiousness, Pleasant resembles those overly civilized citizens who were excoriated in an essay in *Household Words* for hastily and shamefacedly depositing their refuse in the gutter and turning up their noses, rather than seeing filth as the enriching organic substance it could be, and recycling it.[27] Pleasant would rather not think about what happens to those parrots once she has sold them, nor does she appreciate their value once they have been recycled. She may appreciate the profits of Mr Venus's profession but she is not impressed by the art of it (OMF, 128). However, she does eventually acquiesce to the union, provided that Mr Venus agrees to confine himself to the articulation of men, children and the lower animals (OMF, 853). Pleasant is here demonstrating that other nineteenth-century ideal and Dickensian bugaboo – enlightened self-interest. Once she has been assured that Mr Venus will not practice his craft on women, that is, that she herself will not fall victim to the consummation of her husband's artistic desires, the marriage goes ahead.

I have said that *Our Mutual Friend* is about disintegration and dispersal, and such is the most obvious thrust of its metaphors. But the novel does not necessarily define dispersal as bad. Money, for instance, when dispensed as largesse is a good, but when hoarded by misers is an evil. Because the degenerative processes in the novel are also transformative they suggest rebirth and regeneration. Death becomes not an end in itself but a beginning of something else. Death provides the raw material for others to use, much as scrap and dust do. In effect all of the novel's symbols of disintegration end by alluding to regeneration. In this sense they serve as analogues to heredity.

For instance, Mr Venus is not the only craftsman in the novel who is in the business of animating the lifeless, nor yet the only one to make a living from the art of stuffing. This is Jenny Wren's speciality too. Jenny Wren is a doll's dressmaker, and Mr Venus's female counterpart. She not only stuffs her dolls to give them the appearance of life, she also creates them out of bits and pieces. Her dolls are effigies of the high society women whose clothing Jenny copies and reproduces. This is another form of trafficking in human bodies and creating illusions of animation out of pieces of scrap and waste. Both Jenny Wren and Mr Venus use refuse as their raw material, the difference being that her bits and pieces derive from inorganic matter while his were once alive. The occupations of both of these characters appear to parallel the workings of heredity, which also functions as a form of reassembly. The hereditable contributions of both parents are the raw material out of which is created a new being. Heredity too bespeaks a relationship of mix and match, of dissolution and regeneration.

But that is as far as the similarity goes. Mr Venus's creations, because man-made, are fated never to be complete, never to be alive, and always to be flawed. The same is true for Jenny's dolls. No matter how skillful the creator, the result is always only an illusion, only an approximation of life. This inherent flaw is illustrated by the case of the French gentleman, a skeleton on which Mr Venus is at work throughout the course of the novel. When we first encounter him, the French gentleman consists of nothing but ribs, but over the course of the novel he acquires a head, legs and all other bony appurtenances, except the arms. Mr Venus can never get quite the right arms for him, and so the French gentleman is condemned to remain incomplete, a silent testament to the fact that Venus's art is doomed to be inferior to the processes of Nature. But while the French gentleman's skeleton remains an imperfect approximation of a reconstituted human being, it is also a reminder that human beings are as amenable to being dissolved, dispersed, and disassembled as any other form of matter, animate or not. What is more, flaws of construction are not exclusively man-made, witness the crippled back of Jenny Wren.

John Carey has written that Dickens's imagination is most engaged in "the border country between people and things"[28] and nowhere is this more evident than in *Our Mutual Friend*, where dispersal and reassembly occur to the living as well as to the dead, confounding the inanimate with the human, and subjecting all to the processes of regeneration.

Yet none of these processes is hereditary, no matter how closely the activities of Mr Venus and Jenny Wren seem to mimic creation. It is tempting to see hereditary concerns behind the novel's theme of resurrection – resurrection being but a spiritual restatement of regeneration. The resurrection motif in this novel applies to the two heroes. John Harmon is supposedly drowned in the Thames, but emerges from the river alive and adopts a disguise the better to test the young woman whom his father's will has named as his bride. Eugene Wrayburn falls into the river after being struck by his rival Bradley Headstone. He is rescued by Lizzie Hexam and returns to life a less cynical individual, ready to marry his lower-class sweetheart instead of merely toying with her. (The maiming of Wrayburn before he is permitted to marry beneath his social station is reminiscent of the blinding of Rochester in *Jane Eyre* and carries the same unpleasant connotations of physical diminishment.)

Resurrection and regeneration are related to heredity in the sense that they define matter as circular and regenerative in much the same way as Dickens once defined time as cyclical and repetitive by naming the coming generation after the present one. One could argue that in *Our Mutual Friend* the relationship between dispersal and reconstruction, death and life, dust and money, eating and excrement becomes a substitute for the kind of natural regeneration which Dickens has elsewhere associated with heredity. But that is to understand heredity in such a broad sense as to render it meaningless. Heredity represents a relationship in which life grows out of life. Inanimate objects cannot inherit, nor can they bequeath their characteristics to the next generation. The process of disintegration and regeneration which so fascinates Dickens in *Our Mutual Friend* may substitute for his earlier interest in heredity, but cannot replace it. Darwin relegated Man to the margins of creation in *The Origin of Species*. Dickens, as a novelist, can do no such thing. Because he requires the human at the center of his fiction, he requires as well the notion of heredity, to which he returns in his last novel.

The Mystery of Edwin Drood (1870): the return to heredity

In many ways, *The Mystery of Edwin Drood* represents a return to the thematic preoccupations of Dickens's earlier work. Written ten years after the publication of Darwin's *The Origin of Species*, this novel reverts to earlier Dickensian concerns with heredity and the dynamics of family inheritance and interaction, but heredity in this novel is tied to celibacy, and therefore to extinction. The novel seems to have been intended as the psychological exploration of the mind of a murderer, the murder in question being that of a nephew by his uncle.[29] Thus the crime is woven into the structure of a family drama and set against the backdrop of kinship relations, inviting a return to Dickens's earlier preoccupation with issues of resemblance and descent.

The family relationships portrayed here are full of ambiguity, mixing affection with jealousy, intimacy with claustrophobia. In this novel, uncle and nephew vie for the love of an orphan, a struggle which ends in homicide. By way of bracketing this central incident of family violence, Dickens resurrects the incest motif that had so appealed to him in his earlier fiction, parceling it out between a brother–sister pair on the one hand, and a parent–child pair on the other. This means that hereditary issues once more affect the plot, but they are here subsumed to a darker vision linking sex and death.

The most striking thing about *The Mystery of Edwin Drood* is the description of the cathedral town of Cloisterham in which the novel is set. We are introduced to Cloisterham in the novel's very first paragraph which takes place within the mind of John Jasper, an opium addict and the cathedral's choir master. Jasper's hallucination confuses the English Cloisterham with the violent and seductive lands of the East, thereby providing an alternative reality for a city which, in Dickens's description, is haunted by death.

Cloisterham, is "a monotonous silent city," a place of presumptive spirituality, which is nevertheless permeated by an "earthy flavor throughout" (MED, 51). This earthy flavor, deriving from the Cathedral crypt, disseminates its influence over all of Cloisterham, establishing the presence of death as an integral part of the cityscape. But it is death in its fleshy, not its spiritual aspect. It is death as disintegration and dissolution. In one striking passage, Dickens describes the fear of death as "the innate shrinking of dust with the breath of life in it from dust out of which the breath of life has passed" (MED, 153). This proleptic vision suggests that the living are nothing more than collections of dust waiting to decompose. Yet, as he did in *Our Mutual Friend*, Dickens also defines such disintegration as the first step towards physical, if not spiritual regeneration. The bodies in the cathedral crypt belong to the clergy. In fact, Cloisterham is a city

> ... so abounding in vestiges of monastic graves, that the Cloisterham children grow small salad in the dust of abbots and abbesses, and make dirt-pies of nuns and friars; while every ploughman in its outlying fields renders to once puissant Lord Treasurers, Archbishops, Bishops, and such-like, the attention which the Ogre in the story-book desired to render to his unbidden visitor, and grinds their bones to make his bread. (MED, 51)

This passage, with its unholy application of fairy-tale barbarism to the sanctified remains of Christian clergy, alludes to the cannibalization, both literal and metaphoric, of the past by the present. The cannibalization extends beyond food into the realm of architecture and from there passes into the human mind. We are told that fragments of old wall, saint's chapel, chapter house, convent, and monastery have got "incongruously or obstructively built into many of [Cloisterham's] houses and gardens, much as kindred jumbled notions have become incorporated into many of its citizens' minds" (MED, 52). This is a statement of the effects of environment on the human mind, and attributes a simultaneous confusion and obsolescence to the mental processes of the citizens of Cloisterham. In Cloisterham, where all things are of the past and reek of death, "the most abundant and the most agreeable evidences of progressing life" (MED, 52) can be found, not among human beings, but among the vegetable life of the city's many gardens – which are themselves the fruit and offspring of death.

The reference to gardens introduces the notion of sex into the grey atmosphere of a city suffering from an all-pervasive form of Tombatism – a word coined by the stonemason Durdles to describe rheumatism caught from graves. Sex in its varying forms is the leaven of the plot. It is depicted as the ungovernable force, bursting out from the proscriptions and confinements of religion to dominate the world of Nature in an uneasy alliance with death. In Cloisterham, the former Nuns' House has become a Seminary for Young Ladies, but the only change is that the former atmosphere of church-sanctioned repression has given way to the restrictions of social decorum. The result in both cases is a doomed attempt to banish sexuality, which amounts, in effect, to banishing life. The narrator makes the equation abundantly clear when he speculates on the fate of nuns who were walled up alive for "having some ineradicable leaven of busy mother Nature in them which has kept the fermenting world alive ever since" (MED, 52), a metaphor which harks back to the earlier image of the bones of nuns and friars being ground to make bread.

The Young Ladies Seminary, while not taking quite such drastic steps against "the ineradicable leaven" of Mother Nature nevertheless is just as concerned to suppress the irrepressible. Miss Twinkleton, the head of the school, censors love passages in her students' reading, avoids suggestive words like "bosoms," and praises female celibacy. Her charges are no longer walled up, and they may string beads for necklaces rather than telling them as rosaries, but they are no less subject to the wish to control and restrain the imperatives of life. These imperatives stand behind a novel in which sex is allied to death – as in the allusion to fermentation above – to such an extent that sexual jealousy becomes a motive for murder. Standing against this association, dressed incongruously and ironically in the mantle of celibacy, is heredity.

Dickens conceived of *The Mystery of Edwin Drood* as a family drama. As was the case with *Our Mutual Friend*, the plot is set in motion by a will. That will is based on the agreement of two friends that their children should marry when they came of age. Both friends being dead when the action of *Edwin Drood* begins, the will represents a short-sighted and self-centered attempt on the two fathers' part to extend their friendship into the future by imposing its affections and loyalties on the next generation. In fact, the will seeks to take the fathers' intimacy even further by cementing it into a legal union through the agency of their children. Or, in the odd phrasing of Rosa Bud, the intended bride, speaking of the man to whom she is betrothed – "That we might be to one another even much more than they [the fathers] had been to one another" (MED, 114). This way of putting it draws an analogy between the friendship of two men and the marriage of a man and woman as if the two relationships were comparable.

That the future union of Rosa Bud and Edwin Drood should have been based on the friendship of their fathers suggests the extent to which the theme of heredity is tied to futility in this novel. The betrothal falls apart because neither of the young people feels any sexual stirrings for the other. The wish for union had been their fathers', not theirs. Rosa and Edwin part amicably, agreeing to "change to brother and sister from this day forth" (MED, 164). The amicability which the fathers felt for one another will henceforth be repeated by their children, but that is all. The failed union of Rosa and Edwin is only the most central example of how, in this novel, heredity links up to notions of platonic friendship and asexuality rather than to fertility.

To take another example: Rosa Bud is said to resemble her mother who was "a pretty little creature like herself" (MED, 105). The extent of the resemblance causes Mr Grewgious, who is now Rosa's guardian, to be constantly mistaking the daughter for the mother. This is another instance of the past living on in the present, a relationship which is always implicit in the hereditary resemblance between parents and children. Mr Grewgious had loved Rosa's dead mother, and he maintains his fidelity to the mother by protecting the daughter, but this love is, of necessity, platonic. This is so not merely because Grewgious stands *in loco parentis* to the girl, but also because he defines himself as being prematurely aged. This aging is a quality he ascribes to heredity: "... Young ways were never my ways. I was the only offspring of parents far advanced in life, and I half believe I was born advanced in life myself" (MED, 114). Being born advanced in life obviously cuts down on the likelihood of generation. Defining this aged quality as hereditable again underlines the extent to which heredity in this novel exists within the sphere of celibacy and infertility.

The same point is made when the hereditary relationship is that between brother and sister. The siblings in *The Mystery of Edwin Drood* are the Landless twins, whose resemblance to one another is physical, emotional, and psychic. Dickens stresses the twins' similarity in a comment by Mr Crisparkle to Helena Landless: "Miss Helena, you and your brother were twin children. You came into this world with the same dispositions, and you passed your younger days together surrounded by the same adverse circumstances" (MED, 130). The statement neatly confounds environmental conditions with hereditary ones. Granting that Dickens may not have known that male and female twins are always fraternal rather than identical – therefore do not necessarily inherit the same dispositions – the fact remains that he hedges his bets by equating the influence of environment with that of heredity. That Helena and Neville so resemble each other in looks suggests masculine and feminine versions of the same character type, although in this instance – as was the case with the Brasses in *The Old Curiosity Shop* – the resemblance is predicated on the sister assuming masculine characteristics. According to Neville, not only is Helena the fiercer and more resilient of the two, but she has actually passed herself off as a boy:

> ... Nothing in our misery ever subdued her, though it often cowed me. When we ran away from [home] (we ran away four times in six years, to be soon brought back and cruelly punished), the flight was always of her planning and leading. Each time she dressed as a boy and showed the daring of a man.
>
> (MED, 90)

Helena and her brother are alike in certain intuitive ways as well. They seem to read each other's minds, and Canon Crisparkle is aware that in teaching Neville, he is simultaneously teaching Helena, even though she is not physically present during the lessons. Helena, in particular, seems to be gifted with psychic powers. For instance, she senses Rosa's fear of Jasper as well as the fact that Jasper loves Rosa.[30] These psychic powers are related to the fact that the twins, who are so devoted to one another, hail from the East, and appear to be of foreign blood, as if some element of the supernatural adhered by inherent right to those with Oriental ancestry. Brother and sister look very much alike, "both very dark, and very rich in colour; she of almost the gipsy type; something untamed about them both; a certain air upon them of hunter and huntress; yet withal a certain air of being the objects of the chase, rather than the followers" (MED, 85). These allusions to the primal in their make-up – Neville describes himself as having something tigerish in his blood – the suggestion of being simultaneously hunter and hunted, of being untamed and yet civilized, demonstrates again how the sexual element in this novel is just barely held in check. Brother and sister with their dark colouring and untamed air represent the primitive and emotional, at the same time as their relationship stands as an example of the most chaste and altruistic devotion.

Because Dickens never lived to finish *The Mystery of Edwin Drood*, it is difficult to ascertain what role precisely he intended to assign to this brother–sister pair who bear the suggestive family name of Landless. What is clear is that on the thematic level, the twins play a mirroring role, expanding the metaphoric possibilities of doubling, especially as these relate to the double life of Jasper. Dickens liked mirroring effects and often achieved these by multiplying the representatives of certain key themes in his novels. The most obvious example of this occurs in *David Copperfield*, where many of the characters are, like David himself, orphans with a single surviving parent. The four pairs of fathers and daughters in *Our Mutual Friend* are another example of the same tendency. A similar attempt at mirroring appears to lie behind the presence of the twins in *Edwin Drood*. Not only do we get the Landless twins, but Mrs Crisparkle, the mother of the Minor Canon, also seems to be a twin since Dickens describes her sister as "matching her so neatly that they would have made a delightful pair of ornaments for the two ends of any capacious old-fashioned chimney piece, and by right should never have been seen apart . . ." (MED, 82).

This twinning motif finds an echo in a related theme, which I have alluded to earlier – that of the nurturing daughter. In *Edwin Drood*, the daughter has become a son, and the father she cares for is now a mother. Nevertheless, the dynamics of this relationship are just as ambiguous and just as fraught with incestuous overtones as any of its earlier manifestations.

The Reverend Septimus Crisparkle derives his given name from being the seventh of seven brothers and the only one to survive – an echo of Pip's five dead baby brothers in *Great Expectations*. Crisparkle himself appears to be a throwback to such benevolent characters as Mr Jarndyce in *Bleak House,* or the Cheeryble brothers in *Nicholas Nickleby.* He is not only good-natured, but "his radiant features teemed with innocence," an innocence which is further enhanced by the fact that he lives with his mother. We are informed of Crisparkle's living arrangements through a little authorial slight of hand: Mrs Crisparkle is first introduced by title and name, and only secondly as "mother not wife, of the Reverend Septimus" (MED, 78). This in turn draws attention to the conflation of the two roles, since both mother and wife – if there were a wife – would be designated "Mrs Crisparkle."

The Reverend Septimus, a Minor Canon, is "within five years of forty." This means that he is 35 years old, yet Dickens's roundabout manner of stipulating his age puts the emphasis on "forty," making Crisparkle appear five years older than he is. At the same time as premature age is suggested, it is also contradicted. The reverend is portrayed as the epitome of healthy masculinity, a man in the prime of life. He goes swimming in the frozen weir, then shadowboxes in front of the mirror to restore his circulation. These activities are clearly meant to balance what might otherwise be a suspicion of namby-pambiness in his relationship to his mother. As in the following:

> ... The Reverend Septimus left off at this very moment to take the pretty old lady's entering face between his boxing-gloves and kiss it. Having done so with tenderness, the Reverend Septimus turned to again, countering with his left, and putting in his right, in a tremendous manner. (MED, 78)

The juxtaposition here between the ultra-masculine activity of boxing and the tenderness of kissing his mother's face makes for odd resonances, which are only enhanced in the following passage:

What is prettier than an old lady – except a young lady – when her eyes are bright, when her figure is trim and compact, when her face is cheerful and calm, when her dress is as the dress of a china shepherdess: so dainty in its colours, so individually assorted to herself, so neatly moulded on her? Nothing is prettier, thought the good Minor Canon frequently, when taking his seat at table opposite his long-widowed mother. Her thoughts at such times may be condensed into two words that oftenest did duty together in all her conversations: "My Sept!"

(MED, 79)

It is difficult to know the extent to which Dickens is here conforming to Victorian sentimentality on the subject of mothers and sons, and the extent to which he is aware of the undercurrents in the relationship which he is describing. What is beyond doubt is that we are meant to understand the Minor Canon as a good man, and that this picture of his celibacy combined with his athletic pursuits and love for his mother are intended to enhance a portrait of virtue unspotted by the slightest hint of sexual taint.

The portrayal of the relationship between the Reverend Septimus and his mother also has a bearing on another underlying motif in the novel, which has to do with the twisting of time out of its proper sequence. I have suggested that the Darwinian conception of time – slow-moving and progressive, encompassing small changes over long periods, never cyclical and never reverting to what has gone before – is a problem for Dickens, who tends to find comfort in conceptions of recurrent time, such as those embodied in notions of regeneration, resurrection, and preformation. In *Great Expectations*, Dickens – under the recent influence of Darwin – seems to adopt historical time and to define it as a positive. But in *Our Mutual Friend* with its insistence on regeneration, and its theme of life living off death, the definition of time seems once again to be sliding back towards a cyclical formulation.

There are echoes of progressive time in Dickens's description of the history of Cloisterham, which was once known by another name to the Druids, and still other names to the Romans, the Saxons, and the Normans. But this progression, which contains the author's admission that Cloisterham is his own invented name for the city (the original is Rochester), evokes historical time in order to cancel it. The implication is that every succeeding era has called Cloisterham by another name, but Cloisterham in its essence has always remained the same. Or, as the narrator puts it, ". . . A name more or less in the course of many centuries can be of little moment to its dusty chronicles" (MED, 51).

This is just one of several instances in which the novel distorts or undermines the chronological development of time. In fact, the narrative begins with such a distortion, when the "ancient English Cathedral town" dissolves into a scene of Eastern exoticism. This confusion of West and East occurs within the "scattered consciousness" of an opium addict, and serves as an apt introduction to a novel in which time is regularly scattered by being deprived of its accustomed chronology.

In the case of the Reverend Crisparkle and his mother, the relationship depicted is one in which time has stood still. The reverend and his mother both act as if he were still a boy. For instance, he is regularly dosed with medicine from her "herbaceous penitentiary" for the good of his health. He submits to this treatment out of a wish to humour and indulge his mother, but the way to achieve this indulgence appears to be for an adult man to adopt the submissiveness of a child.

Conversely, in order to feed his mother's vanity in other matters, the reverend must pretend to be older and frailer than she. For instance, Mrs Crisparkle is very proud of the fact that, despite her age, her "bright eyes" are still so clear that she can read without glasses. In order that she might more fully enjoy this invincibility to the ravages of time, her son affects short-sightedness and consequently puts on spectacles whenever he needs to read. He thereby reverses the customary sequential relationship between parent and child by making himself appear the elder and the one more in need of artificial aid. But this pretense is dishonest. So wary is Dickens of attributing the least suggestion of weakness to the reverend, that not only are we assured that the Minor Canon can, in reality, read without glasses, but that the reverend Mr Crisparkle "had the eyes of microscope and telescope combined, when they were unassisted" (MED, 80). To which is added the further irony that with spectacles, this paragon of vision has trouble seeing. Thus, in this small episode, we find compressed several modes of distortion, including the distortion of truth.

There are other examples of time being twisted out of its expected order. For instance, John Jasper is only six years older than his nephew Edwin. This means that the usual generational difference between an uncle and nephew does not exist here. Jasper and

Drood are near-contemporaries, both young, and both potential rivals for the affection of Rosa Bud, to whom Edwin is engaged. Dickens deliberately draws attention to the similarity of their ages when he has Jasper say: "Uncles as a rule, Ned, are so much older than their nephews," to which Edwin replies: "... And some uncles, in large families, are even younger than their nephews" (MED, 45). Balancing this erasure of time difference where we might expect to find it is the fact that Jasper, who at 26 is a young man, looks much older than his years, a circumstance which the narrator attributes to his dark colouring.

Other confusions of chronology occur throughout the novel. For instance, Mrs Crisparkle's prettiness places her aesthetically on a par with the two young heroines, Rosa Bud and Helena Landless, whose beauty is the beauty of youth. While the description of Mrs Crisparkle's attractions is intended to represent the thoughts of her devoted and indulgent son, and so is not objective, the narrator concurs with the reverend's estimation. Old Mrs Crisparkle is several times referred to as "the china shepherdess," thereby evoking the immutable prettiness of porcelain. This dwelling on the comeliness of Mrs Crisparkle is a first for Dickens, who nowhere else emphasizes the attractiveness of elderly women. The fact that he does so in this final novel suggests the extent to which bending time out of its sequential shape is a crucial element in his thematic design.

The effects of this bending are everywhere, from the round-about designation of the Reverend Crisparkle's age to the damaging effects of the prearranged betrothal on Rosa Bud and Edwin Drood. Their courtship has gone flat, we are told, because its outcome is known beforehand (MED, 50). Edwin is contemptuous and patronizing of Rosa since he need not exert himself to win her, while she is petulant and coy with him. That they have been required to love each other beforehand, by parental fiat, has ensured that they cannot love each other in the fullness of time, and their engagement is doomed from the start.

Other oddities of time are concentrated in the language. Rosa remembers her mother, who was drowned when her daughter was six years old, as "a pretty little creature like herself (not much older than herself, it seemed to her), who had been brought home in her father's arms, drowned" (MED, 105). It is unclear whether the parenthetical remark alludes to Rosa's age at present or to her age when her mother drowned. Either way, the view of time here is regressive, shrinking the mother back to a youthfulness which would seem to preclude the existence of the daughter.

Time is not the only quality which is distorted in this novel; so, to a lesser extent, is space, and the relative properties of what belongs where. This distortion goes beyond the dreamy confusions of the opening hallucination to include the actual topography of London, which Rosa reaches, travelling by train over the housetops, and where she is introduced to magic gardens that grow in the air (MED, 247). London appears to Rosa to be always waiting for something which never comes, a statement of time as an endless continuum of expectations destined to be frustrated.

Against the perceived irregularities of time and space which afflict the living is placed the permanence of inanimate objects. These are represented first and foremost by the engagement ring given Edwin Drood by Mr Grewgious. According to Forster, Dickens intended this ring to unmask Jasper as Edwin's murderer, since it would be the only part of the young man's body which would not dissolve in the quicklime pit into which Jasper planned to throw Edwin after the murder. The ring is an heirloom, a token of the past, with far greater powers of survival than its owners. It was taken from the finger of Rosa's drowned mother and given into the safekeeping of Mr Grewgious as Rosa's guardian, who in turn gives it to Edwin as Rosa's intended. The ring thus passes from one generation to the next and one hand to the next, outliving the dead and demonstrating the transitory quality of human life, a point brought home by Mr Grewgious:

> See how bright these stones shine! . . . And yet the eyes that were so much brighter, and that so often looked upon them with a light and a proud heart, have been ashes among ashes, and dust among dust, some years! If I had any imagination . . . I might imagine that the lasting beauty of these stones was almost cruel. (MED, 144)

That the permanence of stone outlasts the evanescence of life is one point made by the jewels in the ring. "In their very beauty they were . . . almost a cruel satire on the loves, hopes, plans, of humanity, which are able to forecast nothing, and are so much brittle dust" (MED, 168). To highlight the ephemeral nature of human striving is thus one purpose of the ring, but this is a novel in which, ironically, stone is neither immutable nor inanimate, but is always in the process of being turned into something else, just as the walls of ancient Cloisterham find their way into the newer houses and gardens of today. Even jewelry is subject to the circularity of time.

> [Edwin] would restore [the stones] to [Rosa's] guardian when he came down; he in his turn would restore them to the cabinet from which he had unwillingly taken them; and there, like old letters or old vows, or other records of old aspirations come to nothing, they would be disregarded, until, being valuable, they were sold into circulation again, to repeat their former round.
>
> (MED, 168–9)

The impermanent quality of stone is further demonstrated by the young delinquent called Deputy, whose game is to throw stones at whatever he sees, including among his targets the stonemason Durdles and a pent-up sheep. Lacking a living victim, Deputy is quite as pleased to throw stones at the dead through the railings of the churchyard. It's all the same to him – stoning the living or stoning the dead, especially since "the tall headstones are sufficiently like themselves, on their beat in the dark, to justify the delicious fancy that they are hurt when hit" (MED, 276). Stone here stands for the living because it is a sign of the dead. Similarly the ring is an heirloom from a drowning victim to her daughter. It will also serve to identify the body of a murder victim. There is even a kind of life in stone, as when Durdles draws from the cold hard wall a spark "of that mysterious fire which lurks in everything" (MED, 156).

Durdles, the stonemason, is one of the the novel's two dubious artists (the other is the villain Jasper, who cannot sing a false note). Durdles is an artist of death, so closely identified with his creations that he is the same colour as the tombstones. He plays the part in this novel that Mr Venus does in *Our Mutual Friend*, and is portrayed with the same irony although with less affection. When he is in the graveyard, Durdles is "surrounded by his works, like a poplar [*sic*] Author" (MED, 73). Durdles is responsible for all the headstones in Cloisterham, and it is he who demonstrates that there is life within stone when he makes the round of the cathedral crypt sounding and tapping the walls to discover where the "old 'uns" are buried. Durdles's claim that he suffers from Tombatism, a disease brought on by a lifetime's exposure to tombs, is a joke with universal implications. In this novel of death, everything which lives will sooner or later suffer from this affliction.

If the ring symbolizes both death and the circularity of time, it
also has another metaphoric dimension. Dickens links it to the idea
of fate as embodied in a single link of a chain, an image which he
had used earlier in *Great Expectations*. Here the imagery is
universalized: "Among the mighty store of wonderful chains that
are forever forging, day and night, in the iron-works of time and
circumstance, there was one chain forged in the moment of that
small conclusion, riveted to the foundation of heaven and earth,
and gifted with invisible force to hold and drag" (MED, 169). The
overt reference is to Edwin's decision to hold onto the ring which
Grewgious had entrusted to him, even after the dissolution of his
betrothal to Rosa. But the further implications of these portentous
lines and their ramifications for the working out of the plot can
only be guessed at, because Dickens never lived to supply an ending. And so the meaning of this link which he expected eventually
to elucidate hangs forever in the air, subject to endless speculation
in a novel whose lack of closure turns all interpretation into
conjecture.

So to add to all of *Edwin Drood*'s many distortions of time there
is one other. Because it is unfinished *The Mystery of Edwin Drood*
must exist forever within the frame of cyclical time. It permanently
exists in the form of process rather than completion. Most of what
has been written about this novel has been an attempt to resolve
the mysteries of its plot, mysteries that doubtless would have been
far less intriguing had Dickens lived to explicate them. But he did
not live long enough to do that, with the result that what he has
bequeathed to all future generations of readers is a novel constantly
in the process of unraveling itself and never succeeding. There can
be no finer tribute to the notion of time as cyclical and incomplete.

A Few Last Words . . .

The foregoing has been an attempt to approach the vast edifice of Dickens's work from one particular point of view, rather like using a flashlight to illuminate a palace. Nevertheless, even a flashlight may illuminate, and it is my hope that my concentration on this oddly central and oddly marginal topic of heredity has cast some light on a hitherto little explored corner of the Dickensian mansion.

I began this project with the wish to determine what Dickens understood by heredity and why he was so insistent on drawing attention to hereditary relationships in his novels. Once begun, however, the subject assumed a complexity I had not anticipated. Certain things I had wondered about fell into place – for instance, why Dickens is so insistent on an absolute resemblance between parents and children. But other things – such as the link between hanging, dissection, and artistry – diverse matters which I would never have thought to yoke together before, suddenly acquired a vital connection, once filtered through the thematics of heredity. In fact, the closer I looked, the more complex and intriguing the subject of heredity became, and the broader its potential scope, both literary and philosophical.

What was more, because heredity sits on the thin edge between science and popular belief, it permitted an approach to literature from a point of view outside the purely literary. Investigating nineteenth-century attitudes made studying heredity's equivocal position *vis-à-vis* science and culture all the more rewarding, because I was looking at a time when the actual mechanics of genetic transmission were unknown. This meant that there was no firm division between what was known and what was conjectured; all propositions were equally viable – and all were grist for Dickens's mill.

My general thesis has been that Dickens's attitude towards heredity changed as he matured and his career evolved, that he forsook the simple determinism of his early novels, in which he defined identity as a thing inborn, wholly subject to bloodline and impervious to external conditions. I have tried to show that this rather simple view of human nature – or more specifically, of the nature of the protagonist – gave way to a more complex formulation in such novels from Dickens's middle period as *Dombey and Son* and *David*

Copperfield, until, under the impetus of the Darwinian revolution, Dickens forsook heredity altogether as a factor in the formation of the self.

The great Dickensian motif of the middle novels, that of connection, of hidden threads of relationship running through all strands of society, represents a broadening of the metaphoric potential of heredity. The hidden consanguinity of Hugh the Bastard and John Chester the nobleman in *Barnaby Rudge* expands metaphorically in *Dombey and Son*, and yet again in *A Tale of Two Cities*. But under the influence of Darwin, Dickens lost both interest and faith in heredity, and his novels forsake this theme of hidden connection and interrelation. In *Great Expectations*, this results in a demonstration that what binds one human being to another is a share in the same elemental nature. In *Our Mutual Friend* and *The Mystery of Edwin Drood*, the notion of integrity usually associated with heredity is replaced by images of dissolution and disintegration.

This, in broad outline, is what I have argued in the preceding chapters. What remains unexpressed under all attempts at cool analytic prose is the debt that any one reader owes to any one writer. That essentially is what I feel for Dickens – a gratitude for his having constructed such a huge pleasure palace for the likes of me to wander in, and, what is more, for having done it with the most vibrant, imaginative and sparkling prose in the language, so that each rereading of each heavy tome is always more of a delight than a burden.

Notes

All references to and quotations from Dickens's novels are to the following Penguin editions and are noted in the text:

The Pickwick Papers (PP) (1986)
Oliver Twist (OT) (1985)
Nicholas Nickleby (NN) (1986)
The Old Curiosity Shop (OCS) (1985)
Barnaby Rudge (BR) (1984)
Martin Chuzzlewit (MC) (1985)
Dombey and Son (DS) (1984)
David Copperfield (DC) (1986)
Bleak House (BH) (1986)
Hard Times (HT) (1982)
Little Dorrit (LD) (1985)
A Tale of Two Cities (TTC) (1985)
Great Expectations (GE) (1987)
Our Mutual Friend (OMF) (1977)
The Mystery of Edwin Drood (MED) (1980)

Chapter 1   Whatever Lives Inherits: a Historical Overview of the Hereditary Puzzle

1   Q. D. Leavis, "Dickens and Tolstoy: The Case for a Serious View of David Copperfield," *Dickens the Novelist* (Harmondsworth: Penguin, 1983), 87.
2   The relevant quote is from Leviticus 19: 19: "Thou shalt not let thy cattle gender with a diverse kind: thou shalt not sow thy field with two kinds of seeds." Deuteronomy 22: 9–11 makes a similar point. These injunctions against mixing are in keeping with the Hebrew Bible's general tendency to guard the distinctness of things and to define mixing as a form of contamination. The laws of kashrut and the prohibition against wearing clothing made from two varieties of fabric are other examples of this.
3   Until the end of the Enlightenment, medical science considered the female orgasm as indispensable to ensure conception. See Thomas Laqueur, *Making Sex: Body and Gender from the Greeks to Freud* (Cambridge, MA: Harvard University Press, 1990), 2–3, 45–6.
4   Quoted in Laqueur, 47.
5   Quoted in Laqueur, 56.
6   For a fuller discussion of Aristotle's views on generation and anatomy, see Laqueur, 28–32.

7 Michel Eyquem de Montaigne, *Essays*, I, 8, vol. I trans. E. J. Trechmann (Oxford: Oxford University Press, 1927), 26.

8 Sir William Harvey, "Introduction," *On the Generation of Animals*, in *Great Books of the Western World*, vol. 28, ed R. M. Hutchins (Chicago: University of Chicago Press, 1952), 331.

9 This is the general thesis of Laqueur's book. For more on the confusions of nomenclature for male and female reproductive organs, see Laqueur, 4–5, 96–7.

10 François Jacob, *The Logic of Life: A History of Heredity*, trans. Betty E. Spillmann (New York: Pantheon, 1973), 20.

11 Jacob, 21.

12 Quoted in Jacob, 26.

13 See Marvin Carlson, "Ibsen, Strindberg, and Telegony," *PMLA*, 100, 5 (October 1985), 774. Marie-Hélène Huet's *Monstrous Imagination* (Cambridge, MA: Harvard University Press, 1993) provides a detailed examination of the belief in maternal impressions, extending the implications of this theory into the realm of artistic and literary endeavor in the nineteenth century. The information on Empedocles may be found on page 4 of her book.

14 Maggie Kilgour speaks of a "crude system of values" which defines what is outside the territory of the self as bad, and what is inside as good, a polarization which may be expanded to comprehend more sophisticated notions of social inclusion and exclusion. Maggie Kilgour, *From Communion to Cannibalism: An Anatomy of Metaphors of Incorporation* (Princeton, NJ: Princeton University Press, 1990), 4.

15 Jacob, 27.

16 For more on this, see Jacob, 28.

17 Jacob, 33. There were, of course, those who dissented from the prevailing view: the eighteenth-century French scientist and man-of-letters Bernard le Bovier de Fontenelle took exception to the idea that living things were machines. He suggested that if a dog machine were placed next to a bitch machine, the result would eventually be a puppy machine, but if two watches were placed side by side they would never, in all their lives, yield a third. Fontenelle is quoted in Jacob, 63.

18 Elizabeth B. Gasking, *Investigations into Generation 1651–1828* (Baltimore, MD: Johns Hopkins University Press, 1967), 42.

19 For a detailed account of the intellectual and ideological conflict between the ovists, who believed the germ was located in the egg, and the animalcultists, see Clara Pinto-Correia, *The Ovary of Eve: Egg and Sperm and Preformation* (Chicago: University of Chicago Press, 1997).

20 Peter Bowler, *Evolution: The History of an Idea* (Los Angeles: University of California Press, 1989), 30.

21 Stephen J. Gould, *The Flamingo's Smile: Reflections in Natural History* (New York: Norton, 1985), 144. For a more extensive late twentieth-century defense of the theory of preformation, see Clara Pinto-Correia's *The Ovary of Eve: Egg and Sperm and Preformation*.

22 The story appears in Jacob, 54.

23 Jacob, 62.

24 Gasking, 124.

25 Quoted in Gasking, 76.
26 In his essay on Maupertuis and *Vénus physique*, Stephen Jay Gould rejects
    the idea that Maupertuis was a precursor of Darwin, calling it "an un-
    fair and anachronistic assessment, based on a few fleeting passages that
    abstract Maupertuis from the concerns of his time." See Gould, "For
    Want of a Metaphor," *The Flamingo's Smile: Reflections in Natural His-
    tory*, 142.
27 Gasking suggests that the majority of the particulate theories which
    appeared after 1750 were variants of Buffon's views. Particulate inherit-
    ance implies the transmission to offspring of distinctive traits from both
    the father and the mother. See Gasking, 91.
28 Gould, "For Want of a Metaphor," *The Flamingo's Smile: Reflections in
    Natural History*, 143. For more on the difference between these two theories
    see Clara Pinto-Correia's *The Ovary of Eve: Egg and Sperm and Preformation*.
29 Jacob, 85.
30 Gasking, 149–50.
31 For more on the difference between these two camps, see Gould, "Just in
    the Middle," in *The Flamingo's Smile: Reflections in Natural History*, 377–92.
32 For more on the effects of Romanticism on the study of biology see
    J. A. V. Chapple, *Science and Literature in the Nineteenth Century* (London:
    Macmillan, 1986), 3; see also Gasking, 161.
33 Loren Eiseley, *Darwin's Century* (New York: Anchor, 1961), 8.
34 An English rabbi, writing in the early twentieth century, suggested that
    Jews had particular reason to doubt the inheritance of acquired charac-
    teristics since Jewish fathers in every generation have been circumcised,
    yet Jewish sons continue to be born with foreskins. See W. M. Feldman,
    The Jewish Child: Its History, Folklore, Biology and Sociology (London: Baillière,
    Tindall, Cox, 1917).
       In fact, however, the theory has not yet been laid to rest, and there
    is new evidence that it is not necessarily false under all circumstances.
    Viruses, for instance, may inject themselves into the genetic material
    of a bacterium and be passed along to offspring as part of the bacterial
    chromosome. See Stephen J. Gould, "Shades of Lamarck," *The Panda's
    Thumb: More Reflections in Natural History* (New York: Norton, 1980),
    79. An article by John Rennie, "DNA's New Twists" in *Scientific Ameri-
    can* (March, 1993), 122–32, makes a similar point, arguing that when it
    comes to the inheritance of acquired characteristics, science has been
    guilty of throwing the baby out with the bath water. See also, in the
    same issue, a brief essay by Otto Landman, "Inheritance of Acquired
    Characteristics," p. 150. Landman writes that the abuses of the Soviet
    scientist Trofim Lysenko, who exploited Lamarck's ideas of inheritance
    for ideological purposes, have so prejudiced modern scientists against
    the theory of acquired characteristics that they "refuse to recognize
    that an understanding of the role of acquired characteristics opens a
    perspective on genetics and evolution."
35 Gasking dates the obsolescence of the term "generation" from the begin-
    ning of the nineteenth century. Gasking, 7.
36 The word first occurs in a memoir by Réaumur published in 1712, where
    it is applied to the regeneration of amputated limbs. This meaning was

retained throughout the eighteenth century. Buffon was the first to use "reproduction" to mean generation in general in his *Natural History of Animals* (1748), although he too retained its more specific use for the reconstitution of amputated limbs.

37 Desmond also attributes Darwin's secrecy during this decade to the contentious atmosphere surrounding all questions of origin and evolution. See Adrian Desmond, *The Politics of Evolution* (Chicago: University of Chicago Press, 1989), 2–3.

38 In 1819, Sir William Lawrence, co-founder of the medical journal *The Lancet* and the man credited with introducing the word "biology" into English, caused a furor when he published two volumes of lectures in which he equated the existence of races among humans with the breeds found among domestic animals. Using this analogy, Lawrence argued that all human races are merely different strains within one species. He also asserted that the human brain functioned on principles identical to those of animal brains. Both claims came dangerously close to asserting that humans were merely another form of animal. The storm of controversy that followed forced Lawrence to suppress his own book. For more on Lawrence, see Kentwood Wells, "Sir William Lawrence (1783–1867): A Study of Pre-Darwinian Ideas on Heredity and Variation" in *Journal of the History of Biology*, 4, 2 (Fall 1971), 324.

39 Jacob, 190.

40 See John Farley's *Gametes and Spores: Ideas about Sexual Reproduction 1750–1914* (Baltimore, MD: Johns Hopkins University Press, 1982), and especially the chapter, "The Cult of Sexlessness."

41 See Farley, 111.

42 J. Hillis Miller, *The Form of Victorian Fiction* (Notre Dame, IN: University of Notre Dame Press, 1970), 65.

43 For a detailed account of the contentious atmosphere in scientific circles during the early decades of the nineteenth century, which reached its climax in the 1830s, see Adrian Desmond, *The Politics of Evolution*. Desmond is particularly instructive with regard to the political ramifications of these scientific struggles, especially the attempt to democratize the entrenched and reactionary medical establishment of Oxbridge.

44 See Lois N. Magner, *A History of the Life Sciences* (New York: Marcel Dekker, 1979), 406–7.

45 Leonard Barkan, *The Gods Made Flesh* (New Haven, CT: Yale University Press, 1986), 89.

46 Gillian Beer, *Darwin's Plots* (London: Ark Paperbacks, 1985), 111.

47 See Kilgour, 41.

48 M. M. Bakhtin, "Forms of Time and of the Chronotope in the Novel," *The Dialogic Imagination* (Austin: University of Texas Press, 1981), 90.

49 Bakhtin, 95.

50 Quoted in Laqueur, 57–8.

51 "Genealogy," *Encyclopedia Judaica*, 1972 edn.

52 When François Jacob claims that not until the Darwinian revolution had time been measured by generations, he is clearly in error. The idea of a generation as a measurement of time is as old as the Bible itself. See Jacob, 171.

53 *Brewer's Dictionary of Phrase and Fable* (revised edn) (London: Cassell, 1965), 833.
54 Beer, 63.

Chapter 2   The Inheritance of Goodness: the Early Books

1 John Carey, *The Violent Effigy* (London: Faber & Faber, 1973), 101.
2 Juliet McMaster, *Dickens the Designer* (Totowa, NJ: Barnes & Noble, 1987), 4–7.
3 Cates Baldridge suggests that Dickens is here grafting onto his middle-class characters the same concern with the preservation of "blue blood" as was current among the aristocracy. See Cates Baldridge, "The Instabilities of Inheritance in *Oliver Twist*," *Studies in the Novel*, 25 (1993), 189. It is certainly true that the plot of hidden identity which Dickens uses as the underpinning of *Oliver Twist* traditionally portrays royal lineage as the concealed element, for instance in the legend of Oedipus, or in Shakespeare's *The Winter's Tale*, where Princess Perdita is brought up by a shepherd. Baldridge's fine article is marred by the assumption that the Victorian understanding of heredity was similar to ours. This leads him into anachronisms. For instance, he refers repeatedly to "genetic inheritance" and "geneticism" during the course of his discussion. The term "gene" does not occur prior to the twentieth century – the OED gives 1917 as its earliest citation. The modern sense of the word "genetics," which refers to the theory of particulate inheritance, likewise dates from the twentieth century. While Carlyle and Darwin both used "genetic," their meaning was closer to the meaning of generation than to what we mean by the term today.
4 See Stephen Kern, "Explosive Intimacy: Psychodynamics of the Victorian Family," *The New Psychohistory* (New York: Psychohistory Press, 1975), 31.
5 Author's preface to *Oliver Twist* (Penguin, 1985), 33.
6 Kerry McSweeney uses this same scene to indicate Dickens's lack of sophistication in handling memory in *Oliver Twist*, since the only rational explanation of Oliver's sense of connection to the painting of his mother is to posit that he remembers her face from infancy. See McSweeney, "*David Copperfield* and the Music of Memory," *Dickens Studies Annual*, 23 (New York: AMS Press, 1994), 98. I would suggest, however, that the instinctive connection that Oliver feels towards the portrait has less to do with an actual memory than with the boy's intuitive sense that he is in the reproduced presence of someone to whom he is intimately connected.
7 Marie-Hélène Huet suggests that the link between painting and procreation is part of an ancient tradition according to which works of art are privileged metaphors for the process of generation. See Marie-Hélène Huet, *Monstrous Imagination* (Cambridge, MA: Harvard University Press, 1993), 96.
8 See Kern, 31–2.

9 Quoted in Kentwood Wells, "Sir William Lawrence (1783–1867). A Study of Pre-Darwinian Ideas on Heredity and Variation," in *Journal of the History of Biology*, 4, 2 (Fall 1971), 323.

10 McMaster, *Designer*, 4–5.

11 McMaster, *Designer*, 45.

12 A similar point about the transforming effect of clothes on identity is made in chapter 6 of *Dombey and Son*, when Florence's rich clothes are stolen by Good Mrs Brown and Florence is made to dress in rags instead. The wealthy but neglected Florence dressed in rags is a living embodiment of the poor little rich girl. For more on this, see Harry Stone, *Dickens and the Invisible World* (Bloomington: Indiana University Press, 1979), 181.

For a fascinating essay on the significance of pocket handkerchiefs in *Oliver Twist*, which he sees as Dickens's attempt to articulate "a philosophy of clothing," see John O. Jordan's "The Purloined Handkerchief," in *Dickens Studies Annual*, 18 (New York: AMS Press, 1989), 1–17.

13 Baldridge, 190.

14 See Huet, 217. Marie Tussaud died in 1850, which means that she was still very much alive when Dickens was writing *The Old Curiosity Shop*.

15 Huet, 217.

16 All quotes are from Steven Marcus, *Dickens from Pickwick to Dombey* (New York: Norton, 1965), 162.

17 McMaster, *Designer*, 112.

18 See Patricia Marks, "Dombey and the Milk of Human Kindness," *Dickens Quarterly*, 11, 1 (March 1994), 16.

19 Catherine Waters, "Ambiguous Intimacy: Brother and Sister Relationships in *Dombey and Son*," *Dickensian*, 84 (Spring 1988), 11.

20 A more psychological interpretation of the effects of his mother on Paul's personality can be found in Joseph A. Boone and Deborah E. Nord, "Brother and Sister: The Seductions of Siblinghood in Dickens, Eliot and Brontë," *Western Humanities Review*, 46, 2 (1992), 169–70.

21 For more on Dickens's decision to allow Little Nell to die, see Malcolm Andrews, "Introduction" to *The Old Curiosity Shop* (Harmondsworth: Penguin, 1985), 14.

22 Marcus, 351–2. Marcus suggests that the difference in the way grace functions in *Oliver Twist* and in *Dombey and Son* indicates a difference in Dickens's conception of God. That may be, but my own feeling is that what has changed is the way Dickens conceives of heredity.

23 Marks, 17.

24 See Lawrence Stone, *The Family, Sex and Marriage* (New York: Harper & Row, 1979), 160. See also Harriet Ritvo, *The Animal Estate* (Cambridge: Harvard University Press, 1987) on the enthusiasm for livestock breeding in the nineteenth century and the abuses to which this could lead, such as cattle so heavy they could scarcely support their own weight. The idea of choosing a mate with regard to bloodline is not new. As noted in Chapter 1, the Talmud was advocating just such an approach almost two thousand years ago. What does seem to have changed by the early nineteenth century was a new awareness of the potential for

  manipulating heredity to produce certain specific qualities through the breeding of animals, and consequently of humans.

25 See Harry Stone, *Dickens and the Invisible World*, 148, 166.

26 Barbara Leckie, *Infidelity, the Novel and the Law* (unpublished diss., McGill University, 1991), 34, 37.

27 Quoted in Bernard Grebanier, *The Truth About Shylock* (New York: Random House, 1962), 79.

28 This is the point made by Boone and Nord who argue that *Dombey and Son* is not so much a critique of patriarchal values as an attempt to reform them through harnessing Florence's reproductive powers to the dynastic cause. See Boone and Nord, 171.

29 Kathleen Tillotson, *Novels of the Eighteen-Forties* (Oxford: Clarendon Press, 1965), 108.

30 In his 1882 treatise on hereditary traits, Richard Proctor notes that Roman family names were doubly hereditary: not only did they serve to designate the line of descent, but they also enshrined certain physical characteristics as being hereditary within a particular family. For instance, the Nasones (the Big-nosed), the Labeones (the Thick-lipped), the Capitones (the Big-headed) and the Buccones (the Swollen-cheeked). Richard A. Proctor, "Hereditary Traits," *Humboldt Library of Popular Science Literature*, II, 32 (May, 1882), 2.

31 Dianne Sadoff, *Monsters of Affection* (Baltimore, MD: Johns Hopkins University Press, 1982), 60.

Chapter 3 The Inheritance of Goodness: David Copperfield and Pip

1 Alexander Welsh suggests that Dickens's emphasis on the private domain in *David Copperfield* is an attempt to direct attention away from the real theme of his novel, which is the rise of a successful man despite unpromising beginnings. In this reading, David's unhappy childhood may be seen as the attempt to justify the ambition and success of his adult self. See Welsh, *From Copyright to Copperfield* (Cambridge, MA: Harvard University Press, 1987), 158.

2 Of a young man who had fallen into his father's weaknesses without having had the possibility of observing them for imitation, Dickens wrote: "It suggests the strangest consideration as to which of our failings we are really responsible for, and as to which of them we cannot quite reasonably hold ourselves to be so. What A. evidently derives from his father cannot in his case be derived from association and observation, but must be in the very principles of his individuality as a living creature." Quoted in Q. D. Leavis, "Dickens and Tolstoy: The Case for a Serious View of David Copperfield," *Dickens the Novelist* (Harmondsworth: Penguin, 1983), 87–88.

3 The theme of the symbiotic relationship between the dead and the living fascinated Dickens. In 1846, three years before he began serialization of *David Copperfield*, he had written a Christmas book called "The Battle of Life," which is set on an ancient battlefield, now over-

grown and planted with crops. The field owes its unusual fertility to the decomposed bodies of the men and horses buried beneath the growing corn. In *The Night Side of Dickens* (Columbus: Ohio State University Press, 1994), Harry Stone relates this motif of the living battening on the dead to the theme of cannibalism. See Stone, 236–40.

4 Leavis also suggests that David Copperfield's is "a typical male history of that age" (Leavis, 81). It should be noted, however, that it was not typical of Dickens himself, who did not feel particularly close to his mother.

5 Stephen Kern, "Explosive Intimacy: Psychodynamics of the Victorian Family," *The New Psychohistory* (New York: Psychohistory Press, 1975), 39.

6 Joseph Bottum suggests that Murdstone's similarity to David is deepened when we remember that he is left unpunished at the novel's end. See Bottum, "The Gentleman's True Name: David Copperfield and the Philosophy of Naming," *Nineteenth-Century Literature*, 49, 4 (March 1995), 448.

7 In *Parallel Lives: Five Victorian Marriages* (New York: Vintage, 1984), Phyllis Rose notes that *David Copperfield* begins with David asking whether he will turn out to be hero of his own life and ends by making it clear that his wife plays that role. See Rose, 132.

8 Leavis, 82.

9 See Harry Stone, *Dickens and the Invisible World* (Bloomington, IN: Indiana University Press, 1979), 250.

10 Welsh, *Copyright*, 181.

11 Peter Brooks reads Magwitch as "the fearful intrusive figure of future authorship," while Pip himself represents "an existence without a plot," who is necessarily in search of one. Brooks therefore interprets what I call the "tabula rasa" of Pip's identity as an empty page eventually filled by Magwitch. This, of course, would make Magwitch a stand-in for Dickens himself and imply a correlation between authorship and criminality. See Peter Brooks, *Reading for the Plot: Design and Intention in Narrative* (New York: Knopf, 1984), 116–17.

12 It has become a critical commonplace to identify guilt as the crux of *Great Expectations*. One of the most influential views on this topic was articulated by Dorothy Van Ghent in her 1953 essay "On *Great Expectations*" in *The English Novel: Form and Function* (New York: Harper Torchbooks, 1953). There Van Ghent argued that Magwitch functions in the novel as the objective correlative for Pip's sense of guilt. Since then, other principals in the novel have been identified as alter egos for Pip. Julian Moynahan nominates Orlick to play this role in "The Hero's Guilt: The Case of *Great Expectations*" in *Essays in Criticism*, 10 (1960), 60–79. Shuli Barzilai in "Dickens's *Great Expectations*: The Motive for Moral Masochism," in *Modern Critical Views: Charles Dickens* (New York: Chelsea House, 1987) suggests Estella. Such interpretations are primarily psychological and literary in nature; they tend to slight the novel's rather explicit criticism of religion as the source of Pip's overwhelming feeling of guilt.

13 In the early Victorian years, wealth alone did not guarantee the status

of gentleman. It was necessary also to be independent, so that those who lived off investments and property most readily received the title. In the mid-Victorian period the term disintegrated as a description of social position, becoming vague in specific application, and coming to denote, more generally, social approval and moral approbation, usually combined with a reasonably comfortable income. For more on the changing history of the term "gentleman" during the nineteenth century, see Geoffrey Crossick, "From Gentlemen to the Residium: Languages of Social Description in Victorian Britain" in *Language, History and Class* (London: Blackwell, 1991), 163–4.

14 Northrop Frye suggests that Magwitch's symbolic paternity of Pip and his actual fathering of Estella turn Pip and Estella into siblings and this was the reason why Dickens was so reluctant to let the two marry. See Frye, "Dickens and the Comedy of Humours," *The Victorian Novel* (London: Oxford University Press, 1971), 61.

Chapter 4   Illegitimacy and Villainy: the Negative Aspects of Heredity

1 The statistics come from Walter Houghton, *The Victorian Frame of Mind, 1830–1870* (New Haven, CT: Yale University Press, 1985), 366. In *The Demoralization of Society: From Victorian Virtues to Modern Values* (New York: Knopf, 1995), 253n, Gertrude Himmelfarb suggests that the rate of illegitimacy peaked at 7 per cent of the population in 1845.

2 Thomas Laqueur, *Making Sex: Body and Gender from the Greeks to Freud* (Cambridge, MA: Harvard University Press, 1990), 56.

3 Marie-Hélène Huet, *Monstrous Imagination* (Cambridge, MA: Harvard University Press, 1993), 79–82.

4 Steven Marcus, *Dickens from Pickwick to Dombey* (New York: Norton, 1965), 86.

5 See Françoise Barret-Ducrocq, *Love in the Time of Victoria: Sexuality and Desire among Working-Class Men and Women in Nineteenth-Century London*, trans. John Howe (New York: Penguin, 1991), 156.

6 David Grylls, *Guardians and Angels: Parents and Children in Nineteenth-Century Literature* (London: Faber & Faber, 1978), 145.

7 Grylls, 145.

8 Juliet McMaster, *Dickens the Designer* (Totowa, NJ: Barnes & Noble, 1987), 174.

9 For just one example of such an interruption, see chapter 16:

> What connexion can there be, between the place in Lincolnshire, the house in town, the Mercury in powder, and the whereabout of Jo the outlaw with the broom, who had that distant ray of light upon him when he swept the churchyard-step? What connexion can there have been between many people in the innumerable histories of this world, who, from opposite sides of great gulfs, have, nevertheless, been curiously brought together!   (BH, 272)

10 Quoted in John Farley, *Gametes and Spores: Ideas about Sexual Reproduction 1750–1914* (Baltimore, MD: Johns Hopkins University Press, 1982), 63.

11 See Margaret Derry, "Contemporary Attempts to Understand the Cattle Plague of 1865," *Victorian Studies Association Newsletter*, 54 (Fall 1994), 8–13.

12 See Maura Spiegel, "Managing Pain: Suffering and Reader Sympathy in *Bleak House*," *Dickens Quarterly*, 12, 1 (March 1995), 8.

13 Quoted in Barret-Ducrocq, 20.

14 Dickens claimed to be a realist in his fiction, which may account for his insistence on the scientific validity of spontaneous combustion. As George Levine notes, it is strange that "such coherent symbolic significances should seem to require from Dickens a defense of literal truth." George Levine, *Darwin and the Novelists* (Cambridge, MA: Harvard University Press, 1988), 133.

15 The line comes in a speech by Mr Meagles. Meagles is trying to persuade Miss Wade not to inveigle the orphan Tattycoram away from her home with the Meagleses: "If it should happen that you are a woman, who, from whatever cause, has a perverted delight in making a sister-woman as wretched as she is (I am old enough to have heard of such), I warn her against you, and I warn you against yourself" (LD, 379).

16 To take one example, Richard Proctor, writing on hereditary traits in 1882, suggested that the habit of throwing the right leg over the left during sleep was inherited. See Richard A. Proctor, "Hereditary Traits," *Humboldt Library of Popular Science Literature*, II, 32 (May 1882), 8–9.

17 Angus Wilson, in his introduction to the Penguin edition of *Oliver Twist* (p. 25) asserts that Monks suffers from epilepsy, but Baldridge makes as good a case for syphilis. See Cates Baldridge, "The Instabilities of Inheritance in *Oliver Twist*," *Studies in the Novel*, 25 (1993), 192.

18 Kern, 31.

19 Philip Collins, *Dickens and Crime* (Bloomington: Indiana University Press, 1968), 283.

Chapter 5 Heredity, Class, and Race

1 The symbolic nature of the riot leaders has been noted by many commentators. See, for instance, Philip Collins, *Dickens and Crime* (Bloomington, IN: Indiana University Press, 1968), 45. Steven Marcus suggests that the combination of "malice, reactionary impulse and general resentment of whatever is" is a characteristic quality of English radical movements. Steven Marcus, *Dickens from Pickwick to Dombey* (New York: Norton, 1965), 181.

2 In her reading of *Barnaby Rudge* as a meditation on unconscious processes, Juliet McMaster lists the many times in the novel when Hugh can be found sleeping, including the time when he is roused by the sound of the workmen building the gallows on which he is to hang. Juliet McMaster, "'Better To Be Silly': From Vision to Reality in *Barnaby Rudge*," *Dickens Studies Annual*, 13 (1984), 5–6.

3   Northrop Frye, "Dickens and the Comedy of Humours," *The Victorian Novel* Ed. Ian Watt (London: Oxford University Press, 1971), 51.

4   The words are Harry Stone's in *The Night Side of Dickens: Cannibalism, Passion, Necessity*. (Columbus, OH: Ohio State University Press, 1994), 228.

5   There has been a trend among recent writers on Dickens to emphasize his conservatism, his lack of sympathy with the oppressed whenever they threatened to turn their grievances into social agitation. This highlighting of Dickens's conservative tendencies started with Edmund Wilson's *The Wound and The Bow* (New York: Farrar, Straus, Giroux, 1929). Philip Collins's *Dickens and Crime* continued the trend, arguing that Dickens had little sympathy for criminals of any stripe. But Dickens has been just as frequently hailed as a liberal and even as a Marxist. See Simon David Trezise, "The Making of Dickens: The Evolution of Marxist Criticism," *Dickens Quarterly*, 11 (September 1994), 127–37.

6   See Marcus, "Sons and Fathers," in *From Pickwick to Dombey*, 169–213. In his biography of Dickens, Peter Ackroyd suggests that the theme of fathers and sons is so prominent in *Barnaby Rudge* because of the problems that Dickens was having with his own father at the time when he was writing the novel. John Dickens had been giving his famous son's name as security for loans, and Dickens was obliged to take out advertisements denying all responsibility for his father's debts. Ackroyd further suggests that it is no accident that the two most reprehensible fathers in the novel, John Willet and John Chester, both have the same given name as Dickens's father. Peter Ackroyd, *Dickens* (New York: HarperCollins, 1990), 324.

7   Charles Darwin, *The Variation of Animals and Plants under Domestication* (New York: D. Appleton, 1892), II, 19–21.

8   Marie-Hélène Huet, *Monstrous Imagination* (Cambridge, MA: Harvard University Press, 1993), 72.

9   Benjamin Disraeli, *Sybil* (Harmondsworth: Penguin, 1980), 96.

10 Sheila Smith, *The Other Nation* (Oxford: Clarendon, 1980), 70.

11 This is in contrast to the dishonest poor who "won't work." Quoted in Smith, 40.

12 Dickens spells out this attitude in the following exchange between Rosa Dartle and Steerforth from *David Copperfield*:

> "That sort of people – Are they really animals and clods, and beings of another order? I want to know *so* much."
>
> "Why, there's a pretty wide separation between them and us," said Steerforth, with indifference. "They are not to be expected to be as sensitive as we are. Their delicacy is not to be shocked, or hurt easily . . . They have not very fine natures, and they may be thankful that, like their coarse rough skins, they are not easily wounded."
>
> "Really!" said Miss Dartle, "Well, I don't know, now, when I have been better pleased than to hear that. It's so consoling! It's such a delight to know that when they suffer, they don't feel!"   (DC, 352)

13 Dickens's rendition of the scene in which Polly Toodle is interviewed

as a wet-nurse is an accurate depiction of how wet-nurses were hired, as Dickens had reason to know from personal experience. His wife employed wet-nurses for two of their ten children. See Margaret Wiley, "Mother's Milk and Dombey's Son," *Dickens Quarterly*, 13, 4 (December 1996), 223. According to the manuals of the time, the wet-nurse's milk should be examined for color and taste, and her baby for signs of illness. Above all, the manual-writers agreed that the moral qualities and temperament of the wet-nurse were of primary importance, lest her milk transmit undesirable qualities to the foster child. See Patricia Marks, "Paul Dombey and the Milk of Human Kindness," *Dickens Quarterly*, 11, 1 (March 1994), 20.

14 The phrase is from *The Politics and Poetics of Transgression*. For more on the middle-class Victorians' fear of contamination in public places, see Peter Stallybrass and Allon White, *The Politics and Poetics of Transgression* (Ithaca, NY: Cornell University Press, 1986), 136.

15 Writing in 1858, Dr William Acton noted that the world of prostitution represented a microcosm of society at large. "Prostitutes maintain their notions of caste and quality with all the pertinacity of their betters. The greatest amount of income procurable, with the least amount of exertion is with them, as with society, the grand gauge of position." Quoted in Marcus, *The Other Victorians* (New York: Basic Books, 1966), 7. In *Reading for the Plot; Design and Intention in Narrative* (New York: Knopf, 1984) Peter Brooks lists similar attitudes and gradations among French prostitutes, 157–8.

16 Quoted in Patricia Ingham, *Dickens, Women and Language* (Toronto: University of Toronto Press, 1992), 41.

17 Françoise Barret-Ducrocq attributes this to the gradual withdrawal of middle-class women from active life which started in the eighteenth century and ended with the virtual seclusion of middle-class women in the nineteenth. See Barret-Ducrocq, *Love in the Time of Victoria* (New York: Penguin, 1991), 10. For more on the immorality of street life for women, see Catherine Gallagher "The Body Versus the Social Body in Malthus and Mayhew," *The Making of the Modern Body: Sexuality and Society in the Nineteenth Century* (Berkeley: University of California Press, 1987), 101.

18 See Brooks, 157.

19 See Thomas Laqueur, *Making Sex: Body and Gender from the Greeks to Freud* (Cambridge, MA: Harvard University Press, 1990), 232.

20 I am borrowing the term from Dianne F. Sadoff, *Monsters of Affection*, (Baltimore, MD: Johns Hopkins University Press, 1982), 13.

21 The passage from *Little Dorrit* runs as follows:

> There was a classical daughter once – perhaps – who ministered to her father in his prison as her mother had ministered to her. Little Dorrit, though of the unheroic modern stock and mere English, did much more, in comforting her father's wasted heart upon her innocent breast, and turning to it a fountain of love and fidelity that never ran dry or waned through all his years of famine.
>
> (LD, 273–4)

This passage has excited much comment among feminist critics: Dianne Sadoff writes: "The metaphor of nursing sexualizes the father–daughter relationship, makes the father dependent on the daughter, and upsets the generations. Daughter becomes mother to her father." Sadoff, 56.

Patricia Ingham points to the passage as an extreme expression of one of Dickens's favourite metaphoric indulgences, that of comparing nubile girls to food and so defining them as edible. She also makes the point that Dickens's description of Amy Dorrit emphasizes her asexuality. Amy is "little" and at 22 could pass for 11. She is hardly representative of the maternal type which the passage seems to evoke. See Ingham, 121. For more on the imagery of the breast in Dickens, see Paul Schacht, "Dickens and the Uses of Nature," *Victorian Studies*, 34, 1 (Autumn 1990), 87–92.

22   Dianne Sadoff suggests that Dr Manette returns from the dead, not only because he is recalled by his daughter, but narratively and structurally to punish his son-in-law for the sins of his father. Sadoff, 14.

23   For a more psychological reading of what he calls "splitting" in *A Tale of Two Cities*, see Albert D. Hutter, "Nation and Generation in *A Tale of Two Cities*," *PMLA*, 93, 2 (May 1978), 455–8. The discussion of duality in Dickens has been a critical staple going back to Edmund Wilson's classic study "Dickens: The Two Scrooges" in *The Wound and the Bow* (New York: Farrar, Straus, Giroux, 1978). Wilson noted that Dickens always supplied a good and a bad version of every character, often within the same novel. See especially, p. 53.

24   For more on this, see Hutter, 457.

25   In his 1859 preface to *A Tale of Two Cities*, Dickens wrote that he got the idea for the novel from *The Frozen Deep*, the play which he co-wrote with Wilkie Collins. In that play, the hero sacrifices his life to save the future husband of the woman he loves. However, Albert Hutter suggests an alternative source for Carton's actions. This was the incident, recounted in Carlyle's *The French Revolution* – a book which Dickens used as his source for *A Tale of Two Cities* – in which General Loiseroilles died at the guillotine in place of his son. Carlyle suggested that the father had sacrificed himself in order to ensure that the son might live and grow. Carton's assumption that he will live on in his namesakes implies a similar idea and furthers the novel's thematic concern with resurrection and regeneration. See Hutter, 460 n14.

26   The term "race" originally meant a group of persons, animals, or plants connected by common descent, making it a synonym for "stock," "house," "family," or "kindred" (OED). However, it also has a general application to all people of a particular kind, classified according to certain physical, cultural, or ethnic attributes – the races which make up the human race. For a history of the term, especially the confusions of the nineteenth century, see Raymond Williams, *Keywords* (London: Fontana Press, 1983), 248–50.

27   Gillian Beer has suggested that for many Victorian writers the fascination with race was essentially a fascination with class, since both categories raise similar questions of descent, genealogy, mobility, the possibility of development and transformation. Gillian Beer, *Darwin's Plots: Evolu-*

tionary Narrative in Darwin, George Eliot and Nineteenth-Century Fiction (London: Routledge & Kegan Paul, 1983), 202.

28 Patricia Marks suggests that the Major's treatment of his servant may be read as a representation in miniature of the British Empire's relationship to her laborers, both foreign and domestic. See Marks, 17–18.

29 See Lillian Nayder, "Class Consciousness and the Indian Mutiny in Dickens's "The Perils of Certain English Prisoners," *Studies in English Literature*, 32 (1992), 694.

30 Angus Wilson, "Introduction," *The Mystery of Edwin Drood* (Harmondsworth: Penguin, 1974), 25.

31 Charles Dickens, "The Noble Savage," *Selected Journalism: 1850–1870* (London: Penguin, 1997), 560.

32 Nayder, 694.

33 For more on Dickens's fascination with the subject of cannibalism, see the first section of Harry Stone, *The Night Side of Dickens: Cannibalism, Passion, Necessity.*

34 Quoted in Naman, *The Jew in the Victorian Novel* (New York: AMS Press, 1980), 60. For more on Mrs Davis's letter and its effect on Dickens's conception of *Our Mutual Friend*, see Edgar Johnson, *Charles Dickens: His Tragedy and Triumph*, vol. 2 (New York: Simon & Schuster, 1952), 1010–12. The seminal study of Dickens's treatment of the Jews in his fiction is Harry Stone's "Dickens and the Jews," *Victorian Studies*, 2, No. 3 (March 1959), 223–55.

35 For more on the relationship between the stage-typing of the Jew and the national stereotype, see Shearer West, "The Construction of Racial Type: Caricature, Ethnography, and Jewish Physiognomy in Fin-de-Siècle Melodrama," *Nineteenth Century Theatre*, 21, 1 (Summer 1993), 5–37.

36 In a long and provocative essay in *The New York Review of Books* (26 October 1989), Garry Wills suggests that Dickens intended Fagin to be a pederast. According to Wills, the popular anti-Semitism which Dickens assumed in his audience in the 1830s, and which he shared with it, served him as a cover for Fagin's homosexuality, a topic about which he could not write openly. In support of this theory, Wills notes that in later life Dickens removed from his reading text of "Sikes and Nancy" all suggestions that Fagin was a Jew, and that he partially erased the label "The Jew" from later editions of the novel: Wills, 64. For more on the excisions of the Jew label from *Oliver Twist*, see Stone, "Dickens and the Jews," 251–2.

37 Terry Eagleton, "Introduction," *Hard Times* (London: Methuen, 1987), 2.

38 See Stone, "Dickens and the Jews," 233.

39 See, among others, Collins, 262; Naman, 215–16 n5.

40 Juliet McMaster, *Dickens the Designer* (Totowa, NJ: Barnes and Noble Books, 1987), 193.

41 There are several father–daughter pairs in *Our Mutual Friend*: Rogue Riderhood and Pleasant; Mr Dolls and Jenny Wren; Gaffer Hexam and Lizzie Hexam; Reginald (Rumty) Wilfer and Bella Wilfer. But I am distinguishing a hereditary relationship from a familial one. With the exception of Pleasant's swivel eye, inherited from her father, none of

these father–daughter pairs is presented in terms of physical or emotional characteristics passed down from parent to child.

42 Mrs Davis, in thanking Dickens for Riah in a letter dated 13 November 1864, nevertheless drew his attention to certain anomalies with regard to the characterization. Among other things, she suggested that the phrase "generous Christian master" is uncharacteristic of Jews and that no Jew would ever say, as Riah does, "They curse me in Jehovah's name." Dickens clearly had not bothered to do much research into Jewish customs and traditions for his portrayal of Riah, but merely drew on positive stereotypes in much the same way as he had earlier drawn on negative ones for his portrayal of Fagin. His reply to Mrs Davis admitted as much: "The error you point out to me had occurred to me . . . But it will do no harm. The peculiarities of dress and manners are fixed together for the sake of picturesqueness." Quoted in Naman, 80–1.

43 West, 20.

44 This was another "Jewish" gesture which Mrs Davis called into question in her letter. See Naman, 81. The Jew in *Great Expectations*, in addition to using the supplicatory gesture also speaks with a lisp. This too was a convention taken from the stage, where it dated from the eighteenth century. West, 19 n23. The implication behind the convention was to emphasize the foreignness of the Jew by differentiating and mocking his ability to speak the language of the country.

45 Quoted in West, 8.

46 See West, 8–9.

47 Beer, 202–3.

48 Quoted in Beer, 203.

49 West, 8.

Chapter 6   After *The Origin*: the Last Three Novels

1 Charles Darwin, *The Origin of Species by Means of Natural Selection*, 6th edn (London: Watts & Co., 1929), 10.

2 See Thomas Laqueur, *Making Sex: Body and Gender from the Greeks to Freud* (Cambridge, MA: Harvard University Press, 1990), 39.

3 See Peter J. Bowler, *Evolution: The History of an Idea* (Berkeley, CA: University of California Press, 1984), 166.

4 Peter Morton, *The Vital Science: Biology and the Literary Imagination 1860–1900* (London: Allen & Unwin, 1985), 151.

5 For more on Lord Morton's mare, see Marvin Carlson, "Ibsen, Strindberg and Telegony," *PMLA*, 100, 5 (October 1985), 780.

6 See Bowler, 210.

7 Morton, 150.

8 Discussion of *The Origin* was intense during the year after its publication, and was not confined to scientific circles. *The Saturday Review* noted that the controversy had "passed beyond the bounds of the study and lecture-room into the drawing-room and the public street." Thomas Huxley's review of *The Origin* in the *Westminster Review* of April 1860 made a similar point, while George Henry Lewes, writing in *The Cornhill*,

asserted that "Darwin's book is in everyone's hands." All quotes above are from Alvard Ellegard, *Darwin and the General Reader* (Chicago: University of Chicago Press, 1990), 40–1.

9 Gillian Beer, *Darwin's Plots: Evolutionary Narrative in Darwin, George Eliot and Nineteenth-Century Fiction* (London: Routledge & Kegan Paul, 1983), 8. One of the seminal articles on Dickens's use of science in his novels is Ann Y. Wilkinson's *"Bleak House:* From Faraday to Judgment Day," *ELH*, 34 (1967), 225–47. George Levine's essay on *Little Dorrit* in *Darwin and the Novelists* (Cambridge, MA: Harvard University Press, 1988) applies the theory of entropy to that novel. See Levine, 153–77. However, the extent to which scientific ideas actually influenced Dickens's fiction has recently been questioned by K. J. Fielding in his article "Dickens and Science?" *Dickens Quarterly*, 13, 4 (December 1996), 201–17.

10 Beer, 68.

11 Quoted in J. A. V. Chapple, *Science and Literature in the Nineteenth Century* (London: Macmillan, 1986), 93.

12 Levine, 145.

13 For this discussion of Darwinian time, I am indebted to Beer's *Darwin's Plots*, especially p. 205.

14 Beer, 43.

15 Beer, 63.

16 Sylvère Monod, *Dickens the Novelist* (Norman: University of Oklahoma Press, 1968), 477. Monod was typical of his time in objecting to the over-use of coincidence in Dickens's work, and in the novel generally. The more recent tendency has been to understand coincidence as a part of the novelistic convention. George Levine, for instance, defends Dickens's use of coincidence as a necessary way of giving shape to and imposing order on the profusion and chaos that is so often depicted in the Dickensian novel. See Levine, 130.

17 See Harriet Ritvo, *The Animal Estate: The English and Other Creatures in the Victorian Age* (Cambridge, MA: Harvard University Press, 1987), 40. Gillian Beer suggests that Man is a "determining absence" in the *Origin*. Beer, 10.

18 See James Paradis, "Darwin and Landscape," *Victorian Science and Victorian Values* (New Brunswick, NJ: Rutgers University Press, 1985), 85–111.

19 Ritvo, 40.

20 The phrase "the survival of the fittest" was coined by Herbert Spencer and not by Darwin. Nevertheless, the idea of fitness as suitability – rather than its other meaning of qualified, competent, worthy (OED) – does seem to descend logically from Darwin's theorizing about adaptability.

21 Dickens carried the recycling tendency into his own life, naming his third daughter, born in the year of *David Copperfield*'s serialization, Dora Annie. It was not a wise choice. Like her fictional namesake, Dora Annie died young – after only a year of life.

22 Dickens was at pains to justify the oddity of this will. In the Postscript to *Our Mutual Friend* he writes that those who dispute the probability of such a will should have a look at the hundreds of will cases in the Prerogative Office which are more remarkable than the one he has invented (OMF, 893).

23 Charles Darwin, The Origin of Species, 24.
24 Humphry House, *The Dickens World* (London: Oxford University Press, 1950), 167. The three-way association between the dust heaps, excrement, and money has given rise to a host of Freudian and post-Freudian interpretations equating money with anality, and suggesting that Dickens intended to excoriate the accumulation of wealth. Eve Kosofsky Sedgwick takes this idea further by expanding the metaphoric dimensions of anality to a homosexual reading of the novel. See "Homophobia, Misogyny, and Capital: The Example of *Our Mutual Friend*," *Modern Critical Views: Charles Dickens* (New York: Chelsea, 1987), 245–63. Against this tendency must be placed the strong demur of John Carey, who suggests that Dickens's attitude towards money was not as negative as his critics suppose, given that he himself was a rich man, and that the dust heaps represent no more than Dickens's "genial interest in the resourceful use of junk." See John Carey, *The Violent Effigy: A Study of Dickens' Imagination* (London: Faber and Faber, 1973), 110. What was in fact contained in those dust hills is also a subject of debate. Stephen Gill in his notes to the 1977 Penguin edition of *Our Mutual Friend* (p. 896, note 3) takes issue with House. Basing himself on Mayhew, Gill suggests that the dust heaps of Victorian London were made up of nothing more than ash and refuse, while the lucrative collection of excrement was the job of cesspool workers called nightmen.
25 See Nancy Aycock Metz "The Artistic Reclamation of Waste in *Our Mutual Friend*," *Nineteenth-Century Fiction*, 34, 1 (June 1979), 68, 70.
26 Howard W. Fulweiler, "'A Dismal Swamp': Darwin, Design, and Evolution in Our Mutual Friend," *Nineteenth-Century Literature*, 49, 1 (June 1994), 54. Fulweiler's article gives the fullest discussion to date of the Darwinian elements in *Our Mutual Friend*. For an account of how geology influenced Victorian literature, see Dennis R. Dean, "'Through Science to Despair': Geology and the Victorians," *Victorian Science and Victorian Values* (New Brunswick, NJ: Rutgers University Press, 1985), 111–36.
27 The article was called "Dirty Cleanliness" and appeared in *Household Words*, 24 July 1858.
28 Carey, 101.
29 Forster claimed that the novel was to end in the condemned man's cell with a confession of his crime by Jasper on the eve of his execution. See Peter Ackroyd, *Dickens* (London: Sinclair-Stevenson, 1990), 1050.
30 This has led to the suggestion that in the denouement Dickens intended to have Helena hypnotize Jasper in order to reveal his role in the murder of Edwin Drood. See Philip Collins, *Dickens and Crime* (Bloomington, IN: Indiana University Press, 1968), 303, 307.

Index

Adultery, 27, 58, 60, 85, 129
Africans, 144, 145, 152, 156, 180
Agriculture
  animal breeders, 20, 176, 205n24
  horticulturists, 20
  knowledge of heredity in, 2
Albinoism, 13–14
Animal ancestors, 23
Animal brides or husbands, 23
Animal machine, 8, 201n17
Animals, 23, 36, 79, 164, 167, 181
  cross-mating, 24
  human, 113, 115, 121–2, 169
  in *Our Mutual Friend*, 105–7
  in *The Republic*, 2
  oviparous, 5
Aristotle, 3, 4, 5, 7, 16, 22, 59, 158
Assyrians, 2
Austen, Jane
  Pride and Prejudice, 22

Ballad, folk, 23
Barnaby Rudge, 35, 45, 99, 111–22,
  156, 181, 210n6
  Barnaby Rudge, 112, 113
  Dennis the Hangman, 112, 113,
    119–22, 181
  Hugh, 111–22, 126, 199
  John Chester, 112, 113–17, 199
  see also Paternity in *Barnaby
    Rudge*
Bestiality, 2, 25
Bible, 8, 11, 23, 29, 85, 99, 162
  Hebrew, 27–30, 101, 153, 154;
    Cain, 100; Deuteronomy, 2;
    Eden, 105; fertility in, 29;
    Genesis, 10, 61; genealogy
    in, 28–9; hybridization in, 2;
    Isaiah, 28; levirate marriage,
    159; Leviticus, 2, 200n2; My
    brother's keeper, 117; Sins of
    the fathers, 89–90, 96, 132;
    see also Talmud

New Testament
  The Fall, 103; Judas, 149;
    Pontius Pilate, 167; Virgin
    birth, 90; Virgin Mary, 87, 88;
    see also Jesus; Resurrection,
    theme of
  see also Devil
Bleak House, 41, 72, 86, 88–96,
  127, 145, 177, 191
  Esther Summerson, 86, 88–97
  Lady Dedlock, 91–3, 94
  see also Maternity in *Bleak House*;
    Paternity in *Bleak House*
Blended heredity, 24, 43–4, 158
Blood, 7–8
Bonnet, Charles, 17
Broca, Paul, 154
Buffon, George de, 14, 19, 203n36

Carlyle, Thomas
  The French Revolution, 212n25
Chain of Being, 17–18, 36
Chambers, Robert, 20
Child-wife, 68–70
Children, 12, 21–2, 27, 29, 35, 36,
  39, 43, 50–1, 53–4, 64, 80, 85,
  100
  illegitimate, 86; *see also* illegitimacy
  in *Dombey and Son*, 123–5
  in *The Old Curiosity Shop*, 47
  see also Maternity; Paternity
Christ
  see Jesus
Christianity, 69, 75, 103, 154, 156,
  161–2
  Original Sin, 30, 75
Chromosomes, 18
Class, social, 82, 94–5, 104–6,
  111–42, 143, 146, 155, 166,
  168, 175, 185, 212n27
Colonialism, 56, 144–6, 181
Contagion, 77–8, 93–6, 124
  smallpox, 94–5

217